THE ROMAN EMPEROR TITUS AND THE SPOILS OF THE JEWISH TEMPLE

Detail from the Metropolitan Museum's great Gothic tapestry "The Capture of Jerusalem"

THE
PRACTICAL BOOK
OF TAPESTRIES

BY
GEORGE LELAND HUNTER

AUTHOR OF
"DECORATIVE TEXTILES", "DECORATIVE FURNITURE", ETC.

WITH 8 ILLUSTRATIONS IN COLOUR
AND 220 IN DOUBLETONE

PHILADELPHIA & LONDON
J. B. LIPPINCOTT COMPANY
1925

PRINTED BY J. B. LIPPINCOTT COMPANY
AT THE WASHINGTON SQUARE PRESS
PHILADELPHIA, U. S. A.

I DEDICATE THIS BOOK TO

FRANCE, THE MOTHER OF TAPESTRIES

IN RECOGNITION OF THE FACT THAT IN PARIS
AND ARRAS, IN THE FOURTEENTH CENTURY, THE
ART OF TAPESTRY WEAVING WAS DEVELOPED
FROM PRIMITIVE TO PERFECTED

FOREWORD

GREATLY have I been helped by Mr. Clarence H. Mackay, the Duke of Alba, Sir Joseph Duveen. Whatever merit this book has is largely due to their friendly coöperation, and to that of the others named below.

Greatly am I under obligation to Mr. John D. Rockefeller, Jr., Mr. Joseph Widener, Mr. William Randolph Hearst, Mrs. Alexander Hamilton Rice, Mrs. F. F. Prentiss, Mr. John L. Severance, Mrs. F. T. Bradbury, Mr. W. Hinckle Smith, Mrs. C. Wheaton Vaughan, Mrs. William Hayward, Mr. George Blumenthal, Mr. Otto Kahn, Mr. James L. Breese, Mr. Edson Bradley, Mr. Philip Lehman, Mrs. E. H. Harriman, Mr. H. E. Huntington, Mr. Archer Huntington, Mr. Harry Payne Whitney, Mr. J. Pierpont Morgan, Mrs. E. Parmelee Prentice, Mrs. Harold I. Pratt, Mrs. Edward F. Hutton, Mrs. Nicolas F. Brady, Mr. E. J. Berwind, Mrs. Stanford White, Mr. John J. Albright, Mr. Cyrus H. McCormick, Miss Lilla P. Wheeler, Mr. John D. McIlhenny, Mr. Philip Hiss, Mr. Edward Robinson, Mr. Joseph Breck, Mr. H. W. Kent, Mr. W. H. Clifford, Dr. Bashford H. Dean, Miss Robinson, Mrs. Frances Seaver, Mrs. Ansley Wilcox, Mr. Willis O. Chapin, Mrs. Cornelia Sage-Quinton, Mr. Edwin Atlee Barber, Mr. F. Allen Whiting, Mr. Edward R. Smith, Sir Cecil Smith, Sir Charles Allom, Mr. Harvey Watts, Miss Nancy McClelland, Mr. H. D. Eberlein, Dr. W. R. Valentiner, Mr. Frank G. Macomber, Miss Sarah G. Flint, Mrs. H. M. Wilmarth, Mr. Augustus Eddy, Mrs. Hugh Birch, Mr. and Mrs. Robert McCormick, Mr. Spencer Eddy, Mr. Emile Baumgarten, Mr. Thomas H. Kirby, Mr. Paul Baumgarten, Mr. Robert Baumgarten, Mr. Philip Rice, Mr. Giles Whiting, Mr. Robert Underwood Johnson, Mr. Edwin H. Blashfield, Mr. George G. Booth, Mr. Ralph Booth, The Republic of Austria, Brookline Trust Co., Mr. Paul Drey, Fraulein Bach, Mr. John Lane, Mr. Walter Johnson, Messrs. Halm & Goldmann, Brentano's, Monsieur Edouard Champion, Mr. E. Weyhe, Mr. William Helburn, and Mr. John A. Moffitt.

Especially do I wish to express my gratitude to His Majesty, the King of Spain, Alfonso XIII, for permission and opportunity to study the finest collection of tapestries in the world, and to have special photographs made of the incomparable Virgin set; also, to the Spanish Ambassador at Paris, Quiñones de Leon; the Duke of Fernan-Nuñez, the Marquis de la Torrecilla, the Duke of Medinaceli, the Duchess of Aliaga, the Viscount de Ronda, the Marquis de la Vega Inclán, Señor Vives of the Istituto Valencia, Don Livinio Stuyck, Director of the Royal Spanish Tapestry Factory; and to the Private Secretary of the King, Don Emilio Maria de Torre, whose letters of introduction opened for me the treasures of the Spanish cathedrals.

Warmly I thank the dealers who have allowed me to illustrate tapestries in their possession, and have helped me secure photographs, with permission to publish, of tapestries sold by them: Duveen Brothers, P. W. French & Co., Jacques Seligmann & Son, Demotte, Morris & Co., Wildenstein & Co., Arnold Seligmann, Rey & Company, Lewis & Simmons, Wm. Baumgarten & Co., Alavoine & Co., Richard W. Lehne, Dikran G. Kelekian, Harding, Dawson, Hayden Co., H. S. Souhami, F. Maluf, Hampton Shops, Charles, Frank Partridge, Larcade, Jonas, Jansen, Edgewater Tapestry Looms, Herter Looms, Pollak & Winternitz.

Affectionately I acknowledge my indebtedness for inspiration and guidance to Jules Guiffrey, Joseph Destrée, Eugène Mâle, Georges Doutrepont, Petit de Julleville, L. Farcy,

Seymour de Ricci, Jean Guiffrey, Marquet de Vasselot, Stanford White, G. J. Demotte, Achille Jubinal, Eugène Muntz, E. Soil, Maurice Fenaille, Tormo Monzó, Sanchez Cantón, Gustave Migeon, E. Bertaux, Gomez-Moreño, Alan S. Cole, H. S. Marillier, W. G. Thomson, Max J. Friedländer, Eberhard Bodenhausen, Rudolf F. Burckhardt, R. M. Riefstahl, Hermann Schmidt, Heinrich Göbel, Jules Badin, Gustave Geoffroi, Jean Ajalbert, John Böttiger, Harry Wearne, Henry W. Frohne; and last but not least to E. S. Holloway of the J. B. Lippincott Company.

GEORGE LELAND HUNTER

NEW YORK CITY
JULY 1, 1925

NOTE

Besides the regular edition of this volume, there has been issued, in a special binding and at an advanced price, a Limited Subscribers' Edition which, in addition to the contents of the regular edition, has four full-page plates in colour, and sixteen full-page plates in doubletone, of Tapestry Masterpieces now in America. Reference to these illustrations will be found in the text of both editions. Reference will also be found to *Hunter 1912* and other volumes. These references have been made for the convenience of students who may wish help in consulting the illustrations of other books, especially of my first book on Tapestries, now out of print.

CONTENTS

ILLUSTRATIONS

THE PLATES ARE EASY TO LOCATE AS THEY ARE NEXT THE CHAPTER
THEY ILLUSTRATE, ALL II PLATES WITH CHAPTER II, ALL III PLATES
WITH CHAPTER III, ETC. THE SMALL LETTERS SHOW THE SEQUENCE

ILLUSTRATIONS

ILLUSTRATIONS

2

THE PRACTICAL BOOK
OF TAPESTRIES

CHAPTER I

INTRODUCTION

THIS is a practical book. It sticks to the facts. It is based, not on other books, but on tapestries that I have seen and know. It wastes little space on unimportant tapestries, or on tapestries that have ceased to exist.

I dedicate the book "TO FRANCE, THE MOTHER OF TAPESTRIES" in recognition of the fact that Perfected Tapestries are a French art based on French literature and painting, and developed at Arras and Paris in the fourteenth century. All great Gothic tapestries are French Gothic, whether woven in Northern France or in the French Netherlands.

The Van Eycks, and Robert Campin, and Jacques Daret, and Roger van der Weyden, were French-Flemish painters forming part of the artistic entourage of the French Duke of Burgundy, ruler of the Netherlands. Their paintings like the tapestries related to them, might be called French-Burgundian Gothic. I think it clearer to use the term French-Flemish.

During a large part of the fifteenth century, French-Flemish was the dominant part of French art. Under Philip the Good, Bruges and Ghent and Tournai and Brussels were capital cities of French culture. For the Duke of Burgundy were created the finest French manuscripts, the finest French paintings, the finest French tapestries. Compared with him, his suzerains and relatives the kings of France, Charles VI and Charles VII, were artistically unimportant. The Hun-

1

dred Years' War and the Anglo-Burgundian alliance exalted a French duke above the French king, in wealth and in power.

As in architecture and in furniture so in tapestry there are four important groups. These groups are: (1) Gothic, (2) Renaissance, (3) Baroque, (4) Rococo and Classic Revival. The later groups are child, grandchild, and great-grandchild of Gothic.

Most surviving Gothic tapestries date from the fifteenth century. Most Renaissance tapestries date from the six-teenth century. Most Baroque tapestries date from the seven-teenth century. Most Rococo and Classic Revival tapestries date from the eighteenth century.

But two of the groups lap over into the following century. That is to say, many Gothic tapestries were woven during the first fifteen years of the sixteenth century; many Renais-sance tapestries during the first fifteen years of the seven-teenth century.

Of Gothic tapestries as a whole it may be said that they are vastly superior to later tapestries. Gothic design is closer to tapestry texture, and more completely utilizes the extra-ordinary abilities of tapestry bobbins and loom.

The finest Gothic tapestries are those made before 1480; and those rich with gold, made in Brussels at the end of the fifteenth century, when Philip the Handsome and Joanna the Mad reigned over the Netherlands (1496–1506). Close to these come the Early Renaissance tapestries designed by Bernard van Orley, made at Brussels between 1515 and 1535, and also rich with gold.

Next to Gothics, rank the tapestries woven at Beauvais in the middle third of the eighteenth century, after the designs of François Boucher, with subjects that are far from religious and without gold. Next to Beauvais-Bouchers are the Gobelin-Bouchers and the Gobelin-Coypels.

Altogether magnificent and splendid are the tapestries originated under the direction of Charles Lebrun at the Gobelins during the reign of Louis XIV, many of them with gold, and many created on high-warp looms. They are almost as complete an interpretation of their period as Gothics of theirs.

Inferior to all of these are most Renaissance tapestries, although some of the sets rich with gold in the Royal Spanish collection dazzle with their brilliancy, and although Raphael's "Acts of the Apostles," and many of the sets based on the designs of Giulio Romano and Bernard van Orley and their successors, compel our admiration.

Late Renaissance tapestries, that is to say tapestries woven after 1570, are much inferior to Early Renaissance tapestries. The decadence of tapestry weaving was largely due to the religious troubles of the Netherlands. The attempt of Archdukes Albert and Isabella to revive the industry early in the seventeenth century was only moderately successful.

Many of the Flemish tapestries woven in the seventeenth century are unattractive. The sculptural exaggerations of Baroque are foreign to the genius of tapestry. This applies quite as much to the designs of Rubens as to the designs of his imitators and successors.

Tapestries of the four great groups are comparatively easy to distinguish. Renaissance and Baroque tapestries have wide borders; Gothic and eighteenth century tapestries have narrow borders or none. Baroque tapestries have heavy shadow-and-light bands just inside the border.

Gothic tapestries excel in reds, Renaissance tapestries in whites and golden yellows, Baroque tapestries in blues, Rococo tapestries in roses, while Classic Revival colours are weak and pale. The dark reds of Flemish Baroque tapestries have usually faded, changing to yellows and browns.

Gothic tapestries may be described as "line" tapestries,

Renaissance as "paint" tapestries, Baroque as "sculptural" tapestries, Rococo and Classic Revival as "paint" tapestries. This means that Gothic tapestries tend to accentuate line effects, especially the vertical line effects which are the dominant feature of Gothic decorative art. Renaissance tapestries accentuate horizontal effects, and develop paint-style modeling, *moderately*. Baroque tapestries sacrifice other qualities in the effort to over-accentuate sculptural modeling, and break both vertical and horizontal lines in the effort to secure variety and be emphatic. Rococo has many points in common with fifteenth century Gothic, and is sympathetic in a small way with tapestry texture. Rococo tapestry designers learned much from Chinese paintings and embroideries, that were the great inspiration of Western Europe in the eighteenth century.

To distinguish tapestries of the four great groups is easy. What is hard, is to distinguish tapestries from objects that are not tapestries, or that are not the kind of tapestries which make the subject of this book.

Tapestry is a broad word. If you ask for tapestries in one shop, they will show you "petit points" made with needle. In another, tapestry wall-papers. In another, printed cloths patterned like tapestry wall-papers. In another, silk tapestries with woven pattern resembling that of "petit points." In another, Jacquard verdures and picture panels. In another, tapestry rugs and carpeting. In another, painted imitations of "real tapestries." In another, block-printed imitations. In another, double-warp tapestries. With none of these have we anything to do. We shall treat only of cloths that are tapestry in the proper and primary sense—bobbin-made with surface consisting entirely of weft threads, usually a ribbed or "rep" weave, with coarse hard warps and fine soft wefts, and with open slits left where colours meet parallel with the warps.

Of these, the most important and those that form the main subject of this book are the Picture tapestries developed and brought to perfection in France and the French Netherlands in the fourteenth and fifteenth centuries. The less highly developed tapestries, which resemble rugs, damasks, brocades and other figured weaves in lacking the power to express pictures fully and effectively on a large scale, I have grouped under the heading "Primitive Tapestries" (Chapter II).

The most obvious feature of both Primitive and Perfected Tapestries are the open slits. It is they that especially distinguish tapestries from damasks and brocades and other weaves. It is they that give tapestries the lace-like quality so apparent in the finest pieces (Plate XVII, f.). They are the most important distinguishing feature not only of Perfected Tapestries, but also of Primitive Tapestries.

CHAPTER II

PRIMITIVE TAPESTRIES

EGYPTIAN, GREEK, ROMAN, SARACENIC, GERMAN, PERUVIAN, CHINESE
LITERARY EVIDENCE: HOMER, OVID, MARTIAL

EGYPT is the great-grandmother of us all. The oldest tapestries in existence are Egyptian. In Egyptian graves have been preserved more ancient textiles than survive from all other sources previous to Gothic.

Many of these Ancient Egyptian textiles were woven, not only before the time of Christ, but even before the Trojan War, and some of them even before the Third millenium B. C., when the Pyramids were built.

Of the extant textiles that precede the Trojan War, several are tapestries, notably three from the grave of the Egyptian Pharaoh Thutmose IV. These pieces are described in Volume XV of the catalogue of the Cairo Museum. They are made entirely of linen, with ground in plain weave, and with coloured ornaments inserted in tapestry weave.

The largest of these pieces is 11 inches high by 17 inches wide. The left half of it is illustrated on Plate II, a. The cartouche in the lower left quarter of the illustration, is that of Amenhotep II, father of Thutmose IV. On each side of the cartouche are sacred *uraeus* serpents emblematic of Egyptian royalty. The one on the right bears the white crown of Upper Egypt. The one on the left bears the red crown of Lower Egypt. The field of the tapestry is figured with alternating lotus and papyrus. The border on the left is figured with alternating lotus buds and flowers.

The colours are red, blue, green, yellow, brown-black and gray. The reds and blues are still bright, the brown-blacks are mostly gone, leaving the warps bare. Both sides of the

7

tapestry are alike, no threads having been left floating.   The
weave shows great freedom.   When helpful to the expression
of the design, warps are curved and wefts inserted oblique to
warp.   The weft threads are considerably thicker than the
warp threads.

This tapestry is extraordinarily fine of texture, much finer
than the finest Gobelins, and four or five times as fine as the
great Gothics.   However, the excellence of tapestries does not
depend upon fineness of texture.*   We have no evidence to
show that Perfected Tapestries were ever woven in Ancient
Egypt.   All of those that have survived belong to the Primitive group, without suggestion of an understanding of the
picture possibilities of slits and hatchings artfully combined
with each other and with ribs, producing the greatest contrasts possible in any form of flat art.   Doctor Breasted
whose "History of Egypt" is a classic, and for whose scholar-
ship and ability to humanize it in written form I have the
most profound admiration, was misled when he wrote regarding the palace of Amenhotep:

"The walls were covered with woven tapestry of workmanship so fine
and colour and design so exquisite that skilled judges have declared it equal
to the best modern work."

Pieces of Ancient Greek tapestry that remain are fragments of dress materials in the Museum of the Hermitage,
from the tomb of the Seven Brothers in the Russian province
of Kuban, on the northern shore of the Black Sea.   The tomb
dates from the third or fourth century before Christ.   One of
the fragments is figured with ducks, another with floral stripes.
Both belong to the group of Primitive Tapestries.

The only Ancient Roman tapestries that remain are Egyp-
tian-Roman, woven in Egypt from the second to the fifth centuries.   These are often called Coptic, Coptic being loosely
used for Egyptian after the time of Christ and to include

---

* The whole technique of tapestry-weaving is fully discussed in later chapters
of this book.

Greek-Egyptian, Greco-Roman Egyptian, Byzantine Egyptian, and even Saracenic Egyptian. Most of these Coptic tapestries are dress trimmings, woven in wool and linen on all-linen ground as part of the garment, or woven separately for *appliqué*.

What I regard as the finest tapestry that has survived from the pre-Gothic period is the altar piece of which a detail is illustrated on Plate II, b. This tapestry is 3 feet 7 inches high by 4 feet 5 inches wide, and the detail illustrated is 18 inches high. The polychrome parts, reds, greens, and green-blacks, are in wool; the écru parts and reddish écru flesh tones are in linen. The subject is Blessed Vesta (εστια πολυολβος), with attendants (αρετη, προχοπη, *et al.*).

This tapestry was probably an altar piece, either in a temple of Vesta or in a private residence. Vesta was one of the Great Gods of Olympus, and the eldest sister of Jupiter, Juno, Neptune, Pluto and Ceres. She was especially the divinity of the home, the virgin goddess who presided over the burning hearth. In her temple at Rome six Vestal Virgins kept the sacred fire continuously burning.

While the design and composition of this tapestry are interesting, it is the superiority of weave that causes me to give it such high rank. Here we have a technique superior to that of some of the smaller Gothic tapestries of the fifteenth century and of many tapestries since. If I have decided to class it in the Primitive group, it is not from lack of appreciation of its merits. If the weaver had been guided and inspired by painted cartoons equal to those of the fourteenth and fifteenth centuries, it is possible that he might have passed the line which separate Picture Tapestries of the Perfected type from those of the Primitive type.

This Ancient Egyptian weaver had gone far on the road which leads to perfection. While his *hatchings* are immensely inferior to the hatchings developed by the French in the fourteenth century, and his *ribs* lack the definiteness and strength of Gothic ribs, because the warps are too close together, he has utilized many of the possibilities of *slits*. The modeling of the face, especially of the nose and eyebrows, is largely due to holes, intentionally and artfully introduced by the weaver. Note also the effective use of series of tiny slits in the necklace of the goddess.

One device the weaver has employed far more freely than it was employed later in Gothic tapestries. Seemingly he worked on a loom that enabled him to have more complete control over the warps and their tension than is possible on a two-roller loom. Perhaps he was working on a loom of the Ancient Greek type, with pendant warps weighted at the bottom, separately or in small groups, the weights taking the place of the second roller. Perhaps he was working on a frame similar to an embroidery frame. At any rate, both warps and wefts show variations from the horizontal and the perpendicular, artfully controlled to express the design.

It will be noticed that the shadows on the face are employed arbitrarily and heavily, as was the Roman fashion. This shadowing is interesting to compare with that of the Boscoreale frescoes in the Metropolitan Museum of Art.

The design of the tapestry as a whole suggests mosaic, which is not strange considering the widespread use of mosaic on floors and walls throughout the Roman Empire.

Interesting details of the design are the halo, the pomegranates over the head of Vesta, her coiffure, the jewel on her forehead, her elaborate earrings and necklace.

A wealth of the Later-Egyptian (the so-called Coptic) textiles, including many tapestries, is to be found in the Cairo Museum, Berlin Kunstgewerbe Museum, Victoria and Albert Museum, British Museum, Boston Museum of Fine Arts, and Metropolitan Museum of Art. Indeed, without these Coptic textiles our knowledge of ancient weaves would be meager.

Plate II, c, with its jeweled cross in orange and yellow and its four blue-green ducks, and double warps exposed where the dark wool has disappeared, admirably illustrates the texture of some of the cruder Coptic tapestries. The background is a loosely covered weft rep, and the square block of tapestry insert is a well-covered warp rep. The contrast between the vertical ribs of the warp rep and the horizontal ribs of the weft rep lifts the tapestry insert into bold prominence against its background. The contrast is still further accentuated by the occasional introduction in the background of heavy ribs formed by grouping several wefts together. The background is all in natural linen. The tapestry insert is in natural linen and coloured wool. The tapestry insert is woven, not on the regular weft threads which are allowed to float loose on the back, but on *extra* wefts blocked in on *double* warps. (See the illustration.)

Plate II, d, with its picture of Mercury (Greek ЕРМНС= Hermes) is interesting to compare with Plate II, b. The technique of II, d, is vastly inferior to that of II, b, although indicating familiarity with superior weaves. It will be noticed that the vertical ribs of II, d, deform the face of Mercury, while the ribs of II, b, which are horizontal as in all important European tapestries, lend themselves to the accurate expression of the outlines of the face. (Compare Plates XVII, a, aa.)

Many of the most interesting of the later Egyptian tapestries show Saracenic influence, having been woven after the Mohammedan conquest of Egypt in the seventh century.

An interesting example is that in the Victoria and Albert Museum (Plate II, da), in natural linen with design outlined in red silk, and with Arabic inscription also in red silk.

Among Saracenic all-silk tapestries is one in the Cluny Museum, the stole of a twelfth century Bishop, found at Bayonne when his tomb was opened in 1863 (No. 6526 of the catalogue, 1883). When I first saw this tapestry in 1907, it was labeled " soie brochée " and was in bad condition. It has Arabic lettering.

These medieval Saracenic silk tapestries, whether Spanish

or African or Egyptian or Syrian or Persian, resemble Chinese silk tapestries in technique. I am inclined to believe that all western silk weaving, Egyptian and Byzantine, as well as Persian, received its technique largely from China. Certainly, Saracenic silk tapestries, making allowance for the different style of the design, might almost have been woven by Chinese weavers, and like Chinese silk tapestries belong definitely to the group of Primitive Tapestries.

All-silk tapestries are as a rule uninteresting and apt to be inferior to cloths of similar design in damask, brocade or embroidery. Without wool, tapestry technique of great effectiveness seems impossible.

Modern Aubusson tapestry furniture-coverings in all-silk are much inferior to those that have the proper proportion of wool. Yet many Americans seem to regard all-silk as a virtue.

Plate II, ea, shows a Chinese picture tapestry which, in spite of the elaboration of the design, must be classed with Primitive Tapestries because of the failure to employ slits and hatchings and ribs skilfully to force contrasts beyond the possibilities of paint. Indeed, Chinese tapestries are apt to be inferior to the paintings that inspired them, instead of superior.

I noticed in looking over two of Mr. Freer's silk tapestries attributed to the Sung period, that the ribs were vertical, while the paintings of the period that he showed me were executed on silk horizontally ribbed. So that there was a distortion in the tapestry pictures that did not exist in the painted pictures.

Even the Chinese tapestries inspired by Gobelin tapestries, fail to display sufficiently the virtues of tapestries of the Perfected group—for example, Mr. Severance's Chinese tapestry illustrated and described in the *Burlington Magazine* of June 15, 1914, and the Chinese copy of a Beauvais-Boucher now in New York.

Also to the Primitive group belong the German-Byzantine St. Gereon fragments, which are now in the Lyons Museum (Plate II, e), Nuremburg Museum, Victoria and Albert Museum, and Berlin Kunstgewerbe Museum. These are copies in tapestry-weave of Byzantine silk damasks, and their especial merit is fidelity to the original. The design shows a large wheel with eagle, griffin and bull grouped inside, one on top of the other. The slits have been used with considerable skill and in a manner that indicates the remote influence of tapestries like Blessed Vesta. The weft is of wool, the warp of linen.

Also to the Primitive group belong the German-Romanesque tapestries, the most important of which are those preserved in the Cathedral of Halberstadt. One of these, nearly square with several inches missing from the top, picturing Charlemagne and four Philosophers, I have illustrated on Plate II, f. Just as Blessed Vesta, Plate II, b, suggested mosaic, so this suggests primitive stained glass. Charlemagne (KAROLVS REX.) sits on his throne, sceptre in hand framed in a panel diamond-shaped. In the lower corners sit Cato and Seneca, with identity made certain by their names woven above their heads. Cato says: DENIGRAT MERITUM DANTIS MORA (Delay in giving spoils the merit of the service). Seneca replies: QUI CITO DAT BIS DAT (He who gives quickly gives twice). In the upper corners of the tapestry are Socrates and Plato, incomplete.

Other German-Romanesque tapestries preserved in the Cathedral of Halberstadt are the two friezes, 3 feet 7 inches high, long narrow bands for hanging above the choir stalls. One shows Abraham and the three angels, the sacrifice of Isaac, the archangel Michael and the Dragon. The other shows Christ and the Apostles.

At this point I should like to emphasize the fact that there is nothing marvelous or tremendously admirable about Primitive Tapestries. Many of them would be much more effective in embroidery. The small silk ones would be equally good in damask or brocade. As for Oriental kelims, which since time immemorial have been woven in Asiatic Turkey, Persia, the Russian Caucasus, and Russian Central Asia, though some of the Sehnas are attractive, most of the others are stupid. Even the silk kelims of Persia, the wonderfully rich ones, with gold or silver, made in the sixteenth century and seventeenth century are not great works of art. The finest of them impress one as rather weak copies of Persian knotted rugs.

The weave of Primitive Tapestries has been practiced by almost all primitive weavers, in almost all countries of the world, at all ages. It is the easiest and most natural way to introduce coloured figures on a loom that lacks shuttle and treadle, and that has not been at all developed in the direction of repeat and of speed. The largest group of American Primitive Tapestries comes from Peru. The weave resembles that of the more Primitive Coptic tapestries, but the designs are inferior.

LITERARY EVIDENCE

The literary evidence regarding Greek and Roman tapestries given us by Homer, Ovid, Martial and other Classic writers, is suggestive, but does not indicate that any Ancient Greek or Roman tapestries achieved the excellences which set European Perfected Tapestries in a class by themselves.

In Homeric Greece, tapestry weaving was a feminine duty and accomplishment. Penelope wove a shroud for Laertes, which secretly she unraveled by night in order to postpone the second marriage towards which the suitors were pressing her. As for Helen of Troy, when Iris was sent to call her to see the combat between Menelaus and Paris:

Her in the palace at her loom she found;
The golden web her own sad story crown'd,
The Trojan wars she weav'd (herself the prize),
And the dire triumphs of her fatal eyes.

The tapestries described by Ovid as created in the famous weaving contest between Minerva and Arachne were evidently small pieces, intricate and elaborate but belonging to the Primitive group. Minerva, otherwise Pallas Athene, pictured the council of the Gods that met to decide from whom the city of Athens should receive its name. Arachne pictured the Loves of the Gods. Both used strong reds as well as lighter colours, and both used pliant threads of gold. Minerva introduced separate small scenes in the corner of her tapestry, and gave it an olive-leaf border. Arachne bordered her tapestry with flowers and ivy.

Apparently tapestries in the period of Roman supremacy were distinctively the product of Egypt, while embroideries were distinctively the product of Mesopotamia. In the second half of the first century A. D. the Roman poet Martial wrote:

"Now the needle of Babylon has been conquered by the comb of the Nile."

The great picture-cloths of the Early Middle Ages were embroideries.

PLATE II, a.—DETAIL OF AN ANCIENT EGYPTIAN TAPESTRY OF THE
FIFTEENTH CENTURY B. C., FIGURED WITH LOTUS AND PAPYRUS, AND BEAR-
ING THE NAME OF AMENHOTEP II.   CAIRO MUSEUM

ΕΣΤΙΑ ΠΟΛΥΟΛΒΟΣ

PLATE II, b.—BLESSED VESTA, DETAIL OF THE FINEST SPECIMEN OF
TAPESTRY WEAVING THAT HAS COME DOWN TO US FROM THE PRE—GOTHIC
PERIOD. GRECO—ROMAN EGYPTIAN OF THE SECOND CENTURY A. D.

D. G. KELEKIAN

PLATE II, C.—COPTIC TAPESTRY OF THE FIFTH CENTURY A. D., SHOW-
ING A JEWELLED CROSS IN ORANGE AND YELLOW AND FOUR BLUE–GREEN
DUCKS INSIDE OF CIRCLE AND SQUARE. THE WHITE PARTS IN NATURAL
LINEN, THE DARK PARTS IN COLORED WOOL. FROM AN ANCIENT TOMB AT
AKHMIM, EGYPT. VICTORIA AND ALBERT MUSEUM. (SEE CHAPTER XVII FOR
DISCUSSION OF THE TEXTURE)

PLATE II, da.—SARACENIC TAPESTRY IN NATURAL LINEN WITH DESIGN OUTLINED IN RED SILK, AND ARABIC INSCRIPTION IN RED SILK, FROM AN ANCIENT TOMB AT ERMENT, EGYPT. DATES FROM ABOUT THE TENTH CENTURY. VICTORIA AND ALBERT MUSEUM

PLATE II, d.—COPTIC TAPESTRY OF THE THIRD CENTURY A. D. FROM AKHMIM, EGYPT, SHOWING HERMES INSIDE OF A FLORAL BORDER. VICTORIA AND ALBERT MUSEUM

PLATE II, e.—DETAIL OF A GERMAN–BYZANTINE TENTH CENTURY TAPES–
TRY IN IVORY AND BROWNISH BLUE WOOL, FORMERLY AT THE CHURCH OF ST.
GEREON IN COLOGNE, NOW IN THE LYONS MUSEUM

PLATE II, ea.—THE DRAGON PROCESSION, A CHINESE SILK TAPESTRY
(*kossu*) WOVEN IN THE EIGHTEENTH CENTURY. ABOUT FOUR FEET WIDE.
VICTORIA AND ALBERT MUSEUM

PLATE II, f.—CHARLEMAGNE AND FOUR PHILOSOPHERS, A GERMAN TAPESTRY OF THE
THIRTEENTH CENTURY IN THE CATHEDRAL OF HALBERSTADT

PLATE III, a.—PORTRAIT OF ARTHUR, ANCIENT HERO KING OF GREAT BRITAIN, AS PICTURED IN
MR. MACKAY'S UNIQUE FOURTEENTH CENTURY TAPESTRY

CHAPTER III

EARLY GOTHIC PICTURE TAPESTRIES

KING ARTHUR, APOCALYPSE, PRESENTATION, ST. PIAT AND ST. ELEUTHERE, JOURDAIN DE BLAYE, ANNUNCIATION, HUNTING TAPESTRY

FRANCE is the mother of Gothic tapestries. The development from Primitive to Perfected took place on high-warp looms in the French cities of Arras and Paris in the fourteenth century. During the Middle Ages, before the fourteenth century, damasks rivaled and embroideries surpassed tapestries as a medium for the interpretation of pictures. After the middle of the fourteenth century, tapestries became the form of art most prized by kings and nobles, as is shown by the inventories of the period. Damasks and embroideries and paintings were thrown far into the background.

The fourteenth century development of tapestries was, however, dependent upon the fourteenth century development of French painting. Without strong and brilliant painted cartoons, tapestries like King Arthur and the Apocalypse set would have been impossible.

Nevertheless, important as was the development of design, the development of weave was vastly more important. The weave is the distinctive characteristic feature of Perfected Tapestries. The weave distinguishes them vastly more from Primitive Tapestries, than does the weave of Primitive Tapestries distinguish Primitive Tapestries from damasks and brocades.

The earliest tapestries that display fully the possibilities of the Perfected Tapestry weave, are Mr. Mackay's "King Arthur" (Plates III, a, and b) and the Angers "Apocalypse" series (Plates III, c, ca, cb, cc, d). All of these tapestries excel in both design and weave, and all of them also excel in Story interest. All of them are immeasurably superior to the Brussels Museum's "Presentation," (Plate III, g) and to the "Saint Piat and Saint Eleuthère" series of the Cathedral of Tournai (Plates III, e, and III, f).

The King Arthur pictured in Mr. Mackay's tapestry is not the dim and uncertain King Arthur of history. He is the great and glorious King Arthur of the French twelfth century quickened into the romantic life of the period of the Crusades by the same French genius and French chivalric enthusiasm that made Charlemagne and his contemporaries live again in the "Chanson de Roland" and other *chansons de geste*. Perhaps never was history brought down to earth and contemporized to the same extent as by medieval Frenchmen. Charlemagne and Arthur and David and Hector were represented as real contemporary personages, clad in Medieval costumes, living in Medieval fashion, talking Medieval French. Such was the inventive art of French poets in the eleventh and twelfth centuries, who were trammeled by facts quite as little as the scenario composers of to-day.

Typical creations of Medieval romance are the Nine Preux (Heroes)

    I. Three Bible heroes, Joshua, David, Judas Maccabeus.

    II. Three Pagan heroes, Hector, Alexander, Caesar.

    III. Three Christian heroes, Arthur, Charlemagne, Godfrey de Bouillon.

Inventories and other literary records show that the Nine Preux were a favorite subject of tapestry makers in the fourteenth and fifteenth centuries. Charles V, King of France from 1364 to 1380 had two tapestries picturing the Nine Heroes, and his brother Louis, Duke of Anjou, had one. Similar tapestries were also owned by the King's other brothers, the Dukes of Burgundy and Berri, but with a tenth Preux added, the contemporary Hero of the war against England, Bertrand du Guesclin.

One of the earliest pictured representations of the Nine

Preux that have survived is in a manuscript of the Bibliothèque Nationale, containing arms of the French Nobility. The author was Gilles de Bouvier, called Berry, who was appointed Herald to Charles VII in 1420. At the end of the volume are three large wood engravings (Plates XVIII, a, aa, ab) each occupying a double quarto page, each showing three of the Nine Preux on horseback, each Preux under a separate arch. These engravings, slightly illuminated and contemporary with the manuscript of which they seem always to have been a part, give the Preux costumes and armor like those of the contemporary Frènch Nobility. Each one of the Preux has below him a six line stanza with letters engraved on the same wood block as the pictures.

The verses that describe Arthur are:

> Je fu roy de Bretaigne, d'Escoche et d'Engleterre.
> Maint roialme je vos par ma force conquerre.
> Le grant gaiant Zusto fis morir et deffaire.
> Sus le mont saint Miciel 1 aultre en alai querre.
> Je vis le sang Greal, mes la mort me fist guerre,
> Qui m'ochit vc ans puis que Dieu vint sur terre.

which as translated reads:

> I was King of Britanny, Scotland and England.
> Many a realm I sought by my strength to conquer.
> The great giant Zusto I killed and defeated.
> Upon mount Saint Michel another I went to seek.
> I saw the Holy Grail. Then death made war on me,
> And killed me 600 years after God came on earth.

As the king of three countries, Britanny, Scotland and England, Arthur had on his coat-of-arms three crowns, the three crowns that are shown on his breast as well as on his pennant, in Mr. Mackay's tapestry.

Among Late Gothic tapestries showing Arthur with this coat-of-arms are, the "Triumph of Christ" in the Brussels Museum (Plate 370 of *Hunter 1912*); the duplicate "Triumph of Christ" in the collection of the Saragossa Cathedrals; "The

Story of Charlemagne" in the collection of Mr. George Blumenthal (Plate 371 of *Hunter 1912*) ; the fragment of a Swiss Nine Preux tapestry in the Bâle Museum. (Plate XIV, c.) King Arthur also appears with his three crowns in the crude French Renaissance series of Preux from Saint Maixent, now in the Château de Langeais. There are several duplicates, or near duplicates, of these Saint Maixent tapestries now in America.

The weave of Mr. Mackay's "King Arthur" is splendid. King Arthur's face is delineated with an art difficult to equal and impossible to surpass, (See Plate III, a). While the technique does not possess some of the refinements of the greatest Late Gothic gold tapestries, it makes stronger, bolder and more effective use than they of slits and stepped slits. Note carefully the black holes, in the actual tapestry vastly blacker and deeper and stronger than any painted holes could be, which model King Arthur's brow and eyes and nose and separate his fingers. Those that give actuality to King Arthur's beard and hair and jeweled crown, though quite as important, are unfortunately not equally clear in our illustration.

The composition of the tapestry is simple and effective, and completely architectural. Fourteenth century Gothic columns and arches and canopies frame each of the seven personages. The superior dignity of Arthur is emphasized by his superior size, the lesser characters occupying only half the vertical space alloted to him. The resemblance between Arthur and the two-story personages who introduce the Apocalypse tapestries is striking.

Just as the main personage in each tapestry of the Apocalypse set occupies the full height of the tapestry, while the other scenes are in two rows one above the other, so here, Arthur occupies the full height of the tapestry, and on each side of him are lesser personages arranged in double tier; above, two archbishops standing in the balconies with archepiscopal cross on staff; below, two bishops seated with episcopal crozier (derived not from the cross but from the shepherd's staff).

Noteworthy are the jewels displayed by the bishops and archbishops, on their mitres, fastening their cloaks, and on the backs of their hands.

Arthur, like the two lesser warriors on the extreme left, has a long flowing beard and long wavy hair of the same type as seen on the personages of the Apocalypse.

All in all, the resemblance between the King Arthur tapestry and the Apocalypse series is so close as to compel one to believe that they were woven under similar conditions at about the same time, probably in the same place.

THE ANGERS APOCALYPSE

One of the greatest art treasures in the world is the Apocalypse set of French Gothic tapestries at Angers (Plates III, c and d). It is the only fourteenth century set that remains. All the other famous sets mentioned in the inventories of the period have disappeared.

Fortunately, as a result of the studies of Farcy and Guiffrey, we have much information about the orgin of these tapestries (see *Farcy Angers,* and *Guiffrey Seizième*). The Duke of Anjou, brother of Charles V, King of France, had them made in Paris by Nicolas Bataille in the last half of the fourteenth century, to hang in the chapel of his château at Angers. The cartoonist was Hennequin de Bruges, also called Jean de Bruges, Charles V's court painter, whom the Duke of Anjou borrowed for the purpose, together with an illustrated manuscript of the Apocalypse, which is now in the public library of the city of Cambrai. The painter received instructions to follow the manuscript illustrations closely, and did so, executing the cartoons on large pieces of canvas.

Originally there were ninety separate and distinct scenes, divided among seven tapestries. Five of the tapestries had on the left a bearded personage reading (Plate III, d), with fourteen scenes extending in double row to the right (Plates III, c, ca, cb, cc). What might have been a sixth tapestry of the same size and arrangement was woven in two separate pieces.

Originally the tapestries were eighteen feet high with a combined length of 472 feet. To-day they are worn away at the top, bottom and in the middle, so that the height is only fourteen feet. Of the original ninety scenes, seventy remain intact, and there are fragments of eight others, while twelve have entirely disappeared. The present total length is 328 feet.

In 1480, the tapestries were presented to the Cathedral of Angers by King René of Anjou, and for several centuries were proudly displayed on great occasions. But when tapestries, especially Gothic tapestries, went out of fashion at the end of the eighteenth century, the canons of the Cathedral decided to sell what was no longer useful. Unable to find a purchaser they retained them against their will. They even regarded them so lightly as to turn them over to base uses, spreading them over the orange trees in the greenhouse to keep these from being frostbitten, cutting some of them up into rugs, nailing strips of one on the stalls of the Bishop's stable to prevent his horses from bruising themselves. Not until the middle of the nineteenth century did anyone seem to suspect that these old rags might really be of some artistic importance. To-day, they are again regarded as the Cathedral's greatest treasure, to see which art lovers make pilgrimages from all over the world.

The details of the four scenes illustrated on Plates III, c, ca, cb, cc, are fascinating and give one a new idea of what people in the fourteenth century thought Saint John meant when he wrote the New Testament book of *Revelation*. Plate III, c, is based on verses 17 and 18 of *Chapter XII:*

And the dragon was wroth with the woman, and went to make war with the remnant of her seed, which keep the commandments of God, and have the testimony of Jesus Christ. And he stood upon the sand of the sea.

Saint John on the left, book in hand, watches the combat between the dragon and the faithful. The vegetation and trees are interesting as an early example of what was to be so richly developed in the Country Life tapestries of the fifteenth century. The *lm* monogram scattered thickly over the background perpetuates the memory of Louis, Duke of Anjou and Marie de Bretagne, his wife.

Plate III, ca (at the right of Plate III, c) is based on verse 1 of *Chapter XI:*

And there was given me a reed like unto a rod: and the angel stood, saying, Rise, and measure the temple of God, and the altar, and them that worship therein.

The ruler that the angel gives Saint John is like those employed by Medieval architects. The altar that Saint John is to measure is a splendid piece of cabinet work, of exquisite design, the arches and ornamentations of which have been forced into extraordinary distinctness by the use of stepped slits combined with strong hatchings contrasting boldly with the horizontal ribs.

Plate III, cb, (below Plate III, c) is based on verses 9, 10 and 11 of *Chapter IV:*

And when those beasts give glory and honour and thanks to him that sat on the throne, who liveth for ever and ever, the four and twenty elders fall down before him that sat on the throne, and worship him that liveth for ever and ever, and cast their crowns before the throne, saying, thou art worthy, O Lord, to receive glory and honour and power: for thou hast created all things, and for thy pleasure they are and were created.

Saint John on the left looking out of his Gothic pavilion, sees the twenty-four aged kings prostrate themselves before Christ. Note the starred background of the pointed oval that enshrines the figure of Christ. Note also the halos of Saint John and of Christ.

Plate III, cc, is based on verses 14, 15 and 16 of *Chapter XIV:*

And I looked, and behold a white cloud, and upon the cloud *one* sat like unto the Son of man, having on his head a golden crown, and in his hand a sharp sickle. And another angel came out of the temple, crying with a loud voice to him that sat on the cloud, Thrust in thy sickle, and reap: for the time is come for thee to reap; for the harvest of the earth is ripe. And he that sat on the cloud thrust in his sickle on the earth; and the earth was reaped.

An interesting feature of the scenes as originally placed in the tapestries, is that the coloured grounds alternated red and blue. Below the double row of scenes was vegetation. Above the double row of scenes were clouds. Below each scene were the verses on which it was based.

Of the Brussels Museum's Presentation (Plate 37 of *Hunter 1912*), contemporary with King Arthur and the Apocalypse, I have illustrated a detail, the head of Saint Joseph, on Plate III, g. Although the tapestry has many of the infirmities of great age, it still shows marvelous technical ability on the part of the weaver. The slits and stepped slits force the modeling of Saint Joseph's face and hands boldly forth, and the hatchings of his robe are boldly and effectively placed. The tapestry was discovered by a Spanish painter Señor Leo y Ecosura whose studio it long adorned. It attracted much attention at the Paris Tapestry Exposition of 1876 and at the Exposition des Primitifs Français of 1904.

ARRAS AND ARAZZI

While the French city of Arras gave its name to tapestries, in the English *arras,* the Italian *arazzi,* and the Spanish *paños de ras,* and must have been the most famous centre of tapestry weaving, at least for export, in the fourteenth and early fifteenth centuries, there remains only one small set of Gothic tapestries which we can positively and definitely attribute to it. This set is the one at the Cathedral of Tournai, picturing the lives and miracles of the locally famous Saints Piat and Eleuthère (Plates III, e, f).

Of the original 18 scenes, only 15 are left, 6 feet 10 inches high with combined length of 71 feet 8 inches.   They are badly hung with later and inappropriate border above and below, and need cleaning and repairing.

The two scenes illustrated on Plate III, e, are from the life of Saint Eleuthère, on the left, Baptising Pagans; on the right, Departure for Rome.   The inscription on the left reads:

When all the Christians of Tournai were crushed, many pagans had themselves baptised in the name of God in the place called Elandaing.

The inscription over the right reads:

Dead is the bishop of Tournai.   Wherefore the Christians of Tournai of true heart send Saint Eleuthère to Rome, and wish no other bishop.

Even on Plate III, e, can be discerned some of the slits that give strength to the design, especially on the horses' manes, while the texture detail on the page opposite brings vividly to the eye the skill with which weavers then employed hatchings to model roofs, and slits to outline the hoops of barrels, and the lines of buildings.   The trees too get their reality from slits aptly placed.

Compared with King Arthur and the Apocalypse, however, the series of Saint Piat and Saint Eleuthère is inferior in both design and weave.   So that if we had to judge the merits of Arras and Paris as ancient tapestry weaving centres by the examples that have survived, Arras would not be in the running.   But if we are to decide on the evidence of the literary records, the two cities rank side by side.   One fact is certain, we do not know enough about Paris and Arras ancient Gothic weaves to be able to tell them apart.   All we are justified in saying is that King Arthur is most like the Apocalypse, which we know from literary records was woven at Paris while the tapestry illustrated on Plate III, h, is most like Saint Piat and Saint Eleuthère, which we know was woven at Arras in 1402, because one of the missing scenes bore an inscription saying so.

JOURDAIN DE BLAYE

The tapestry illustrated on Plate III, h, is the first of a set of tapestries based on a thirteenth century *chanson de geste* that tells the story of Jourdain de Blaye. In the tapestry we see Fromont welcomed at Blaye by his nephew Girard whom he had come to assassinate. The second stanza of the inscription says:

"See Fromont coming by water in ships from Bordeaux to Blaye for the purpose of betraying Girard."

In the first stanza of the inscription the whole of the story of Jourdain de Blaye is suggested, how Fromont assassinated Girard, and tried to get hold of Girard's son Jourdain, who had been given into the keeping of Girard's faithful follower Renier; how Renier delivered his own son to die in Jourdain's place, and brought up Jourdain as his own son; how Jourdain, learning the secret of his birth when he grew up, avenged the death of his father by killing Fromont, and recovered his paternal estates that had been seized by Fromont.

Blaye, it should be remarked, is a French town on the Gironde, about twenty-five miles from Bordeaux, famous in the Middle Ages for possessing the tombs of Roland and Oliver, and the beautiful Aude. The floriation and animals of this tapestry are interesting to compare with those of the Saragossa Crucifixion (Plate IV, e, ea), which was woven a little later.

Mrs. Harold Pratt's Annunciation illustrated on Plate III, i, combines excellence of design with perfection of weave. It marks a distinct advance in the development of tapestry art. The weave of the architecture, the foliage (Plate XVII, c), of Gabriel's wings, of the Virgin's hair and halo, shows refinements that are a liberal education in the possibilities of tapestry technique. The texture effects are extraordinarily real. The surfaces of different materials stand apart from each other as in nature. Flesh and foliage and wood and pottery and

marble and draperies retain their distinctive qualities.   The
contrasts are far beyond the power of a painter's brush.

A glorious hunting tapestry is that of which two details
are illustrated on Plate III, k, ka.   Personages and horses
and dogs and wild boar and other animals are warm with
life.   The modeling of horses and draperies by the use of
hatchings is vigorous.

The tapestry illustrated on Plate III, j, is the largest and
best of its group, of which there are five in the Musée des
Arts Décoratifs, one in the Louvre, one in the Victoria and
Albert Museum, one in the collection of Mr. Frederick Pratt,
one in Mr. Kahn's collection.   Only the middle part of those
in the Musée des Arts Décoratifs is original, the top and bottom being restorations badly done.   But the personages making love and music and courteously picnicking by brook and
among trees are full of grace, with adorable costumes.   The
one in Mr. Pratt's collection is an immediate ancestor of the
"Training the Falcon" tapestry illustrated on Plate VI, k,
and was illustrated and described by my friend Joseph
Destrée in 1912 in the Annales de la Société Royale d'Arch-
éologie de Bruxelles.   Mr. Kahn's is almost entirely silk
enriched with gold.   It may be of a little later date than the
style of its foliage, being a provincial product, as is indicated
by the crudity of design of the faces of John the Baptist,
Saint Martin, and Saint Hugo.   The foliage and birds and
flowing waters of the duck-laden brook show great skill on the
part of the weaver, and great freedom in the manipulation of
wefts which are often curved and given irregular angles.

PLATE III, b.—KING ARTHUR, EARLY GOTHIC TAPESTRY OF MR. CLARENCE H. MACKAY, MADE AT PARIS IN

PLATES III. c, c, ca, cb, cc.—FOUR SCENES FROM THE GREAT APOCALYPSE AT ANGERS, THE ONLY FOURTEENTH CENTURY SET OF

PLATE III, d.—ONE OF THE PERSONAGES INTRODUCING THE
GROUPS OF SCENES IN DOUBLE ROW OF THE ANGERS APOCALYPSE.
THE BUTTERFLIES BEAR ON ONE WING THE ARMS OF ANJOU, ON
THE OTHER THAT OF BRITTANY. THE DUKE OF ANJOU'S WIFE
WAS MARIE OF BRITTANY

PLATE III, f.—DETAIL, SHOWING TEXTURE OF A SECTION OF TAPESTRY PICTURED OPPOSITE

PLATE III, g.—DETAIL SHOWING TEXTURE AND HEAD OF SAINT JOSEPH, IN THE BRUS-
SELS MUSEUM'S FOURTEENTH CENTURY PRESENTATION

For illustration of the entire tapestry, see Plate 37 of Hunter 1912

PLATE III, b.—SCENE FROM THE STORY OF JOURDAIN DE BLAYE, AN EARLY GOTHIC TAPESTRY IN

PLATE III, i.—ANNUNCIATION, EARLY GOTHIC TAPESTRY OF MRS. HAROLD I. PRATT

PLATE III, j.—EARLY GOTHIC VERDURE WITH PERSONAGES. INTERESTING TO COM-
PARE WITH THE SIMILAR PIECES IN THE MUSÉE DES ARTS DÉCORATIFS. FORMERLY IN THE
DELANNOY COLLECTION. JANSEN

PLATES III, k, ka.—TWO DETAILS OF A MAGNIFCENT EARLY GOTHIC HUNTING TAPESTRY. NOTE THAT THE LOWER RIGHT QUARTER OF "k" IS THE SAME AS THE UPPER LEFT QUARTER OF "ka." DEMOTTE

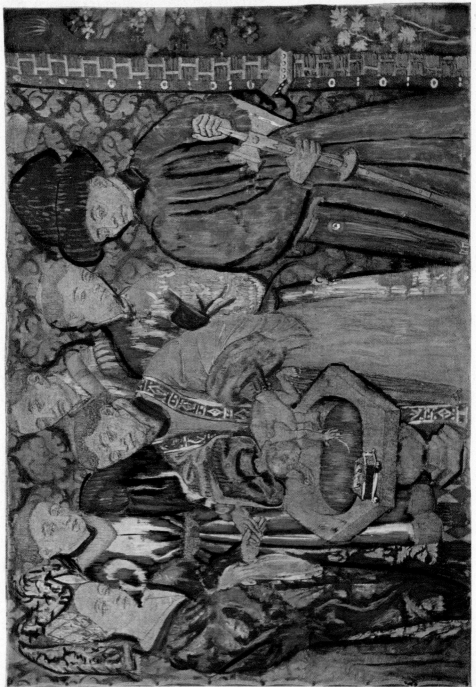

CHAPTER IV

GOTHIC RELIGIOUS AND ALLEGORICAL TAPESTRIES

CREDO AND SALVATION, PRODIGAL SON, VIRTUES AND VICES, SIBYLS
CRUCIFIXION AND PASSION, SEVEN SACRAMENTS, HOLY CROSS, MAGI
TRAJAN AND HERKINBALD, JERUSALEM, ESTHER, JEPTHAH, DAVID
SUSANNA, JUDITH, JOSEPH, PETER, FRENCH PROVINCIAL, TRIUMPHS
OF PETRARCH, BANQUET AND SUPPER, THE CERF FRAGILLE

The Gothic centuries were Christian centuries. Not only
Gothic religion but also Gothic history and romance and art
were passionately Christian.

To the Gothic centuries, all the ancient world before
Christ was the Old Dispensation, and all the world after Christ
was the New Dispensation. The wise men of the Old Dispensation were the Prophets; the wise men of the New Dispensation were the Apostles. Christian priests and theologians
of the Middle Ages searched the Old Testament, phrase by
phrase for verses that might seem to foreshadow or foretell
the events of the New Testament. They crowned their efforts
by dividing the Apostles' Creed into twelve articles, one for
each of the Apostles, and matching the Apostles with Prophets
displaying Latin inscriptions prophetic of the Creed.

For example, the first article of the Creed, *Credo in deum
omnipotentem, creatorem coeli et terrae,* fell to the apostle
Peter. The corresponding prophet was Jeremiah with, *Pat-
rem invocabitis qui terram fecit et condidit coelum.*

The entire list of Credo Apostles and Prophets as it
appears in an ancient illustrated manuscript (*Mâle Fifteenth,*
page 261) is as follows:

I.	God the Father (Creation)	Peter	Jeremiah
II.	Jesus Christ (Baptism)	Andrew	David
III.	Virgin Mary (Nativity)	James the Greater	Isaiah
IV.	Crucifixion	John	Daniel
V.	Descent into Hell and Resur-rection	Thomas	Hosea
VI.	Ascension	James the Less	Amos
VII.	Last Judgment	Philip	Zephaniah
VIII.	Holy Spirit	Bartholomew	Joel
IX.	Holy Catholic Church	Matthew	Micah
X.	Remission of Sins	Simon	Malachi
XI.	Resurrection of the Flesh	Thaddeus (Jude)	Zechariah
XII.	Life Everlasting	Matthias	Ezekiel

CREDO TAPESTRIES

I do not know of any complete *set* of Credo tapestries, containing all the articles. Possibly the last six articles of the Creed were never included. At any rate, the Credo tapestries listed below include only the first six articles. But in a single tapestry of the Hearst-Morgan collection (Plate XIX of *Ricci Morgan*), crude and provincial in design and weave, the entire Credo is pictured, in fifteen scenes, without prophets or apostles or inscriptions.

1. The Boston Credo (Plate IV, g) pictures the first four articles of the Creed.
2. The Duveen Credo pictures the second three.
3. The Leo XIII Credo pictures the first three.
4. The three Demotte fragments picture the first, parts of the second, the whole of the third, part of the fifth, the whole of the sixth. Two of these fragments were part of a tapestry picturing the first three articles, while the third fragment was part of a tapestry picturing the second three articles.

Of these tapestries the Demotte fragments are the latest (about 1510), the Leo XIII Credo the earliest (about 1475).

Each tapestry of the Credo group contains several scenes from the Credo, with an Apostle in the lower corner of each scene facing a Prophet in the opposite corner. For example, the Boston Credo (Plate IV, g) has four scenes, with a prophet in the lower left corner of each scene, and an apostle in the lower right corner of each scene, four prophets and four apostles in all.

While the Boston Credo pictures the first four articles of the the Apostles' Creed (Creation, Baptism, Nativity, Crucifixion), the Duveen Credo pictures only the second three (Crucifixion, Resurrection, Ascension), but with several subordinate scenes one of which is shown on Plate IV, h. These scenes subordinate to Crucifixion are: (1) Pilate washing his hands (2) Christ staggering with the Cross, with Envy pulling him roughly along, and Humility and Charity regarding pitifully (3) the Entombment. The scenes subordinate to Resurrection are: (1) Christ opening the gates of Hell (2) Christ followed by the released Prophets and Patriarchs, meeting Elijah and Enoch at the gates of Heaven. The scenes subordinate to Ascension are: (1) Christ taking leave of his Mother (*Plate IV, h*) (2) Christ in Heaven seated at the right hand of the Father Almighty, with the Holy Spirit at the left hand. The Boston Credo has no subordinate scenes.

The article of the Creed common to the Boston and the Duveen tapestries is Crucifixion. In both tapestries we have John as the Crucifixion apostle; but in the Boston tapestry we have Isaiah as the Crucifixion prophet, while in the Duveen tapestry we have Zechariah, and the ancient illustrated manuscript I quoted above presents Daniel as the personage. So it is evident there was considerable difference of opinion regarding who actually was the Crucifixion prophet.

Let us turn again to the Boston Credo (*Plate IV, g*). In the lower left corner of the four scenes (1) Creation (2) Baptism (3) Nativity (4) Crucifixion, we have the four Prophets (1) Jeremiah (2) Daniel (3) Isaiah (4) Hosea. In the lower right corner of the four scenes, we have the four Apostles (1) Peter (2) Andrew (3) James the Greater (4) John.

Each of the four Apostles bears his article of the Creed. For example:

4

(4) John, Crucifixion, *Passus sub poncio pylato. crucifixus. mortuus et sepultus, johannes.*

Each of the four Prophets bears his prophetic text. For example:

(4) Hosea, Crucifixion (*Hos. XIII,* 14), *O mors ero mors tua. morsus tuus ero inferne* (O Death I will be thy death; O grave I will be thy destruction.

It is interesting to note that in the Boston Credo the scene selected to illustrate Creation is the "Birth of Eve from the rib of Adam." The Creation scene of the Leo XIII Credo is much more comprehensive.

THE SALVATION GROUP

Of the salvation group I have illustrated five, two of which are in the collection of Mr. William Randolph Hearst (*Plates IV, j, ja*), one in the Château de Haar (*Plate IV, i*), one in the Louvre (*Plate IV, jb*), and one at Hampton Court (*Plate IV, k, ka*). The first four of these were formerly in the famous Berwick and Alba collection offered for sale in Paris in 1877. (See the illustrated catalogue).

At this point, I wish to acknowledge my indebtedness to Mr. D. T. B. Wood for his splendid articles on the Salvation and Credo tapestries, published in the *Burlington Magazine* in 1912 and 1914. His was the first serious attempt to bring order out of chaos.

The most important tapestries of the Salvation group still in existence are:

1. Creation. Haar-Alba (Plate 281 of *Hunter 1912*). Hearst-Toledo.
2. Redemption, design A. Hampton Court (Plates IV, k, ka). Burgos, Morgan-Knole (the left half).
2. Redemption, design B. Palencia. Hearst-Toledo. Saragossa.
3. Baptism. Hearst-Alba (Plate IV, j). Palencia. Hampton Court-Anglesey (the right half, Plate 17, *Hunter* 1912).
4. Nativity, design A. Burgos.
4. Nativity, design B. Palencia. Demotte (almost complete in two fragments).

5. Crucifixion. Haar-Alba (Plate IV, i). Hearst-Toledo. Burgos.
6. Resurrection. Hearst-Alba. Hearst-Toledo.
7. Ascension. Haar-Alba (Plate IV, ja). Palencia.
8. Last Judgment. Louvre-Alba (Plate IV, jb). Demotte.

Among small fragments are one from Creation in the
C. B. Alexander collection; one from Redemption in the Kelekian collection and another in the Victoria and Albert Museum;
one from Crucifixion in the Lawrence collection sold at auction
in New York, 1920.

The plan of the Salvation group is radically different from
that of the Credo group. Each Salvation tapestry has only
two Prophets and no Apostles (Plates IV, i, j, ja, k, ka).
For example, the Château de Haar Crucifixion (Plate IV, i)
has in the lower left corner Isaiah with the inscription (*Isai.
XXXV, 4*), *Ipse veniet et salvabit vos,* and in the lower right
corner Zechariah with the inscription (*Zech. XIII, 6*), *His
plagatus sum,* there wrongly attributed to *Isaie XIII.* The
Hampton Court Redemption has on the left Jeremiah with the
inscription (*Jer. IX, 21*), *Ascendit mors per fenestras,* and on
the right Moses with the inscription (*Deut. XXXI, 41*), *Reddam ulcionem hostibus.* The Hearst-Toledo Redemption has
on the left a prophet with scroll fast rolled up in his hand, and
on the right Jeremiah with the inscription (*Jer. IV, 1*), *Ejice
illos e facie mea* (Cast them out of my sight).

BAPTISM

Each Salvation tapestry also has several subordinate
scenes supplementing and explaining the titular scene, which
does not always occupy the centre of the tapestry or have the
prominence one might expect. For example, the titular scene
of Baptism (Plate IV, j) is on the left, "Christ baptized by
John the Baptist, with God in Heaven above." On the right
of the titular scene, John preaches to Homo, Natura, Abraham,
etc., while on the left Salome receives John's head. The
middle of the tapestry is occupied by the Resurrection of

Lazarus, which is symbolic of Baptism that is regarded as a sacrament conferring New Life. In the lower corners are prophets as usual. The one on the right is David with a Latin inscription which translated reads: (*Psalms XLV,* 4) "Gird thyself with thy sword upon thy thigh, O thou most mighty." On the left of David are grouped beautiful, crowned ladies symbolic of the Virtues and Vices. The Virtue with shield bearing the pelican that gives its blood for its young, just as Christ gave his blood for Humanity, is Charity. With her left hand she points to the scene in the tower where Judas sells His Master for thirty pieces of silver, while her right hand passes the gauntlet of combat to the Seven Vices, among them *invidia* (Envy) who receives the gauntlet, *superbia* (Pride), and *luxuria* (Luxury). On the right of the Judas scene, the Tempter with a spiked club holds as prisoners *natura* (Nature) in chains, *homo* (man), *Jan* (John the Baptist), *Abraha* (Abraham). Still farther to the right, in the upper right corner of the tapestry, Christ as a Christian knight in armor receives from Charity a banner bearing the Five Wounds, and from Humility a helmet with Crown of Thorns.

CRUCIFIXION

The continuation of this last scene is found in Crucifixion (Plate IV, i) where Christ as a Christian knight in armor, and mounted, leads the Virtues in battle against the Vices. As this battle indicates, Gothic Christianity is full of Symbolism. The Crucifixion, to the Christian mind, was to be taken not only literally, but also symbolically. It was to be regarded not only as the Passion of Christ but also as the Battle of Christ, in the glorious struggle of Good against Evil. The scrolls held by the angels on each side of the Cross in our Crucifixion tapestry bear an inscription reading: *Pange, lingua, gloriosi prelium certaminis* (Sing, tongue, the battle of the glorious conflict), which is the *first* line of a Latin hymn composed in the sixth century A. D. by Fortunatus, Bishop of

Poitiers. The *second* line of the hymn is: "Describe the noble triumph on the Cross, symbolic."

The seven Virtues that attend the armored Christ are Affection, Humility with a cross, Patience, Chastity holding a lily and riding a mule, Sobriety, Devotion to God riding a deer, Charity riding a lion and pouring freely from her pitcher. The seven Vices opposing Christ are: Pride mounted on a camel, brandishing a sword, and crested with a peacock; Envy with flaming spear, mounted on a dragon of hideous mien; Avarice carrying a rake and riding a goat; Luxury, holding a mirror and riding a pig, with a nude woman pictured on her shield; Laziness, Anger, and another.

In the lower corners of the the tapestry are the two prophets: on the left, Isaiah whose scroll reads, (*Isaiah, XXXV,* 4) *Ecce veniet et salvabit vos* (Behold he will come and save you); on the right Zechariah, whose scroll reads (*Zech. XIII,* 6), *His plagatus sum* (Those with which I was wounded). The verse refers to the wounds of Christ, and the meaning is made clear by quoting the whole: "And one shall say unto him, what are these wounds in thine hands? Then he shall answer, those with which I was wounded in the house of my friends."

In the upper corner of the tapestry are two allegorical figures representing the two Testaments that by Christ were reconciled: on the left, standing on Mount Sinai, the Old Testament (*vetus testamentum*), with banner bearing the Mosaic tables several times repeated, pendant from her trumpet; on the right, the New Testament (*novum testamentum*), with banner bearing the Cup of the Eucharist.

REDEMPTION

The most human tapestry of the Salvation group is Redemption. It comes in two different designs. The Hampton Court and Burgos Redemptions have design A; the Palencia, Hearst-Toledo and Saragossa Redemptions have design B.

The upper middle part of design A (Plate IV, k, ka) is occupied by the enthroned Trinity, surrounded by angels, and with clouds separating them from the Earth below. The Trinity are represented as three crowned kings, with sceptre and symbolic globe, all alike except that the globe of Christ is underfoot in sign of Humility, and His sceptre pointed down in sign of Mercy.

Just below the Trinity, we see the Virtues arguing for and against Man, Mercy and Peace opposing Justice and Truth. Justice carries a sword, Truth a book, Mercy a lily branch, Peace an olive branch. This is the famous "Paradise Law Suit" so often presented on the stage in the fifteenth century. It was the vital and introductory act of Arnoul Greban's famous Passion. Adam in Purgatory prays God for release. Justice in Heaven maintains that Man does not deserve pity. Mercy admits that Man has sinned but pleads extenuating circumstances. The case after long argument is finally won by Mercy, and God consents to sacrifice his only Son for the Salvation of Man. Then follows the Annunciation.

At the left of the Trinity scene is a Gothic pavilion, the Temple of the Virtues, two of whom display a picture symbolic of Luxury, which is also illustrated by the group still farther to the left.

At the right of the Trinity, *homo* (man) is assailed by the three armored Vices, *luxuria* (Luxury) who pierces his heart, *avaricia* (Avarice), *gula* (Gluttony), and by *temptator* (the Tempter) with trumpet, and is defended by *spes* (Hope).

Still farther to the right, sits Christ attended by the Virtues.

In the foreground of the tapestry, on the left, Mercy restrains Justice from running her sword into Man who has fallen a victim to *luxuria* (Luxury) and other Vices. In the foreground, on the right, Man is made a Christian knight by the Virtues, *gracia dei* (Grace of God) giving him a breastplate, and *pax* (Peace) giving him a helmet, while *misericordia* (Mercy) administers the oath.

The prophets in the lower corners of the tapestry are: Jeremiah at the left with (*Jer. IX*, 21) *ascendit mors per fenestras* (Death is come up unto our windows); and Moses on the right with (*Deut. XXXII*, 41) *reddam ulcionem hostibus* (I will render vengeance to mine enemies).

Design B is utterly unlike design A. The Trinity scene much modified has been transferred to the left of the tapestry and its place in the middle is taken by the enthroned Vices. Between the two thrones is Man seated beside Nature while Work offers him a shovel, Nature of course being the part of Man that tends to lead him astray unless restrained by Work. Beneath the enthroned Vices is the Tempter scene. In the upper right corner of the tapestry, Luxury sits enthroned alone, immodestly unclothed for conquest, while Man is conducted towards her by Flesh, Nature, Sin, and Enticement. Pleasure sits at the right of the throne. The prophets in design B are Jeremiah on the left (*Jer. XV*, 1) *Ejice illos e facie mea* (Cast them out of my sight), and David on the right with scroll not yet unrolled.

L'UN ET L'AUTRE

The famous Paradise Law Suit mentioned above was sometimes developed and presented separately (Page 425 of Volume II of *Julleville Mystères*). The "Law Suit between Mercy and Justice," a short mystery of about 2000 verses, though copied largely from Greban's Passion, is evidently an attempt at rejuvenation, and contains some new elements. The action opens with a dialogue inspired by Lucretius rather than by the Bible. Earth begins by explaining magniloquently the secrets of germination performed in her breast by Nature. Two tiny nude personages, *l'un* and *l'autre* (lower left quarter of a Late Gothic Tournai tapestry belonging to Bernheimer of Munich, and illustrated on Plate XIV

of *Koch Kunstwerke*) complain to the Earth that they have
been thrown into the world naked.   Earth explains that it is
the fault of Adam.   Suddenly are heard the groans of Adam
in Purgatory, and the scene changes to Heaven.

NATIVITY

The design of the Burgos Nativity is utterly unlike that
of the Palencia Nativity.   The Nativity scene is on the right
of the Burgos panel but in the middle of the Palencia panel.
Scenes of the Palencia panel that do not appear in the Burgos
panel·are: the Circumcision of Jesus, Augustus and the Sibyl,
the Presentation of Jesus, the Meeting of Jesus and John the
Baptist as Children.   The Demotte Nativity, in two fragments, is like the Palencia Nativity.

STORY OF MAN

A splendid tapestry in the Stroganoff collection, Rome,
presents the Story of Man in four scenes.   In the upper corners trumpeting angels celebrate Man's eventual victory.
Scene one shows *homo* (Man) consecrated to Christian life by
a bishop, while Virtues look approvingly on.   In Scene two,
Man in armor with a wealth of plumes springing from his
helmet and bearing a lily branch, sets forth encouraged by
fortitudo (Bravery) and *sapiencia* (Wisdom) but discouraged by *invidia* (Envy).   In Scene three, we see pictured
the struggle between Good and Bad in Man as represented by
Virtues and Vices.   In Scene four, Man having fought the
good fight, kneels before the Trinity, while angels with organ,
and from manuscript music, make sweet harmony.

MUSIC AND DANCING

Among other tapestries without prophets developed from
the Redemption subject are two in the Saragossa cathedrals,
one with Music, the other with Dancing, as the principal subject.   Music shows Christ enthroned in Heaven, with Mercy

and Peace opposing Justice and Truth in the Earth below, but the main and titular scene consists of a group of musicians attacked by Justice.   The musician in most immediate danger is Man with a flute, but the lady with the mandolin is evidently frightened.   The lady at the organ, the lady with the harp, and the man with the drum, do not seem yet to have seen the enemy any more than have the gentleman and lady at the table on the extreme left, she singing while he plays the flute.   In the foreground of the tapestry appears the same scene as in Redemption, but more extended, Man on the ground threatened by Justice whom Mercy and Peace restrain.

There are duplicates of this Music tapestry in the cathedral at Palencia and in Hampton Court Palace.   The Hampton Court one has Latin verses below in Gothic letters which read translated: "Before the judge in the presence of the Virtues, Justice and Mercy argue.   Guilt is threatened by Justice but reconciled by Mercy. When blessed Fortitude appears, the Faults always leave the field.   The Sins eternally are chastised by the Virtues who do not die."

The Saragossa Dancing shows a pair of lightly clad ladies posing rhythmically in the foreground, with Vices mounted on weird animals riding up from the right, and groups of musicians and lovers throughout the rest of the panel.   There is a duplicate of this tapestry in the Cathedral of Palencia, and at Hampton Court a modified version of the right half of it, with Latin verses below which read translated: "Sin beginning at first as a trifle, becomes deadly and profane. The Seven Sins just as they are generated in the World, here fly figuratively."   A pig bears *luxuria,* a camel *impenitentia,* a donkey *invidia,* etc.

HUNOLSTEIN VIRTUES AND VICES

Also inspired by the Salvation group are the famous Hunolstein Virtues and Vices, a set of four tapestries now in the collection of Mr. William Randolph Hearst, exhibited in

Paris in 1880 and called by Eugene Müntz "this priceless set, as beautiful as it is little known." The dominant characters of each of the four tapestries, high on a throne in the middle (with supplementary and explanatory scenes divided into panels by Gothic columns and arches) are: (1) *fortitudo* (Bravery), (2) *Caritas* (Charity), (3) *Superbia* (Pride), (4) *Ira* (Anger), two of them Virtues and two of them Vices. Originally there may have been a set of fourteen, seven Virtues and seven Vices.

THE PRODIGAL SON

Closely related to the Redemption subject is that of the Prodigal Son. One of the finest of the Brussels Late Gothic "Prodigal Son" tapestries showing the influence of the Salvation group, hangs in the country residence of Mrs. Nicholas F. Brady (Plate IV, 1). In the lower left corner of the tapestry Luxury and Dissipation and Worldliness tempt the youth to enjoy with them pleasures forbidden at home. Above, the youth distinguished by a massive, twisted golden necklace, receives his inheritance from his aged father and sets forth upon his career of independence. In the middle foreground, the youth seated beside Dissipation, hands her a purseful of money, while a page with wonderful plumed hat ransacks the treasure chest for other gifts. On the left, below, Luxury holds the youth's attention. On the right, below, Gluttony brings him a dish of cherries, pears and plums, while round cakes and a goblet of wine stand on the damask-covered table before him. In the middle of the tapestry, at the top, the three Virtues who will ultimately rescue him, Repentance, Humility, and Mercy, read the Book of Knowledge. On the left, Luxury and her sister Vices beguile him and his gay companions. On the right, music helps lead him astray. The column that separates the scene in the upper left corner from the rest of the tapestry is adorned with a wreath expressive of the young man's glee at emancipation from parental control.

Similar to the Brady tapestry, but differing in details, is the Prodigal Son in the Cathedral of Palencia.

Another Brussels version of the Prodigal Son story is pictured on a tapestry exhibited by Leo Nardus at Brussels. (Plate VII of *Destrée Brussels*, 1905.) In the middle foreground under a Gothic canopy the Son receives his inheritance, while the Author of the tapestry is seen through a window on the left. In the lower left corner of the tapestry the Father addresses good advice to his Son whom *Mundus* (the World) already has hold of. In the lower right corner, the Son influenced by *amor sui* (Self-love) embraces Luxury. The pendant of this tapestry, showing the Ruin, Reform, and Rehabilitation of the Prodigal Son, was exhibited at Bruges in 1902.

In the upper right corner of a Brussels Prodigal Son tapestry formerly in the J. Lowengard collection the connection with the Bible is emphasized. Christ attended by Mercy with a ring and by Compassion welcomes Adam who like the Prodigal Son, is symbolic of Man in general. The scroll over Adam's head reads (*Luke XV*, 19 and also 21) *Non sum dignus vocari filius tuus* (I am not worthy to be called thy son). The scroll over Christ's head reads (*Luke XV*, 22) *Cito proferte stolam primam* (Quickly bring forth the best robe). An angel holds the robe richly embroidered with stars.

Much more human and closer to life (but inferior in design and weave) is the Tournai Prodigal Son tapestry in the Cluny Museum.

THE WORLD

Crude and much repaired but entertaining because they are so obviously sermons, are the three World tapestries made in Tournai about 1520, now in the Museé des Arts Décoratifs, with French inscription above and French names on the personages, all in Gothic lettering. The inscription of one reads translated: "The World hangs only by a thread because of the Sins that are seen at present to reign. But the

Church humbly pacifies the Divine Wrath that wishes to cut down the tree.''

The main scene shows a tree from which hangs a globe symbolizing the World. On the right *ire divin* swings an axe while on the left kneel *l'église, oraison,* and *abstinence.* The wickedness of the world in the first quarter of the sixteenth century is pictured by *Convoitise* who refuses her treasures to *mendiant;* by *vanite* who works at her mirror, by *apetit desordone* and *friandise* whose pleasure is the table, by *fol amour* and *jonesse* who give themselves to music and flirtation.

THE PRINCE OF WICKEDNESS

In the Salvation group all the Virtues and all the Vices except Tempter are feminine. In the three Tournai World tapestries, the Virtues and part of the Vices are feminine. In Edson Bradley's magnificent *prince de malice* (Prince of Wickedness, Plates s, h, of the *Subscribers' Edition*), 11 feet 4 by 15 feet 5, made about 1460, and formerly lent to the Metropolitan Museum of Art, while the seven Virtues are feminine, the eighteen Vices are all masculine. This tapestry contrasts the Vices with the Virtues by displaying on the right the Castle of the Prince of Wickedness, and at the extreme left, part of the Castle of Goodness. Trees separate the two castles. The architectural development is superb. Gothic columns and arches and towers and tiled floor and leaded windows set the personages forth. The Prince of Wickedness with long beard and hair, both elaborately curled, elaborate crown, and pomegranate-brocaded robe, sits high on a jeweled throne. His courtiers (Vices) as well as those of the Court of Goodness (Angels and Virtues) are also richly clad. The attendants nearest the Prince of Wickedness are *avarice* with jeweled cup, *orgoeul* with mirror, *flaterie,* and *gloutonnerie.* In the foreground Sin (*pechee*) is talking eloquently to Wrath (*yre*) while *envie* listens impatiently.   Vices in the background are *luxure, ipocrisie, barat,* and *trayson;* on the right, and on the left, *faux report, discort, despit,* and *malebouche.*   Two of the Vices, *yre* and *avarice* wear beards.   The others are clean shaven.   In the adjacent but hostile Castle of Goodness, three warrior maidens in full armor are on guard.   Their names are *prudence, carite, atempranse* (Temperance).   Peaceful Virtues are *castite, sobresce, bonte, humilite.*   At the upper left are three Angels.

THE SIBYLS

In developing the New Dispensation out of the Old Dispensation, the Middle Ages employed the authority not only of Jewish Prophets but also of Pagan Sibyls.   The Pagan world like the Jewish world was part of the Old Dispensation. The Sibyls of the Pagan world correspond to the Prophets of the Jewish world.   In the Pagan world the Sibyls were the oracles of God.   Princes and potentates sought their advice on affairs of state, and endeavored from their answers to forecast the future.   The Sibylline books were the Bible and the ultimate authority of the Roman Kingdom, and continued so after it grew into the Roman Republic and into the Roman Empire.   It was the Cumaean Sibyl who brought to Tarquin the Proud nine books written in Greek which she offered for a certain price.   When he refused, she burned three, and offered the remaining six at the same price.   When he again refused, she burned three more, and offered the remaining three at the same price.   Impressed by her pertinacity, Tarquin bought them.   They were preserved in the temple of Jupiter on the Capitol, and a college of curators assisted by Greek interpreters, was appointed to consult them, on command of the Senate, regarding religious observances necessary to avert pestilence, earthquakes, and other extraordinary calamities, and to expiate prodigies.   Through the Sibylline books, the religion and civilization of Rome were guided along lines fundamentally Greek.

When the Roman Empire became Christian, the Sibyls also became Christian. They were a favorite subject of Gothic painters. Eight of the Sibyls are pictured on the walls of a chapel in the Cathedral of Amiens, with inscriptions in both Latin and French.

The Sibyl scene that appears most often in tapestries is that of "Augustus and the Tiburtine Sibyl" found in the Mazarin and other Triumphs of Christ (Chapter VII); and in the Nativity (design B) of the Salvation series. There were also tapestries devoted exclusively to the Sibyls. Two panels of such a set made in Tournai at the beginning of the sixteenth century, are in the Duveen collection. Each panel has a canopied fountain in the middle, with a Sibyl on either side. One panel pictures the Erythraean and Cumaean Sibyls; the other panel pictures the Tiburtine and Delphic Sibyls. The Tiburtine Sibyl is accompanied by peacock above and lion below; the Delphic Sibyl by deer above and centaur below; the Erythraean Sibyl by unicorn below; the Cumaean Sibyl by falcon above and griffin below. The Erythraean Sibyl holds in her hand a sprouting twig symbolic of the rod of Jesse, and hence of the maternity of the Virgin. The Sibyl's Latin scroll reads translated:

In the last age, God shall humble himself, the divine offspring shall become human, divinity and humanity shall be united, he shall lie on hay, etc.

The Cumaean Sibyl holds a towel symbolic of the Birth of Christ. Her scroll reads:

The Cumaean Sibyl foretold the sign of Judgment. The Earth shall be moist with sweat, the King shall come from heaven to reign throughout the centuries actually present in the flesh, etc.

Even more dramatic seems to me the Latin inscription that accompanies the painted Cumaean Sibyl at Amiens, an inscription taken from Virgil's Fourth Eclogue, and hence seeming to enroll Virgil himself as one of those announcing Christ. It reads :

Magnus ab integro seculorum nascitur ordo
Jam redit et virgo, redeunt saturnia regna,
Jam nova progenies celo demittitur alto.

The great cycle of the ages is born anew.
Now returns the Virgin and the rule of Saturn.
Now from lofty heaven a new race descends.

CRUCIFIXION TAPESTRIES

The earliest large Crucifixion tapestries in existence are the two in the marvelous collection of the Saragossa cathedrals, 13 feet 8 inches high by 27 feet 7 inches wide, dating from about 1440.   Both tapestries once belonged to Ferdinand the Catholic, who bequeathed them to his son Archbishop Alonso, who bequeathed them to the Cathedral of La Seo. The one of the two that is best preserved I have illustrated on Plates IV, e, ea.   The Crucifixion is in the middle, with the Road to Calvary on the left, and the Descent into Hell, and Resurrection, on the right.   Above, the souls of the two thieves are seen being carried away, the soul of the repentant Thief on the left, by an angel up to Heaven; the soul of the unrepentant Thief on the right, by a devil down in Hell.   At the foot of the Cross, the soldiers throw dice for Christ's robe.

Similar to these two tapestries in plan and general arrangement is the great Crucifixion of the Brussels Cinquentenaire Museum (13 feet 11 by 29 feet 11), but later in date (about 1460) with foliage and costumes more highly developed.   Still a little later (about 1480) but rather archaic in details, is the set of four Passion tapestries at the Cathedral of Angers, which Time has treated harshly.   Still later in date (about 1515) is the small Crucifixion rich with gold from the Dreicer-Hainauer collection, now in the Metropolitan Museum of Art.   All of these tapestries except the last are typically French in design (Page 22 of *Destrée Cinquenten-*

aire) but I see nothing in design or weave that distinguishes them widely from the great Tournai sets picturing the Trojan War and the stories of Esther, Alexander, and Caesar. There is a duplicate of the middle section of the Brussels Crucifixion in the collection of the Viscount de Roda, Madrid.

INSTRUMENTS OF THE PASSION

Tapestries growing out of the Crucifixion are those picturing the Instruments of the Passion in the Cathedral of Angers, and in Notre Dame de Nantilly at Saumur, made in France at the beginning of the sixteenth century. The former is in three pieces 5 feet 6 inches high with combined length of 56 feet 3 inches. There are seven scenes, each showing an angel with Instrument, (1) the purse of Judas, (2) the lance, (3) the flagellation column and whips, (4) the pitcher and basin from which Pilate washed his hands, (5) the Cross, (6) the pail and sponge from which Our Lord drank gall and vinegar, (7) the shroud. Beside each angel is a large eight-line stanza of French verse in Gothic lettering, except that the first angel has two such stanzas. The background of the scenes is covered with millefleur verdure, birds and animals. Over the inscriptions appears the coat-of-arms of Pierre de Rohan who died in 1513, and who was the father of the Bishop of Angers, François de Rohan.

THE SEVEN SACRAMENTS

The splendid Seven Sacraments tapestry of the Metropolitan Museum (Plates IV, a, b, c) consists of five fragments containing seven scenes. Originally the tapestry contained fourteen scenes, the upper row illustrating the Origin of the Sacraments, the lower row illustrating the Sacraments as Celebrated in the Fifteenth Century.

At first glance several of the scenes, notably those picturing the "Origin of the Sacraments," seems to take one back to the beginning of the fifteenth century. But the costumes of the scenes picturing the ''Seven Sacraments as Celebrated in the Fifteenth Century,'' make it impossible that the tapestry can have been designed much before 1440.

Two of the fragments are mounted wrong side out, which illustrates the fact that, except for difference of direction, tapestry pictures are alike on face and back. Furthermore, as time goes on, tapestries fade more on the face than on the back, and the loose threads that mark the back are apt to disappear, so that it is easy for an ignorant repairer to be led into error. This applies not only to the pictures but also to the French Gothic inscriptions, two of which in the Seven Sacraments are mounted wrong side out.

On Plates 46 and 47 of *Hunter 1912,* I arranged the five fragments (reversing those mounted wrong side out) to show the relative position they occupied in the ancient tapestry. These illustrations also made clear the fact that originally the tapestry had a brick frame with floriation outside, and that round Gothic columns separated the different scenes.

The seven scenes that appear on the five fragments are:

I. Christ baptized by John the Baptist, the Origin of Baptism.
II. Fifteenth century Baptism.
III. Jacob Blessing two Children, the Origin of Confirmation.
IV. Adam and Eve married by God, the Origin of Marriage.
V. Fifteenth century Marriage.
VI. Unction of Honor given to David at Hebron, the Origin of Extreme Unction.
VII. Fifteenth century Extreme Unction.

One of the missing scenes is Confirmation and Tonsure as celebrated in the fifteenth century. Strangely enough, this fragment now hangs in the Victoria and Albert Museum (Plate IV, d).

The inscriptions that remain were of great help in studying the tapestry (See my article in the *Burlington Magazine* of December, 1907). While the inscriptions of Marriage and Extreme Unction are still complete, we have of the Confirma-

5

tion and Tonsure inscription only the first two-thirds, and of the Baptism inscription only the last third. The following illustration shows the way in which these mutilated inscriptions appear at the top of the Origin of Baptism. Below the illustration I have placed the transcription:

Adfin qua vigheur sabandonnent. creatures prelas leur/tores de lescriptures. Confirmacion et tonsure. et de che samblanche en d/t ou sainct baptesme purgies.
jacob le patriarche fist. qui ses mains sur ij enfa/ue de jourdain lauez.

The rhyme helps to complete the lines describing Confirmation and Tonsure. Originally they read as follows:

> *Adfin qua vigheur sabandonnent*
> *Creatures, prelas leur donnent*
> *Confirmacion et tonsure*
> *Et de che samblanche en desure*
> *Jacob le patriarche fist,*
> *Qui ses mains sur deux enfants mist.*

The translation is:

In order that mortals may surrender themselves to strength, prelates give them confirmation and tonsure, and other similar holy offices. Jacob the patriarch did it, who placed his hands on two children (Plates IV, c, d).

The part of the inscription referring to Baptism reads in translation:

> ....riters of scripture
> ....by holy baptism purified
> ....water of Jordan washed

Plate IV, b, shows the fragment containing Marriage and Extreme Unction, as it hangs mounted wrong side out in the Museum. Being mounted wrong side out of course reverses the direction, so that Extreme Unction comes on the left before Marriage, and so that the vertical brick column which should be on the right, at the end of the tapestry, appears

on the left.   Note that the inscriptions above the two scenes
are also reversed and that the repairer has worked the nun's
headdress into the band carrying the inscription.

The two inscriptions read as follows:

Le sacrement de mariage. dont multiplie humain lignage.
moustra dieus quand adam crea. et de sa coste eve fourma.
qui fu des femmes la premiere. et a adam amie chiere.

The sacrament of marriage, by which the human race multiplies, was
instituted by God when he created Adam and from his rib formed Eve, who
was of women the first and sweetheart to Adam.

Mais la derniere unction. qui contre la temptation.
de sa vertu donne vigheur. moustra lunction dhonneur.
faite en ebron a david roi. pour estre de plus fort arroi.

Also extreme unction, which against temptation by its virtue gives
strength, was instituted by the unction of honor given in Hebron to King
David to increase his power.

Plate IV, a, picturing Fifteenth Century Baptism, gives the
colours of this wonderful tapestry, which though in bad condition still retains much of its ancient power.   Even the sections
where dark brown wefts have rotted away leaving warps bare
do not stand out unpleasantly.   But the patches are annoying, especially the large one in Fifteenth Century Marriage,
although it is not only ancient but from another part of the
same tapestry.

Design and weave of the Seven Sacraments tapestry are
wonderfully vigorous.   The faces are full of character and
individuality.   The entire surface is richly patterned and
strongly textured.   The weave is coarse, 12 warps to the inch,
and the ribs are flat as is common in Gothic tapestries
before 1480.

Boldly the garments flow in vertical Gothic folds, folds
quite as interesting in the plain robes as in the rich damasks
and velvets and embroideries and ermine.

Boldly the personages stand forth from damask-patterned wall and tiled floor, and from one another, line contrast being accentuated by mass contrast of reds, blue-greens, golden yellows.

Boldly the different scenes are separated by round Gothic columns with jeweled mouldings and capitals while a woven-brick border with jewels inside and floriation outside frames the whole tapestry, pushing back the damassé background, and giving additional semblance of relief to the personages. Light and shade are artfully employed to increase the rotundity of columns and drapery folds, and the thickness of the enframing bricks.

The border of this great tapestry is one of its most distinctive features. It is the earliest Gothic all-round border that I have found. It is the only Gothic border that is heavily shadowed. Possibly this tapestry is the "Histoire du Sacrament" bought at Bruges in 1440 by Philip the Good, Duke of Burgundy, to decorate the chamber of his son the young Count of Charolais, known to history as Charles the Bold. It hung for centuries in the chapel of Ferdinand and Isabella at Granada, and by 1871 was in such bad repair that the authorities discarded it. It was then purchased by the painter Fortuny and with the other furnishings of Fortuny's studio sold at auction in Paris in 1875.

Possibly the bride and groom in Fifteenth Century Marriage, and the father and mother in Fifteenth Century Baptism, were intended to suggest Philip the Good and his wife Isabella of Portugal. Certainly the bride and mother look strangely like Van Eyck's portrait of Isabella, as copied in the seventeenth century (See Dimier in *La Renaissance de l'Art Français,* September, 1922). Likewise both Philip the Good and his youthful son Charles, as pictured in my manuscript illustration on Plate XVIII, b, remind one of the tapestry husband and father.

THE EXALTATION OF THE HOLY CROSS

Two magnificent tapestries from the middle of the fifteenth century in the collection of the Saragossa cathedrals, one of them 14 feet high by 36 feet long, the other a little smaller through the injuries of time, picture the "Exaltation of the Holy Cross." They were presented to La Seo by Archbishop Dalmau de Mur y Cervellon (1431–1458). The story is told in Latin Gothic inscriptions. The first of the tapestries shows: (1) The Persian King Chosroes riding out of Jerusalem with the Cross; (2) Chosroes seated on his golden throne resigns in favor of his son; (3) Chosroes sits on a magnificent throne built for the purpose, with the Cross beside him, and seeks to be worshipped as God; (4) The Roman Emperor (Byzantine Roman) Heraclius, consecrating himself to God and the Holy Cross, defeats the son of Chosroes in single combat.

The second tapestry shows: (1) Chosroes refusing to become a Christian, Heraclius decapitates him and recovers the Cross. The youngest son of Chosroes is baptized. (2) Heraclius riding in triumph with the Cross, is about to enter Jerusalem, when the gateway suddenly turns to blank wall. Above the gate appears an angel who says, "When the King of Heaven about to receive the sacraments of the Passion, passed through this entrance, he wore no glistening crown and rode no splendid charger, but seated on a humble ass left an example of humility to his disciples." (3) Heraclius barefoot and in chemise carries the Cross through the wall that opens for his passage. (4) Heraclius kneels before an altar on which he has placed the Cross.

THE VENGEANCE OF JESUS CHRIST

A most interesting but rather gruesome Gothic tapestry (See my frontispiece in colour) from the middle of the fifteenth century, at the Metropolitan Museum of Art, pictures the Capture of Jerusalem by Titus in the year 70 A.D. It is one of a group illustrating the "Vengeance of Jesus Christ," and the punishment inflicted upon those responsible for the death of the Saviour. Eight large fragments of the group, from at least three different sets of different design and quality and date, are the two formerly in the Heilbronner collection (Illustrated in the sale catalogue, Paris, 1921); the two in the W. R. Coe collection (Illustrated in the Charles sale catalogue, New York, 1920); the one in the Seligmann-Rey collection; the one in the church of Notre Dame de Nantilly at Saumur (Photo 554 *Archives;* one in the Vienna Museum for Art and Industry (Plate 9 of *Kurt Tournai*); one in the Lyons Museum.

The tapestries arranged in the order of the story are:

I. The Vienna piece shows the reception by Pilate of the messenger sent by Vespasian to secure the Veronica. As the tapestry shows, the voyage of the messenger had been rough.

II. One of the Heilbronner pieces shows on the left Vespasian cured of leprosy by the Veronica (cf. Mr. Philip Lehman's Veronica rich with gold, Plates VII, e, f).

III. The Lyons piece shows Nero on his throne giving instructions to Vespasian, on the left; and on the right, Vespasian and Titus capturing a city in Palestine.

IV. One of the Coe pieces shows the city of Jotopata in Palestine surrendering to Vespasian. After the surrender, its defender, the Jewish historian Josephus, became an ally of the Romans.

V. The Saumur piece shows the coronation of Vespasian as Roman Emperor.

VI. The Seligmann-Rey piece shows some of the cruelties of the siege of Jerusalem, hands being cut off, etc.

VII. The second of the Coe pieces shows the hand-cutting scene with Titus looking on, while starving Jews inside the walls cook and eat little children, and others swallow their money in the effort to save it from the Roman conquerors.

VIII. The second of the Heilbronner pieces shows the Roman soldiers attacking; and a Jewish woman cooking and eating her own child, as told by Josephus in his Jewish Antiquities.

IX. The Metropolitan Museum piece shows Titus triumphant after the fall of Jerusalem, with the Ark of the Convenant and other treasures of the Jewish Temple prominently displayed. In the foreground the Jews who swallowed their money are forced to give it up.

The two Coe tapestries have four-line French Gothic inscriptions at the top, but the upper three lines on one of them do not belong to the tapestry and have been added from a ''Lerian and Laureole'' set.

THE MAGI, TRAJAN AND HERKINBALD

Two extremely important tapestries from the middle of the fifteenth century are the ''Adoration of the Magi'' (Plate XXI, fa) about 12 feet square, and the ''Justice of Trajan and Herkinbald,'' 14 feet high by 41 feet long, at the Museum of Berne. Both bear the sewed-on arms of George of Saluces, Bishop of Lausanne, who died in 1461, and both were transferred from the Cathedral of Lausanne to Berne in 1536. Both are characteristically Tournai in design and weave. The brick wall and the floriation of the Adoration suggest those of the Metropolitan Museum's Seven Sacraments. Above the ox and ass of the Adoration is the inscription *Non redietis ad heroden*. The Trajan and Herkinbald tapestry pictures, in four scenes, the Justice of Trajan and the Justice of Herkinbald, each in two scenes, with long Latin Gothic inscriptions below each scene. Probably the cartoons were based on paintings of Roger van der Weyden, anciently in the Brussels City Hall, but destroyed during the bombardment of 1695. In the first scene, on the left of the tapestry, with Roman double eagle above, Trajan riding at the head of his army, is stopped by a widow who beseeches him to punish her son's murderer. Impatiently Trajan bids her wait until he returns. ''But you will never return,'' cried the widow. Impressed by her words, Trajan dismounts, and as shown in the tapestry has justice done immediately. The widow was right. Trajan never did return. He died on his way back from the Orient. There is a Late Gothic tapestry version of this first picture in the Duveen collection. The second scene shows, on the right, the skull of Trajan presented to Pope Gregory who, moved by the justice of Trajan, prayed (on the left) that the soul of Trajan be admitted to Paradise. The tongue of Trajan was found to be still undecayed, a sign that the prayer was granted.

Just as in the Seven Sacraments, we have the Sacraments as Celebrated in the Fifteenth Century, contrasted with the Origin of the Sacraments, so in this tapestry we have the Mediæval Justice of Herkinbald contrasted with the Ancient Justice of Trajan. The third scene shows Herkinbald, Duke of Brabant, slaying with his own hand his nephew who has been guilty of the crime of rape. In the fourth scene, the justice of Herkinbald's act receives divine sanction. When the Bishop refuses to give him the last sacrament unless he confesses as a murderer, the sacred wafer miraculously passes from the ciborium, and places itself on the tongue of the dying Herkinbald.

About sixty years later is the Herkinbald tapestry in the Brussels Cinquentenaire Museum (Illustrated in *Destrée Cinquentenaire*) which contains some gold. The accounts of the Confrérie du Saint-Sacrement of Saint Pierre, at Louvain, for the year 1513, list in Flemish the payment of 2½ Rhine florins, and 2 pots of wine at 5 sous, to Jan van Brussel (Jean de Bruxelles) for the sketch after which the large cartoon was made; of 13½ florins to Philip the painter for making the large cartoon; also 10 sous to Philip for bringing the large cartoon and hanging it in the church.

While the Berne tapestry is full Gothic the Brussels tapestry is almost Renaissance. The Berne tapestry has no border; it is the antithesis of symmetrical, the left third a confused mass of figures, with nothing to restrain but trees above and flowers and inscription below, the right two-thirds rigidly framed into separate scenes by slender Gothic columns and arches, with trees above and inscriptions below; and it has a plot too subtle for most of those who have written about it.

The Brussels Herkinbald, *with* border, with architecture already Renaissance, and with central composition, is only held on the Gothic side of the line by its long robes and figures arranged in vertical tiers.   Here, the stabbing scene has been crowded into the upper right corner, with the seduction scene added in the upper left corner, for the sake of balance, while the death-bed scene reminds one of Louis XIV giving an audience.   As for the faces, those of the Berne tapestry have individuality and character, while these of the Brussels tapestry are mostly angelic and insipid, borrowed with technical skill but without great intelligence from the great Late Gothic tapestries rich with gold, and from Italy.   In other words, the Berne tapestry, despite the enfeebling work of repairers, is still a great tapestry, while the Brussels Herkinbald is weak.

THE STORY OF ESTHER

Now in the Charles Jairus Martin memorial collection of tapestries of the Minneapolis Institute of Arts, and formerly on loan at the Metropolitan Museum as part of the Morgan-Hoentschel collection, is a fine fragment from the famous Gothic group picturing the story of Esther (Plate 403 of *Hunter 1912*).   The two main scenes are separated by a Gothic column with jeweled moulding, resembling the columns of the Metropolitan Museum's "Seven Sacraments," but square instead of round.   The tiny scenes in the upper left corner show, on the right, Esther learning of the condemnation to death of all Jews; on the left, praying that King Ahasuerus (whom we, following the Greeks, call Xerxes) may pardon her presumption in approaching him unbidden, for in the words of the Bible (*Esther IV*, 11) "Whosoever, whether man or woman, shall come unto the king in the inner court, who is not called, there is one law of his to put him to death, except such to whom the king shall hold out the golden sceptre, that he may live.''

The main scene on the left of the tapestry shows Ahasuerus on his throne holding out his golden sceptre to Esther (*hester*), thus sparing her life. Esther who had succeeded Vashti as Queen, wears her crown. She and her attendants are costumed magnificently. On the right stands the smart courtier and favorite of the King, Haman (*aman*), who also appears on the right of the next scene, but in profile. ''What wilt thou, Queen Esther?'' asked the King, ''and what is thy request? It shall be even given thee to the half of my kingdom.'' And Esther answered, ''If it seems good unto the King, let the King and Haman come this day unto the banquet that I have prepared for him.'' The scene on the right of the tapestry shows the banquet scene, Esther and Ahasuerus looking much as Margaret of York and Charles the Bold must have looked when banqueting, seated at a table royally appointed in fifteenth century style. The story is told in Latin in Gothic letters at the bottom of the tapestry.

ESTHER TAPESTRIES AT SARAGOSSA

The most splendid Gothic Esther tapestries in the world are the three (each about 14 by 26 feet) belonging to the Saragossa cathedrals, which once were the property of Ferdinand the Catholic, who willed them to his son Archbishop Alonso, who willed them to La Seo. They picture the first half of the story of Esther as told in the Bible. The tradition is that they had previously belonged to Charles the Bold, Duke of Burgundy. While they resemble the Minneapolis Esther in style and weave, the design is altogether different, as can be seen by comparing the Minneapolis Esther with the corresponding scenes of the third Saragossa piece. The Latin inscriptions of the Saragossa tapestries are in Gothic letters, at the top.

(1) The main scenes of the first Saragossa tapestry (Plates IV, n, na) are: (a) The feast given by Ahasuerus to the princes and nobles of his empire; (b) The refusal of Queen Vashti (*vasti*) to come when commanded; (c) The divorce and expulsion of Vashti.   It will be noticed that Plate IV, n, illustrates the left two-thirds of the tapestry, while Plate IV, na, illustrates the right two-thirds, thus repeating the middle third.

(2) The main scenes of the second Saragossa tapestry are: (a) Arrest of the two chamberlains whose plot to lay hand on Ahasuerus was exposed by Mordecai (*mardose*); (b) Esther brought to Ahasuerus by Mordecai, in response to the proclamation that fair young virgins should be sought for the king; (c) Esther made Queen. Ahasuerus places her, crowned, on the throne beside him, gives her his ring, and makes a great feast in her honor.

(3) The main scenes of the third Saragossa tapestry are: (a) Haman becomes prime minister and plots the destruction of the Jews, especially of Mordecai who refused to do him reverence; (b) Esther approaches the king at the risk of her life; (c) Esther's first banquet to the king and Haman. Subordinate scenes above show Haman joyfully telling Zeresh his wife that Esther has asked him to another banquet with the king, but lamenting that he still sees "Mordecai the Jew sitting at the king's gate."

The life and vivacity of these three tapestries is extraordinary. Every face is full of expression and every scene is full of action. Hats and gowns and jewels are rich and beautiful. The architectural framework is elaborate and exquisite. The story of Esther is brought completely up to date, and acted out in their own environment by personages of the French Gothic Court of Burgundy.

The first inscription on the first Saragossa tapestry is, *Assuerus rex grande fecit convivium cunctis principibus suis ut ostenderet divicias glorie regni sui* (King Ahasuerus made a great feast for all his princes that he might display the riches of the glory of his kingdom). The inscriptions are based on the Book of Esther, and follow the meaning of the text, but modify and abbreviate the phraseology of the Vulgate.

OTHER ESTHER GOTHIC TAPESTRIES

Besides the Saragossa and Minneapolis Gothic Esther tapestries, there are the following fragments:

(1) Two adjacent scenes at the Nancy Museum, from the booty found in the camp of Charles the Bold after his defeat and death under the walls of Nancy in 1477 (Figs. 10, 11 of *Fondation Piot, 1903*). There are French inscriptions at the top. The scenes are: The Refusal of Vashti, and the Divorce of Vashti. The designs are altogether different from those of the Saragossa set.

(2) One scene without inscription in the Louvre (Fig. 9 of *Fondation Piot, 1903*), a duplicate of the Nancy "Refusal of Vashti."

(3) One scene formerly held by a Brussels dealer (Plate 27 of *Kurt Tournai*), a duplicate of scene c of the second Saragossa tapestry, "Esther Made Queen."

We have then parts of at least four different sets: (A) the Saragossa set; (B) the Brussels set, probably a duplicate of the Saragossa set; (C) the Nancy set; (D) the Louvre set, probably a duplicate of the Nancy set. Possibly the Minneapolis fragment belongs to the C or the D set, which may originally have had Latin inscriptions at the bottom as well as French inscriptions at the top, but I think it more probably was part of a fifth set.

Esther also appears in the Mazarin and other "Triumph of Christ" tapestries, in the Sens "Triumph of the Virgin," in the Somzée "Triumph of the Virgin" now on loan at the Metropolitan Museum of Art, and in the Duveen "Esther and Augustus" (See Chapter VII).

THE STORY OF JEPHTHAH

Another splendid tapestry in the collection of the Saragossa cathedrals, a little earlier in date than the Esther group, pictures the first part of the story of Jephthah (*Judges, XI*). This is the Jephthah who vowed when he went forth

against the Ammonites, that if the Lord delivered the children
of Ammon into his hands, he would on his return offer up for
a burnt offering whatsoever came forth of the doors of his
house to meet him.   The Lord did deliver the Ammonites
into his hands, and he came home victorious to his house in
Mizpah, where he was welcomed by his only daughter with
timbrels and with dances.   At the extreme left of the tapestry the Author delivers his prologue.   Next on the right,
with beautiful ladies in the background, the elders of Gilead
go to the land of Tob to ask the aid of Jephthah who has been
unjustly banished.   Jephthah is crowned king as the Gilead-
ites promised if he would help them.   Next, messengers to
and from the Ammonites.   Last, the battle in which Jephthah
defeated the Ammonites.

THE STORY OF DAVID

One of the best-known and most brilliant sets of Gothic
religious tapestries pictures the Story of David, and hangs
in the Cluny Museum.   It was made in Brussels at the
beginning of the sixteenth century (1505–1510).   It is 14
feet 9 inches high and contains considerable gold, especially
in the brocaded names of *david, bersabee, urias,* etc., but not
enough to bring it into the class of the "rich with gold"
Gothic tapestries of Chapter VII.   The subjects of the ten
tapestries, the story of which is taken from the Bible, *II
Samuel, VI, XI, XII,* are:

   I. David dances before the Ark.
  II. Bathsheba at the Bath.
 III. David and Uriah.
  IV. Uriah with the army at Rabbah.
   V. Joab reports Uriah's Death.
  VI. Marriage of David and Bathsheba.
 VII. David reproached by Nathan.
VIII. Death of the Baby.
  IX. Capture of Rabbah (Plate XVIII, fa).
   X. David crowned at Rabbah.

The scenes follow the Bible text but with minor changes that increase the dramatic effect.

The inscriptions are in Latin, in Gothic letters, but there are only three of them on the whole set, one under the portrait of the Author at the left end of tapestry No. I, one under the portrait of the Author at the right end of tapestry No. IX, one on the scroll held by the personage in the lower left corner of tapestry No. VII.

The presence of Virtues and a Vice in tapestry VII shows the influence of the great Salvation group. In the middle of the tapestry David and Bathsheba sit on a magnificent throne, surrounded by their Court, but disconsolate because of the reproaches of the prophet Nathan who stands in the foreground. In the extreme upper left corner, Nathan kneels in prayer before God visible in the sky above. At the right of this scene, from left to right across the upper third of the tapestry are seven beautiful winged maidens, six Virtues, *contricio* kneeling repentant, *ira dei* brandishing a sword, *misericordia* with lily branch, *justicia* with sword and scales, *sapiencia* with mirror, *penitencia* with sword, and one Vice, *luxuria*, with casket.

Tapestries closely related to the Cluny David set are:

(1) Mr. Edward A. Faust's "David reproached by Nathan," with entirely different design from the corresponding Cluny tapestry, and without the Virtues and Vices. David (with DAVID woven into the hem of his robe) and Bathsheba are not seated, but stand before the throne, and there are subordinate scenes in the upper corners of the tapestry, on the left, David giving Uriah the letter instructing Joab, " Set ye Uriah in the forefront of the hottest battle, and retire ye from him, that he may be smitten, and die;" on the right, Uriah delivering the letter to Joab.

(2) The " Bathsheba at the Bath " belonging to the city of Brussels, formerly in the Somzée collection (Plate XXIII of the sale catalogue).

(3) The three David tapestries rich with gold in the Royal Spanish collection (Plates 9, 10, 11, of *Valencia Spanish*). The "Bathsheba at the Bath," is a reduced version, with some changes, of the Brussels one.

(4) The rather inferior "David, Abigail and Saul" tapestry in the Brussels Cinquentenaire Museum.

(5) The two David tapestries in the collection of Mr. J. E. Aldred.

(6) The somewhat later version of the Spanish "Bathsheba at the Bath" (See No. 3, above), formerly in the collection of French & Co.

(7) The narrow frieze tapestries in the Royal Italian collection at Florence, picturing the Story of David and Bathsheba.

MR. MACKAY'S "DAVID"

Earlier than all of these, is Mr. Mackay's huge tapestry, 15 feet high by 29 feet 4 inches long, that in five scenes pictures the Marriage of David and Bathsheba (Plate S, c, in colour, of the *Subscribers' Edition*). David, it will be noticed (Plate S, o, of the *Subscribers' Edition*) is clean shaven in the style of the fifteenth century instead of being bearded in the style of the sixteenth century, as in the David tapestries previously named. Here we have the ancestor of the group, an ancestor superior to any of its descendants, all of which show the family likeness. In Mr. Mackay's "David," designer and weaver have combined to utilize effectively the wonderful possibilities of tapestry texture, and by contrasts of ribs and hatchings and slits, and silk and wool, and pattern and colour, and light and shade, and columns and arches, to present personages in groups boldly and brilliantly. Admirably does the ancient narrow border fulfil the purpose of its being, which is by contrast to exalt the lines and colours of the scenes that it enshrines. It consists of round leafy clusters growing from the spirals of the sinuous stem that divides it into small compartments.

The architectural framing of the tapestry is unusually simple and symmetrical, and the different members are shaded and hatched and coloured with a skill that sets their intricate ornamentation strongly forth. Just inside the border is a woven frame of sharp mouldings in high relief, accentuated by a row of colored jewelry with intervening pearls in groups of five or six. Upon the inner side of the bottom of the frame stand the five-sided bases of the two middle columns that make the tapestry a triptych, and the four-sided bases of the columns partly engaged in the jeweled frame at each end of the tapestry. The outer wings of the triptych are divided horizontally by round jeweled beams with spiral mouldings. An arched and ribbed canopy springing from slender twisted columns distinguishes David's throne.

Scene I, in the upper left corner, Bathsheba at the Bath, is not at all like Rubens' "Bathsheba at the Bath." Bathsheba on the roof of her house after holding her hands daintily under one of the streams of water falling into the basin of the fountain, is about to wipe them on the towel with knotted fringe, and blue border and cross stripes, which one of her maids holds ready. David, from his palace, looking out through the window with trefoil arch, catches sight of this beautiful woman, and turns to his courtiers to ask who she is. In the words of the Bible (*II Samuel, XI*, 2–3) :

> And it came to pass in an eveningtide, that David arose from off his bed, and walked upon the roof of the king's house; and from the roof he saw a woman washing herself; and the woman was very beautiful. And David inquired after the woman. And one said, Is not this Bath-sheba the daughter of Eliam, the wife of Uriah the Hittite?

Immediately David sent messengers to fetch Bathsheba. Scene II in the lower corner of the tapestry shows how warmly David received her. David's infatuation was such that he arranged to have Uriah killed in battle. After Uriah's death David was in a position to legitimize the situation, and the middle third of the tapestry shows David on his throne welcoming Bathsheba as his wife. Scene IV in the lower right corner shows David and Bathsheba reproached by Nathan. Scene V in the upper right corner, shows Bathsheba lamenting the illness of her baby. In the background is the bed upon which lies the dying child. Outside the door David and his followers join in the lamentation.

SUSANNA, JUDITH, AND JOSEPH

The most important tapestries picturing the Story of Susanna are the set of five in eight scenes described and illustrated by M. Guiffrey (*Guiffrey Susanne*), with French Gothic verses at the top; and the one in the Victoria and Albert Museum (Plate 325 of *Hunter 1912*, with wide border but with no inscription except the name *susenne*.

The most important tapestries picturing the Story of Judith are the one in two scenes in the Somzée sale (Brussels 1901) with short Latin Gothic inscription above (Plate 347 of *Hunter 1912*); and the Tournai one at the Cathedral of Sens (Plates CV, CVI of *Demotte Gothic*), with the fragment of a Story of Ruth tapestry sewed on at the right, and with Latin Gothic inscriptions below. The Wolsey coat-of-arms attached above suggests the possibility of this having come from Hampton Court, and being one of the Judith set made by Arnould Poissonnier and given to the Duke of Suffolk by the city of Tournai in 1516.

Interesting Story of Joseph tapestries are the ones in the collection of Mr. Thomas W. Lamont, " Joseph spurning Pharaoh's crown"; "Pharaoh's Dream" in the Stibbert Museum, Florence; "Triumph of Joseph" at the Cathedral of Tarragona. In the last, two subordinate scenes, "Adoration of the Magi," above on the left, and "Christ Preaching" above on the right show that Joseph is here presented as a forerunner of Christ. Below these two scenes are, on the left, *faro* (Pharaoh) putting his ring on Joseph's finger; on the right *iosap* with sceptre looking out of a window at *puitefer* (Potiphar) and his wife *assonech* who seem to be quarreling. The middle half of the tapestry shows Joseph seated on a throne between Pharaoh and *sapiencia* (Wisdom), who is Joseph's companion in all three scenes. Above the head of Joseph in the middle scene is a dove symbolic of the Holy Spirit.

6

SAINT PETER

In the year 1460, Guillaume de Hellande, Bishop of Beauvais, presented to the Cathedral of Saint Peter at Beauvais, a set of Saint Peter tapestries just completed, probably at Tournai but perhaps at Beauvais, by weavers steeped in Tournai traditions. A major part of the set is still in existence, most of it at the Cathedral of Beauvais (Illustrated by Madam Crick-Kunziger in the *Burlington Magazine,* November, 1924), one piece in the Cluny Museum (Plate 363 of *Hunter 1912*), one piece in the Bacri collection, three pieces in the United States. This may be regarded as the finest that remains to us of the many sets that were made picturing the Lives of the Saints. Furthermore it serves as a concrete example illustrating the type of tapestries that inspired donors, authors, designers, and weavers of the numerous provincial Late Gothic, Gothic Renaissance and Early Renaissance sets made in France, picturing the Lives of the Saints and of Christ and the Virgin, such as the Beaune "Virgin," the Le Mans and the Soissons "Saints Gervais and Protais," the Chaise-Dieu "Christ," the Cluny "Saint Stephen," the Louvre "Saint Quentin," the Plessis-Macé "Eucharist," the Saumur "Saint Florent," the Saumur "Saint Peter," the Angers "Saint Maurille," "Saint Martin," "John the Baptist," and "Saint Saturnin," the Reims "Virgin," the Reims "Saint Rémi," etc. Of these sets, those woven after 1520 have architecture and costumes that are more Renaissance than Gothic, despite many archaicisms, but the inscriptions are in Gothic lettering, with a few minor exceptions, and the general plan and spirit is still Gothic. The Aix-en-Provence "Christ and the Virgin" differs greatly from these French sets in style, and was made in Brussels.

Of the Beauvais "Saint Peter" set, three pieces are now in the United States, one in the Seligmann-Rey collection (Saint Paul beheaded), two in the Andrew W. Mellon collection

(Tabitha raised from the Dead; and Apparition of the Angel to Cornelius). The arrangement of the first of these three pieces, with the coat-of-arms of the donor in two corners, and that of the Bishopric of Beauvais in the other two, with the word *paix* scattered here and there, and with French Gothic two-line inscription at the top, is typical of the set.

The inscription at the top of "Saint Paul beheaded" reads, *Comment saint pol a este decole hors rome, sa teste separee du corps fist troix saulx* (How Saint Paul was beheaded outside Rome. His head after separation from the body, made three bounds). Saint Paul kneels in the foreground behind the huge sword of the executioner. Three pools of water mark the spots where his head has touched the ground. Hence the name of Three Fountains given to the place. The bearded and haloed head still wears the veil of Platilla (Consult the *Golden Legend*), and before the lips are the letters *ihs,* initials of the *Jesus hominum salvator* that issued from Saint Paul's mouth when the head touched the ground. Above is a scroll with the words written by Saint Paul to the Philippians (*I,* 21) *Michi vivere Christus est et mori lucrum* (For me to live is Christ and to die is gain). At the top of the tapestry just beneath the inscription is God receiving the soul of Saint Paul in the form of an infant brought by two angels. The spectators of the main scene are divided into two groups, Pagans on the left, Christians on the right. The central figure of the Pagan group is the Roman Emperor Nero, clean shaven, in golden armor, and with laurel wreath crowning his long hair.

The word Peace (*paix*) that is scattered over all the tapestries has a special significance. For more than a century the Hundred Years' War had raged between France and England. France had been saved from bondage only by the miraculous intervention of Joan of Arc who was condemned by a tribunal presided over by Bishop Guillaume's predecessor. Bishop Guillaume, a loyal Frenchman, disavowed the acts of his predecessor, and was active in the rehabilitation of Joan's name and character. About the time he became Bishop, peace was made between Henry VI of England and Charles VII of France. In the grand celebration of the peace at Paris, Bishop Guillaume played a prominent part. This is the Peace meant by the *paix* on the Saint Peter tapestries.

The Quo Vadis illustrated on Plate XXI, d, formerly in the Blanchet collection, is from another Saint Peter set of similar character, made about fifteen years later.

In my discussion of the Credo and Salvation groups I showed how the idea of the New Dispensation foretold by the Old Dispensation, was developed magnificently by Authors and Designers at Brussels. We will now turn to French provincial tapestries developed crudely from picture books like the Biblia Pauperum (Bible of the Poor) and the Speculum Humanæ Salvationis (Mirror of Human Salvation). The set closest to the Bible of the Poor (Consult *Mâle Fifteenth*) is the Life of Christ at La Chaise Dieu (1518). As in the Bible of the Poor, which became widely circulated and easy of access after it began to be printed from engraved blocks of wood about 1460, so in the Chaise-Dieu tapestries, fourteen of the pictures show some event from the Life of Christ in the centre, flanked by Old Testament scenes, with two prophets above and two prophets below, and with a wealth of Latin Gothic inscriptions. For instance, the Annunciation scene is flanked on the left by the Temptation of Eve and on the right by the Fleece of Gideon, with Isaiah and David above, and Ezekiel and Jeremiah below.

The Life of the Virgin set at Reims, presented to the Cathedral of Reims in 1530 by Archbishop Robert de Lenoncourt whose coat-of-arms appears repeatedly on the tapestries, while owing much to the Bible of the Poor, is vastly superior to the Chaise-Dieu set in design and weave and instead of

four prophets has only two, these in the lower corners. But
the main scene is still flanked by the same Old Testament
scenes (Plate IV, o, showing the Annunciation of the Reims
"Virgin" set) ; on the left, the Temptation of Eve, on the right,
the Fleece of Gideon. In the Temptation of Eve, in the
branches of the tree around which is coiled the human-
headed Serpent, God holds the globe that symbolizes the
Earth. The Latin hexameter inscription above on the left
reads: *Vipera vim perdit, sine vi pariente puella* (The viper
loses his venom, the Virgin becoming a mother without violence). Gideon (GEDEON), having left his companions at the
foot of the mountain, kneels beside the Fleece and asks God
for a sign of victory. The angel above holds a scroll reading:
(*Judges VI*, 12) *Dominus tecum, vir fortissime* (God is with
you, man most brave). Below Gideon is a scroll reading:
Rore madet vellus, permansit arida tellus (The Fleece is wet
with dew, the soil remains dry). In the lower corners of the
tapestry two prophets, Isaiah on the left, David on the right.
Isaiah's inscription reads: (*Isaiah VII*, 14) *Ecce virgo con-
cipiet et pariet filium* (Behold a virgin shall conceive and bear
a son). David's inscription reads (*Psalms LXXI*, 6)
Descendet Dominus sicut pluvia in vellus (The Lord shall
descend like rain upon the Fleece).

In the middle of the tapestry, above the main scene, is
God crowned and surrounded by angels, and separated by
clouds from the Earth below. The inscription on the arch
above him reads: VIRGO SALVTATVR INTACTA MANENS GRAVIDATVR
(The Virgin receives the Annunciation and conceives without
sin). The main scene is the Virgin's chamber, with tile floor,
elaborate Renaissance vase of lilies, Gothic chests, and bed
draped in Gothic manner. Gabriel followed by angels inclines
his sceptre towards the kneeling Virgin and says in the words
of the scroll above: AVE GRACIA PLENA DOMINVS TECVM, the
GRACIA and DOMINVS being abbreviated to GRA and DNS. The
French Gothic verses below read translated:

The vile serpent falsely argued with our Mother, and finally deceived her. The divine angel made the Annunciation to Mary. The son of God humbling himself was conceived. Gideon noble judge received a celestial sign upon the mundane earth, by the rain or dew that fell upon the Fleece in sign of victory.

Another interesting set at Reims, also of Gothic inspiration and also with architecture largely Renaissance, and apparently cartooned by the same painter, are the ten tapestries 16 feet high, one foot less than the Reims Virgin set, picturing the Story of Saint Rémi, presented to the church of Saint Rémi by the same Archbishop Robert de Lenoncourt, in 1531. The inscribed verses are in French Gothic, and the inscribed names in French Roman.

Earlier in date, and also much superior to the Chaise-Dieu Christ and with an attractive millefleur foreground, is the Virgin set at Beaune completed in the year 1500.

Also interesting is the Saint Gervais and Saint Protais set 4 feet 11 inches high at Le Mans, donated to the Cathedral in 1509.

An interesting set 5 feet 9 inches high of which two scenes on one piece are in the United States at the Boston Museum of Fine Arts (Plate 73 of *Hunter 1912*) is the Miracles of the Eucharist, dispersed at the Plessis-Macé sale in 1888. Of the other pieces one is now at the Louvre, two in the museum of the Gobelins, several in the Château de Langeais.

SMALL RELIGIOUS TAPESTRIES

On Plates IV, f, fa, fb, I have grouped three small religious tapestries for the purpose of contrast. One of them (Plate IV, f), the Metropolitan Museum's small Crucifixion, I attribute to the last half of the fourteenth century, despite the opinion of those who would date it 1400 or earlier, and despite the early character of the design. German and other provincial tapestries are usually archaic in weave. They are apt to be still more archaic in design. No tapestry can be earlier than its latest detail of design or weave. The weave of this Crucifixion, even after making allowance for the modification in texture produced by the repairer, is provincial and nearer to that of German and Swiss tapestries than to that of French tapestries. On the other hand, the Metropolitan Museum's charming small Adoration of the Magi (*Plate IV, fa*) is a little earlier than the date usually assigned, probably not later than 1480. The contrast I wish especially to point out is that between the backgrounds of these three small tapestries. The first (Plate IV, f) has a background of large geometrical stars in the style of the fourteenth century; the second (*Plate IV, fa*) has naturalistic presentation of both sky and personages in the style of the last third of the fifteenth century; the third (*Plate IV, fb*) has personages and tower set against a background of Gothic verdure, in the style of the end of the fifteenth century.

TRIUMPHS OF PETRARCH

The only Gothic set of tapestries in the National Austrian collection is the six 13 feet 9 inches high picturing the Triumphs of Petrarch—Love, Chastity, Death, Fame, Time, Eternity—from French designs of Italian inspiration, woven at the end of the fifteenth century, perhaps in Tournai but more probably in France. Comparison of this set with the Brussels Triumphs of Petrarch at Hampton Court and at the Victoria and Albert Museum, develops clearly the marked difference in style between the Late Gothic tapestries of Brussels and of France-Tournai. Incidentally it may be remarked that the French set is much superior in design and weave to the Brussels set.

On Plates 365 and 375 of *Hunter 1912* were illustrated two of these French Triumphs of Petrarch, the first Fame, from the Somzée collection (Sale Catalogue Brussels 1901) with inscription missing but otherwise a duplicate of the Austrian Fame; the second, Love, from the Austrian collection, with French Gothic inscriptions above. Love is personified by Cupid who sits blindfolded on a golden wagon drawn by two doves, two goats, two harpies, and Urania with a harp. Crushed beneath the wheels of the wagon, which is guided by Pleasure (*volupte*) and pushed by Idleness (*oisi-vite*), are Paris and Helen and Jason and Hercules and Solomon and Herodias and Pyramus and Thisbe, all inscribed with their names in French Gothic. The inscriptions read:

> *Par cupido d'amours le dieu immonde*
> *Qui de son arc a faict plusieurs efforts*
> *Sont vaincus les preux hardis et fors*
> *Et les plus grans representant le monde*

In translation:

> By Cupid the impure god of Love,
> Who with his bow has made many shots,
> Are conquered the heroes bold and strong,
> And the world's greatest personages.

Of special interest is the Austrian Triumph of Eternity with all the previous victors under the wheels of the chariot that is drawn by the four Evangelists in their customary symbolic forms (*s. mathieu* as a winged man, *s. marc* as a lion, *s. luc* as an ox, *s. ian* as an eagle, all with halos), while on the chariot, cushioned on clouds and framed with clouds and angels rests a huge globe-and-cross-of-empire bearing the Trinity, Christ nailed to the Cross, the Holy Spirit in the form of a dove; and God the Father, with papal crown, supporting on outstretched hands the horizontal bar of the Cross.

Interest in this set is increased by the fact that there are duplicates of two of the tapestries, Time and Fame, the latter incomplete, in the United States, formerly in the French & Co. collection.

Of the Brussels Triumphs of Petrarch the Victoria and Albert Museum has three, Chastity, Death, and Fame, while Hampton Court has four, Fame, Time, and two of Death, making three Deaths in all, which must have come from three different sets.   Each tapestry has two French Gothic inscriptions in the top border and one Latin Gothic inscription in the bottom border.   The inscribed names are in Roman. Each tapestry has not one scene, but two.   The tapestry Death shows on the left the Fates attacking the unicorn-drawn chariot of Chastity, and on the right the Fates riding triumphant on their buffalo-drawn chariot.   The tapestry Fame shows on the left Fame attacking the buffalo-drawn chariot of the Fates (Death), on the right Fame riding triumphant on her elephant-drawn chariot.

These tapestries were woven in Brussels about 1510.   The Victoria and Albert Chastity bears two dates, 1507 and 1510, which may have been the dates of beginning and completion.

SUPPER AND BANQUET

An allegorical set of five pieces in the museum of Nancy, the Condemnation of Supper and Banquet, pictures the dangers of the table.   Those who have eaten not wisely but too well are attacked by numerous maladies personified. Finally (Plate IV, m) Lady Experience (*dame estperiense*) seated on her throne, with French Gothic inscription above, orders her officers to arrest alluring Supper and Banquet. On the right of the tapestry the officers execute the order. The various personifications are vivid and interesting, and the action as lively as in one of the plays or pageants on which the design of the tapestry was based.   This set was made in Tournai about 1510.

THE CERF FRAGILLE

Five Late Gothic tapestries formerly in the Kermaingant collection (four of them illustrated on *Plates LXXIII and LXXIV of Ganay 1913*) and now in the United States in the collection of Mr. Arthur Lehman, show Man personified as a Gentle Stag (*cerf fragille*) wandering through the forest subject to the attacks of the various infirmities of Human Nature. The story is told in French Gothic verses below.

Developed and enlarged from one of these tapestries, with the inscription above and with the addition of interesting Tournai-style foliage, is the tapestry of the Wildenstein collection showing the Gentle Stag pursued by the dogs of Ignorance—Pride, Will, Haste—while Vanity blows her horn (Plate VI, n).

PLATE IV, b.—TWO OF THE FIVE FRAGMENTS OF THE METROPOLITAN MUSEUM'S "SEVEN SACRAMENTS"
ARE MOUNTED WRONG SIDE OUT. THIS IS ONE OF THEM. IT ILLUSTRATES THE FIFTEENTH CENTURY CELE-
BRATION OF MARRIAGE AND OF EXTREME UNCTION. NOTE THAT THE INSCRIPTIONS ABOVE ARE ALSO WRONG

PLATE IV, C.—THE ORIGIN OF THE SACRAMENT OF CONFIRMATION AND TON-
SURE, JACOB CONFIRMING TWO CHILDREN. ONE OF THE FIVE FRAGMENTS OF THE
METROPOLITAN MUSEUM'S "SEVEN SACRAMENTS"

PLATE IV, D.—CONFIRMATION AND TONSURE AS CELEBRATED IN THE FIFTEENTH CENTURY.
MISSING FRAGMENT OF THE METROPOLITAN MUSEUM'S "SEVEN SACRAMENTS". LENT BY MISS
EṆID DU CANE TO THE VICTORIA AND ALBERT MUSEUM

PLATES IV, e, ea.—CRUCIFIXION, WITH SUBORDINATE SCENES. TAP-
ESTRY OF THE SECOND QUARTER OF THE FIFTEENTH CENTURY, MADE
PROBABLY IN TOURNAI, BEQUEATHED BY FERDINAND THE CATHOLIC TO
HIS SON ARCHBISHOP ALONSO, WHO BEQUEATHED IT TO THE CATHEDRAL
OF LA SEO IN SARAGOSSA, WHERE IT STILL IS

PLATES IV, f, fa, fb.—PLATE IV, f, AT THE TOP OF THE PAGE, EARLY GOTHIC CRUCIFIXION, IN THE METROPOLITAN MUSEUM OF ART. PLATE IV, fa, IN THE MIDDLE OF THE PAGE, LATE GOTHIC ADORATION OF THE MAGI, IN THE METROPOLITAN MUSEUM OF ART. PLATE IV, fb, AT THE BOTTOM OF THE PAGE, THE TWO MARYS AND BARBARA, LATE GOTHIC VERDURE WITH PERSONAGES, LOANED ANONYMOUSLY TO THE METROPOLITAN MUSEUM OF ART

PLATE IV, g.—LATE GOTHIC CREDO TAPESTRY, IN FOUR SCENES, CREATION, BAPTISM, NATIVITY, CRUCIFIXION, AT THE BOSTON MUSEUM OF FINE ARTS

PLATE IV, h.—CHRIST PARTING FROM HIS MOTHER, DETAIL FROM THE MAGNIFICENT
LARGE CREDO TAPESTRY FORMERLY IN THE CATHEDRAL OF TOLEDO. DUVEEN BROS.

PLATE IV, i.—FROM THE FAMOUS SALVATION SERIES, CRUCIFIXION, WITH THE VIRTUES LED BY CHRIST AS A CHRISTIAN KNIGHT IN BATTLE AGAINST THE VICES. FORMERLY IN THE BERWICK AND ALBA COLLECTION, NOW IN THE CHATEAU DE HAAR, HOLLAND

PLATES IV, j, ja, jb.—BAPTISM, ASCENSION, LAST JUDGMENT, FROM
THE FAMOUS SALVATION SERIES. THREE HUGE AND SPLENDID TAPES-
TRIES FORMERLY IN THE BERWICK AND ALBA COLLECTION. THE FIRST
TWO OF THESE ARE NOW IN THE COLLECTION OF MR. WILLIAM R. HEARST,
THE LAST IS IN THE LOUVRE

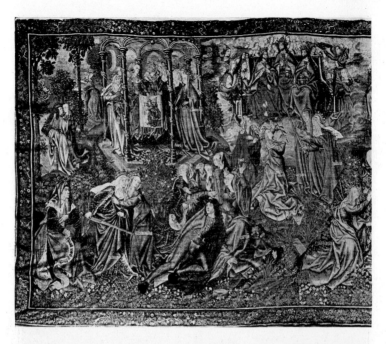

PLATES IV, k, ka.—REDEMPTION, FROM THE FAMOUS SALVATION SERIES.
FORMERLY IN THE COLLECTION OF CARDINAL WOLSEY, AND OF HENRY
VIII, AND STILL AT HAMPTON COURT. NOTE THAT THE MIDDLE OF THE
TAPESTRY APPEARS IN BOTH ILLUSTRATIONS

PLATE IV, 1.—PRODIGAL SON, A LATE GOTHIC TAPESTRY IN THE COLLECTION OF MRS. NICHOLAS F. BRADY

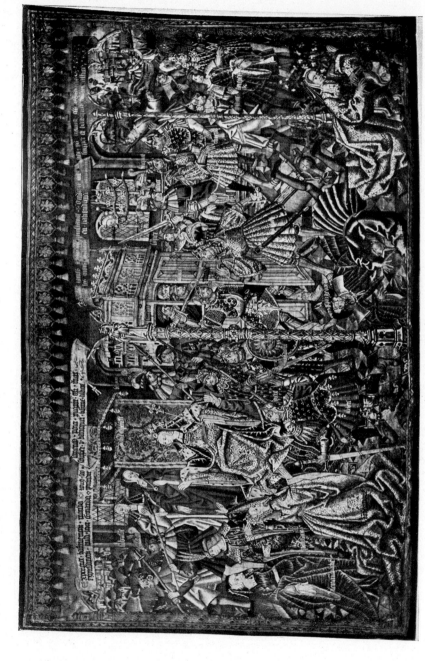

PLATE IV, III.—LADY EXPERIENCE, A LATE GOTHIC TOURNAI TAPESTRY IN THE COLLECTION OF THE DUKE OF FERNAN-
NUÑEZ, MADRID. THIS IS ONE OF THE FAMOUS "BANQUET ET SOUPER" SERIES OF WHICH THERE ARE SEVERAL IN THE
MUSEUM AT NANCY

PLATES IV, n, na.—DISMISSAL OF VASHTI, FROM THE FAMOUS GOTHIC
ESTHER SERIES. ONE OF THE THREE IN THE CATHEDRAL OF LA SEO,
SARAGOSSA, BEQUEATHED BY DON ALONSO DE ARAGON, WHO INHERITED
THEM FROM HIS FATHER, FERDINAND THE CATHOLIC, HUSBAND OF
ISABELLA WHO HELPED COLUMBUS

PLATE IV, ⊕.—ANNUNCIATION, WITH SUBORDINATE SCENES, SEVENTEEN FEET HIGH. ONE OF THE FAMOUS VIRGIN SERIES AT REIMS. GOTHIC—RENAISSANCE TRANSITION, WITH GOTHIC SPIRIT STILL DOMINANT IN THE MIDST OF RENAISSANCE FORMS. NOTE THE RENAISSANCE ORNAMENTATION OF THE BORDER AND OF THE PILASTERS

PLATE V, a.—PORTRAIT OF KING PRIAM, DETAIL FROM MR. MACKAY'S GOTHIC TAPESTRY
"HECTOR AND ANDROMACHE"

CHAPTER V

GOTHIC HISTORICAL AND ROMANTIC TAPESTRIES

THE GREAT TROJAN WAR SET, HERCULES, ALEXANDER THE GREAT IN AIRSHIP AND SUBMARINE, BRITAIN NAMED FROM BRUTUS, TARQUINIUS PRISCUS, BRENNUS SACKS ROME, THE BERNE CAESAR, THE REIMS CLOVIS, CHANSON DE GESTE TAPESTRIES, ROLAND, CHARLEMAGNE, JOURDAIN DE BLAYE, THE SWAN KNIGHT

THE largest and most interesting group of Gothic Historical tapestries that has survived pictures the Story of the Trojan War as told in French verse in the twelfth century, by Benoit de Sainte Maure in his *roman de troie,* and retold by others in Latin and in French, in prose and in verse, (Chapter XVIII). The importance of the set is such that I have devoted to it Plates V, a, b, c, ca, d, e, f, g, h; as well as Plates S, j, k, l, m of the *Subscribers' Edition.*

The finest piece in America is Mr. Mackay's Hector and Andromache; with Andromache appealing to Hector, above; and Priam detaining Hector below; and with the story told in French Gothic verses, above; as well as in Latin Gothic verses, below (Plate V, b). The Latin ten-syllable rhymed verses read:

> *Andromatha deflens cedidium. . Hectoris quod vidit dormiendo*
> *Affert prolem huic in remedium. Priamus hunc vocat retinendo*

And in translation:

> Andromache bewailing the death of Hector seen in her sleep
> Brings her children to prevent it. Priam calls Hector and detains him.

The French ten-syllable rhymed verses read translated:

> Andromache fearing the death of Hector that in her dreams she had bewailed upon her knees, with great lamentation brought her children and besought him not to go out on that day. Despite which Hector had himself armed for battle, and mounted his horse. King Priam made him turn back, because of the pity he felt for Andromache.

The upper scene of this tapestry (Plate V, b; also Plate S, j, of the *Subscribers' Edition*) shows *hector* being armed by his squire for battle. *Andromata* kneels before him with her two children, holding the baby *astronata* (Asternates) in her arms, and clasping the hand of five-year-old Laudamanta who stands before her. Behind Andromache stand *heline* (Helen) and *polixene* (Polyxena) and *heccuba* (Hecuba), and another woman who with her hand wipes a tear from her eye. The picture is exquisite in composition and draftsmanship, with faces and costumes beautifully developed.

The lower scene of the tapestry shows (Plate V, b; also Plates S, k, l, of the *Subscribers' Edition*) *hector de troie* in full armor mounted on his beloved Galatee, whose trappings are magnificent, and noisy with bells pendant from lion heads. King Priam (Plate V, a, in colour), raising his left hand, forbids Hector to go out to battle. Priam's face is full of dignity and power. His hair and beard are patriarchal and superbly delineated and woven. His tall headdress is rich with jewels and circled with fleurs-de-lis. Hector who in the interval between scene one and scene two has lost his moustache (and perhaps his beard) listens unwillingly, almost sullenly. In scene one he listened to Andromache impatiently, even angrily.

The armor of Hector and Galatee, as well as of Hector's mounted followers is an important feature, drawn with spirit and fidelity. From the details shown in scenes one and two it would seem almost possible to reconstruct the different pieces of Hector's suit. No wonder that this tapestry appeals so strongly to the learned and enthusiastic curator of the Arms and Armor department of the Metropolitan Museum of Art.

THE LOUVRE SKETCHES

Comparison of this tapestry with the corresponding Trojan War sketch in the Louvre (Chapter XVIII) indicates that the Louvre sketch is not the original design for the tapestry, but copied from it, or from an inferior version, and perhaps made as we make photographs today, simply as a picture memorandum, or to make a woodcut from. The drawing of the sketch is ridiculously crude, and also *later in style* than Mr. Mackay's tapestry. The groupings of the sketch are absurdly ineffective, and the many differences in detail betray the copyist who did not understand what he was copying. The faces and hands in the sketch are awkward and ugly caricatures. The armor is even worse. In other words while the tapestry is a great work of art, the sketch is crude and weak.

ULYSSES AND DIOMEDES AT PRIAM'S COURT

The next best Trojan War tapestry in America is in the Edson Bradley collection (Plate V, h). It pictures Ulysses and Diomedes at Priam's Court, sent as ambassadors to demand the return of Helen; and in a subordinate scene in the right upper corner King Teuthras (*le roy teutran*) of Mysia, killed by Achilles (*achille*) who had gone with Telephus on a foraging expedition. In the lower right corner of the tapestry Ulysses (*ulixes*) and Diomedes (*diomedes*) stand before the palace door (over which is inscribed *le grant pales de troie*) looking up at the marvelous Golden Tree. The horses from which they have dismounted stand beside them, in the care of a varlet. In the main scene on the left Ulysses and Diomedes present their message to King Priam beside whose throne stand his sons Hector and Paris and Deiphobus and Troilus. The demand of the Greeks is incontinently refused because of the grief felt by Priam at the refusal of the Greeks to return his sister Hesione. The story is told in French Gothic verses above and in Latin Gothic verses below.

Also extremely interesting are Mr. Kahn's three fragments the Funeral of Hector, Palamedes killing Paris, and the Centaur, formerly at the Château de Sully. But the Latin inscriptions are missing, and the French inscriptions that belong above, have been pieced together incorrectly, and applied below at the bottom of the wrong scenes. For example the right two-thirds of the inscription attached below the Funeral of Hector is part of the inscription belonging to the Centaur scene.

THE FUNERAL OF HECTOR

After Achilles killed Hector, not face to face, but catching him off his guard, the Greeks asked for a two months' truce to give time for the recovery of Achilles from his wounds. The Trojans willingly granted the truce, in order to be able to celebrate the funeral of Hector fittingly. For fifteen days the Trojans kept the body of Hector in solemn state at the temple of Jupiter inside the city. Then on the master altar of the rich temple of Apollo, near the gate Timbree, outside the city next the Greeks, they erected a marvelous tabernacle, and inside of it a throne exceeding rich. On the throne they placed the body of Hector, seated and in full armor and supported by a chain from behind (Plate V, d). In Hector's right hand is his drawn sword, as if threatening the Greeks, while his shield, resting on the floor beside him and supported by his left hand, displays his "lion rampant in red on gold." Behind the throne the service is intoned by men with faces made powerfully vivid through masterful use of ribs and hatchings, and of slits both horizontal and stepped (Plate V, g). In front of the throne stand the mourners (Plate V, d), on the right, Hecuba, Polyxena, Andromache, Helen, and others (Plate V, f); on the left, Priam and Troilus and Paris and others (Plate V, e).

The second of Mr. Kahn's Trojan War tapestries shows, above, Palamedes killing Deiphobus and killed by Paris; and below, Calchas urging the discouraged Greeks to fight on. The inscription consists of the first fourth of the odd lines, and the last three-fourths of the even lines, of an inscription referring to these scenes and the one preceding.

The third of Mr. Kahn's Trojan War tapestries showing the Centaur (*sagittaire*) in action (Plate S, m) is a duplicate of the middle half of No. 240 of the Heilbronner collection (Sale catalogue, Paris, 1921). The Heilbronner Centaur still retains the Latin Gothic inscription below, as well as most of the French Gothic inscription above, which reads, with the assistance of the Centaur inscription below Mr. Kahn's Funeral of Hector:

> *Achilles vint impetueusement. En bataille ou tau ung joyant.*
> *Qui combatoit mult vertueusement. Fort terrible nomme hupon le grant.*
> *Le sagitaire orrible et espatant. Polixenar tua en cest effort.*
> *Diomedes vertueux et puissant. Le sagitaire occit et mist a mort.*

In translation:

> Achilles came impetuously into battle, where he killed a giant who fought with great bravery, a terrible man whose name was Hupon le Grand. The Centaur horrible and awful, killed Polixenar in this combat. Diomedes brave and mighty slew and put to death the Centaur.

The upper part of the Heilbronner Centaur shows *achilles* killing *hupon le grand*. In the middle-ground, *diomedes* with uplifted sword is about to strike the Centaur from whose huge bow an arrow flies. Polixenar (PONIPENAR, in Roman lettering), breast pierced by one of the Centaur's arrows, falls from his horse. Beside Polixenar, in the foreground, is his relative Telamon Ajax. In the lower right corner of the tapestry *achilles* and *hector* are having their famous interview, during the three months' truce that followed this eighty days' battle. The conversation, as developed by Benoit de Sainte Maure, makes Hector a much more attractive personality than Achilles.

THE COMPLETE SET

From my study of the Louvre sketches and of the tapestries that have survived, and with the assistance of Gómez-Moreno's splendid article in *Arte Español*, Madrid, 1919, pages 265–289, I conclude that the great Gothic Trojan War series of the French Court of Burgundy consisted of at least twelve tapestries, each 15½ feet high by 31 feet long, (with four French Gothic inscriptions above, and four Latin Gothic inscriptions below, except that the last tapestry of the set had one more inscription above, and one below) making a total length for the set of 372 feet, with 49 French inscriptions and 49 Latin inscriptions. Both French and Latin inscriptions consist of ten-syllable lines woven in double width. The French are octets rhymed a b a b b c b c; the Latin are quatrains rhymed a b a b. The twelve tapestries named from the most striking event in each, are:

> I. Judgment of Paris.
> II. Elopement of Helen.
> III. Ulysses and Diomedes at Priam's Court.
> IV. First Battle.
> V. Fourth Battle.
> VI. Hector and Andromache.
> VII. Hector killed by Achilles.
> VIII. Palamedes killed by Paris.
> IX. Achilles killed by Paris.
> X. Arrival of Penthesilea.
> XI. Penthesilea killed by Pyrrhus.
> XII. Troy Captured.

The designs of Tapestries IV and V have been preserved to us in the Louvre sketches only. The tapestries that survive, as shown by the triplication of parts of Tapestry VI at Zamora and in Mr. Mackay's and Mr. Kahn's collections, belonged to at least three different sets, probably more.

Of the Trojan War tapestries that I have already described, Mr. Kahn's Centaur, the Heilbronner Centaur, and Mr. Mackay's Hector and Andromache are part of Tapestry VI; Mr. Kahn's Funeral of Hector, of Tapestry VII; Mr. Kahn's Palamedes killed by Paris, of Tapestry VIII; Mr. Bradley's Ulysses and Diomedes, of Tapestry III.

TROJAN WAR TAPESTRIES IN EUROPE

The most important Trojan War tapestries in Europe are: in the courthouse of Issoire, the left half of Tapestry I, the left three-fourths of Tapestry VI, three fragments from Tapestry XI; in the Victoria and Albert Museum, the left three-fourths of Tapestry X (Plate 59 of *Hunter 1912*); in the Duke of Alba's palace at Seville, the whole of Tapestry XI; in the Cathedral of Zamora, the whole of Tapestries II, IX, XII, and the right three-fourths of Tapestry VI, the left fourth of which was injured by fire, cut off and sold in 1906. So that the Zamora collection far excels all the others.

Tapestry XII, the Capture of Troy, I have illustrated from the unique example at Zamora, the left three-fifths on Plate V, c, the right three-fifths on Plate V, ca, thus duplicating the middle fifth. The catalogue of the Madrid Exposition 1892–3, Room VI, No. 100, contains a transcription, with minor errors, of the five French and five Latin inscriptions. It is interesting to note that the famous Horse which in Virgil was of wood is here of bronze (*le grant cheval darain*).

The palaces and temples of the city of Troy furnish a splendid architectural background, with the sea in the distance on the extreme left and extreme right. In the upper left corner, on the city wall, stands Helen, her name woven into her headdress, looking towards the sea and the ships of the Greeks. In the foreground on the left, the Horse, and the Greeks making carnage, among them, *Synon, agamemnon,* and *diomedes.*

In the upper middle part of the tapestry, Hecuba, Polyxena, and Antenor. At the right, below, Pyrrhus slaying Priam in the temple of Apollo. Above, to the right, Cassandra, Andromache, and Ajax Telamon. Just below, Hecuba, gone mad at sight of her beautiful daughter Polyxena (below, to the right) being beheaded by Pyrrhus on the tomb of Achilles. This is one of the finest and most dramatic scenes of the whole Trojan

7

War group. The tomb bears in Latin Gothic hexameters, the inscription:

Achilles, conqueror of Hector (in the words of Virgil) fell, his feet pierced by the arrow of Paris.

At the end of the tapestry, is pictured the Author of the tapestries with his two assistants, who says, in the last French inscription:

" Thus ends the piteous story of the city worthy of high renown, Troy the Great."

According to Gómez-Moreno (*Arte Español 1919*) the coats of arms *woven* into the four Zamora Trojan War tapestries are those of the Mendozas granted by the Pope in 1486 to the great Count of Tendilla and his descendants. But the tapestries look earlier. The sewed-on coats of arms are those of the Guzmans, Enriquez, and Toledos, subsequent owners of the tapestries, which in 1608 were presented to the Cathedral of Zamora by Don Antonio Enriquez de Guzman, Count of Alba.

PENTHESILEA KILLED BY PYRRHUS

I am especially indebted to the Duke of Alba for a photograph of, and notes about, his "Penthesilea killed by Pyrrhus," which the hot weather of the summer of 1923 prevented me from going to Seville to examine personally. This tapestry, though badly repaired, is interesting and important. It is the second of the two tapestries (Nos. X, XI) called "Story of the Amazons" in the marriage contract of the Duke of Alba dated 1485, and valued at 44,352 maravedis. The ancient measurements would seem to indicate that the French inscriptions were then already missing. The right half of the tapestry pictures the treachery of Antenor and Æneas.

HELEN OF TROY

We now leave the great Trojan War group a moment for a set of later design and inspiration devoted to Helen of Troy, and illustrated on Plates V, i, ia; and on Plate S, r, of the *Subscribers' Edition*. It is interesting to compare the "Ulysses and Diomedes at the Court of Priam" of this set with the same subject as presented in Mr. Bradley's tapestry (Plate V, h). The faces of this Story of Helen set are in fine condition (Plate S, r) although the names inscribed under the personages are almost invisible. The marriage of Paris and Helen (Plate V, ia) is a composition of especial charm.

HERCULES AND THE TROJAN WAR

While Homer's Iliad begins in the middle of the story, with the quarrel between Agamemnon and Achilles, Benoit de Sainte Maure's Romance of Troy that was the source of the great Trojan War Gothic tapestries, begins with the Expedition of the Argonauts and the First Destruction of Troy, that took place when Laomedon, father of Priam, was King of Troy, and while Priam was absent from home. Consequently it seems probable that three tapestries now in the possession of French & Co. were part of Trojan War sets. Two of them are duplicates, with one extended more to the left, the other extended more to the right. They show a palace with *troiee* (Troy) over the doorway, and a ship labeled *de gresse* (From Greece). Inside the yard of the castle, stands Laomedon, sceptre in hand, surrounded by his courtiers. In front of the castle, just out of the boat that brought them from the ship, stand Jason and Hercules, waiting for the message from Laomedon. One of the two tapestries has a Latin Gothic inscription at the top—one quatrain and part of another. The complete quatrain reads:

> *Iason et hercules euntes in colchon.*
> *in quodam portu troiano quieuerunt.*
> *quod cum compertum regi laomedon fuisset.*
> *iussit per legatum ut sine mora recederent.*

> Jason and Hercules on their way to Colchos
> Stopped at a Trojan port.
> When this became known to King Laomedon
> He ordered them through an officer to leave without delay.

The third of the three tapestries is a battle scene with the city of Troy in the background, and with *erculle* (Hercules) prominent among the mounted warriors. The action is spirited and shows how vigorously fifteenth century knights in armor struggled for victory. This is the battle that resulted in the First Destruction of Troy.

THE STORY OF HERCULES

A Hercules Gothic tapestry, not connected with the Trojan War group, is the incomplete one, with inscriptions missing, in the Brussels Cinquentenaire Museum (Plate 389 of *Hunter 1912*), made at Tournai near the end of the fifteenth century. In the lower left corner, Hercules receives his first bath, while his mother ALCMENA watches from her bed. Above, the infant Hercules strangles the two dragons sent by Juno to kill him. In the middle foreground, Hercules appears at the Court of Eurystheus (ERISTEVS); above, he shoots with bow and arrow; to the right, he engages in a jousting contest.

In the Daniel Guggenheim collection are four Story of Hercules tapestries made at Tournai about 1515, with inscriptions missing. Of one of these there is a duplicate, with French Gothic inscription above, at Hampton Court (Plate LVIII of the catalogue of the Franco-British Exhibition, 1921). It shows the death of Hercules on the pyre he had built and lighted to end the tortures inflicted by the shirt dipped in the blood of the centaur Nessus, which his jealous wife Dejaneira sent him, in order to punish him for his infidelity. In a separate scene in the upper right corner of the tapestry, *dianira* is seen giving the shirt to the messenger. At the left end of the Hampton Court tapestry appears part of a "Diomedes devoured by his Horses" scene, of which there was more when I first saw the tapestry in 1907. A millefleur tapestry in the Musée des Arts Décoratifs shows *hercules* with spiked club standing between a lion that symbolizes Bravery, and Cupid who symbolizes Love. A patch hides the Cupid scene which I suspect is immodest.

NEPTUNE AND MESTRA

Other Gothic mythological tapestries are the two from the end of the fifteenth century in the Brussels Museum of Painting, formerly in the famous Somzée collection (Nos. 531, 532, of the sale catalogue, Brussels, 1901), picturing the Story of Neptune and Mestra, not as told in book VIII of Ovid's Metamorphoses, but based on a different and more extended version. One of the tapestries is inscribed at the top HERESITON. NEPTVM. MESTRA; the other, DEANA. NEPTVNVS. MESTRAM. Erisichthon was punished with insatiable hunger for having cut down a tree sacred to Ceres. The more he ate, the more he wanted. What would be enough for whole cities, was not enough for him. In the effort to satisfy his hunger, he exhausted his fortune, and finally sold his daughter Mestra to get money for more food. Mestra appealed to her sweetheart Neptune, who gave her the power of changing her form at will. Thus she escaped from slavery, and returned to her father, who sold her again and again, until finally in a paroxysm of hunger, he tore and devoured his own flesh, and died.

Part of another Late Gothic mythological set are the two in Mr. Hearst's collection picturing scenes from the Story of Perseus and Andromeda.

ALEXANDER THE GREAT

The Alexander the Great Gothic tapestries, is by no means the actual personage who conquered Darius and against whose father Demosthenes delivered his *philippics*. The Alexander the Great of Gothic tapestries, is even less like the real Alexander, than the Mary of Burgundy of the cinema is like the real Mary of Burgundy. The Alexander the Great of

Gothic tapestries, is a romantic creation of the historical novelists of the Middle Ages, who made ancient history easy to understand by bringing it up to date and by giving free rein to both imagination and memory. In their development of stories that cling and incidents that thrill, they borrowed much from the romantic East. So that the scenarios of Gothic tapestries are crowded with interest.

The most important Alexander the Great tapestries that have survived (Plates V, k, ka are the two in the Palazzo Doria, Rome (Plates VII and VIII of *Kurt Tournai*), each 13 feet high and 33 feet long; and the three fragments in the Petit Palais, Paris, formerly in the Ainard collection. The first Doria tapestry shows on the left, Alexander taming Bucephalus, the horse that had two horns and lived on human flesh and that no one could ride. But no sooner did Bucephalus look at fifteen-year-old Alexander than he knew his master, and in the tapestry we see Alexander riding leisurely out of the stable, the floor of which is deep with human bones. Above, Alexander is congratulated by his proud father and mother. On the right half of the tapestry, Pausanias who had stolen Alexander's mother and mortally wounded his father is captured by the youthful Alexander and brought to his father's bedside to be stabbed by the latter. The last scene shows the coronation of Alexander by his dying father.

The three Petit Palais fragments, from a different set woven later, and showing Bucephalus with one horn instead of two, were originally all part of one tapestry, the smallest piece coming in the 'middle, and the largest piece at the right. While the Doria tapestries have no inscriptions, the two larger Petit Palais fragments have Latin Gothic inscriptions at the bottom. King Nicolas sent messengers to collect tribute from Alexander's father. Alexander thereupon invaded the country of Nicolas, killed him, and captured his capital city of Caesarea. The design of the last scene with many details modified and crudely drawn appears on an ancient colored pen-and-ink sketch in the British Museum (Plate A of an article by A. E. Popham in the *Burlington Magazine* of August, 1924).

ALEXANDER THE GREAT IN AIRSHIP AND SUBMARINE

The second Doria tapestry gets interest not from the battle on the left, but from the scenes on the right which I have illustrated, Alexander in an Airship (Plate V, k) and Alexander in a Submarine (Plate V, ka). The airship made of wood and leather had as motive power four griffins that flew always towards two legs of meat at the end of two poles held by Alexander (See the illustration). As long as Alexander held the meat above their heads the griffins flew up. When he inverted the poles, the griffins descended. Note God in Heaven above watching Alexander ascend, and down below Aristotle and Alexander's other teachers waiting for him to descend, which he did when the upper air got too hot. Plate V, ka, shows not only the trip in the submarine, but also some of the weird creatures Alexander encountered in the desert, notably men with their faces below their shoulders. In the midst of the four boats can be seen the face of Alexander in a barrel of glass suspended from one of the boats by three chains. After Darius died leaving his empire and his daughter to Alexander, the latter, apparently blasé, had said to his companions: "I have conquered Rome, Apulia, Calabria, Africa. I know the inhabitants of the land well enough. I wish to get acquainted with those of the sea." However, all that Alexander seems to have discovered in his submarine was that "the big fish eat the little ones," which he already knew was the rule on terra firma.

A tapestry illustrated by Jubinal, the present location of which I have been unable to discover, had an inscription showing that it pictured Alexander in Italy.

TARQUINIUS PRISCUS

Superior to Alexander in design and weave, is the Story of Tarquin at Zamora. This tapestry bears at the top the same coats-of-arms as the four Zamora Trojan War pieces. It has at the top two long prose Latin Gothic inscriptions with part of a third on the right. These inscriptions were transcribed in the catalogue of the Madrid Exposition 1892–3, Room VI, No. 99. The architectural framework of the tapestry is of extraordinary excellence, with the royal palace in the middle foreground, backgrounded at the sides by the Gothic walls and towers and monumental buildings of ancient Rome, as imagined by French painters of the fifteenth century. Lucinus was a wise and rich Etruscan who emigrated to Rome with all his followers. As the train approached the new home an eagle swooped down and carried away the hat of *lucinus,* afterwards returning it. From this, *tanaqual* wife of Lucinus argued that he was to rise to the summit of power among the Romans. The costumes and faces of Tanaquil and her lady attendant, both mounted, are most attractive. Humorously the artist has given the horse of one of the followers, goat's horns like those of Alexander's Bucephalus. (Compare the Doria Alexander tapestries.) In Rome, on account of the novelty of his coming and the great variety of his riches, Lucinus had his name changed by his fellow citizens to *pristus tarquinus* (Tarquinius Priscus), and when Ancus Martius died, Tarquinius Priscus was crowned King of the Romans. This coronation occupies the middle of the tapestry, with masons in the foreground under the King's direction building the famous Etruscan sewers for the drainage of Rome (among them the Cloaca Maxima). On the right of the tapestry, Tarquin with the first two letters of s. p. q. r. on his shield, leads his troops against the Latins, with whom he afterwards formed a confederation. The archer and the wounded knight falling from his horse, in the foreground, are pictured vividly.

BRITAIN NAMED FROM BRUTUS

A splendid tapestry in the style of the great Trojan War group, is the one at Saragossa, 12 feet high by 26 feet long, picturing part of the Story of Brutus (Plate XLI of *Bertaux Saragossa*). Because of the number of ships shown, this is known as the Ship Tapestry. It has four Latin Gothic inscriptions at the top. Brutus, the grandson of Æneas, is a romantic hero developed in the Middle Ages, from whom Britain was supposed to get its name. Brutus, having killed his father while hunting, was forced to leave Italy for Greece where he found Priam's son Helenus and other Trojans who had been made captives by Achilles' son Pyrrhus. Brutus organized a revolt against the King of the Greeks, Pandrasus, defeated him and made him prisoner. Here the tapestry begins. After marrying *Ignoge* daughter of *pandrasus, brutus* says goodbye to his father-in-law who stands on the shore, and sails forth with the Trojans in search of a new home. Above this scene, to the right, on a deserted island, is the altar of Diana (*diana*) whose oracle told Brutus that he was destined to found a new Troy on a distant island where the sun sets. Sailing west past Gibraltar, Brutus lands in Aquitaine and defeats King Gopharius. The battle is vividly portrayed. Here the tapestry ends. Brutus then sailed to Albion, and on the bank of the Thames founded a new Troy, the name of which in the reign of Lud who fought Julius Caesar, was changed to Ludton (London). Bertaux suggests that the set of tapestries of which this is one may have been woven in honor of the English Princess Margaret of York who married Charles the Bold in 1468.

BRENNUS, BRITISH KING OF GAUL

A little later in date, but rich with the qualities of the middle of the century, is a tapestry now in America (Plate XXI, b) picturing the surrender of Rome to Brennus, British

King of Gaul. Here we see how completely history was rewritten into romance in the Middle Ages. The story of this tapestry is based, not on Livy or Plutarch, or Polybius, but on Geoffrey de Monmouth's *Historia Regum Britanniæ*, or on Wace's *Roman de Brut*, both of the twelfth century, or still more probably on the amplified version found in the fourteenth century French romance of *Perceforest*.

In these romances, Brennus, though King of Gaul, was not a Gaul by birth, but a Briton, of Trojan descent, and in his conquest of Rome had associated with him his elder brother, Belinus, King of Britain. After the conquest, Belinus went back to Britain, but Brennus remained in Italy where he ruled with an iron hand. In the tapestry, Brennus appears twice: once on the right, mounted, and once on the left, with plumed hat instead of crown, but with *brennus* woven into his robe to establish his identity, standing next his crowned brother Belinus who is distributing the ransom paid by the Romans. The other personages in the left half of the tapestry are the Gallic and British knights of Brennus and Belinus. On the right, suppliant before Brennus are the unfortunate citizens of Rome, men and women and a child, headed by their bishop who wears a mitre. The burgher in the extreme foreground brings the keys of the city. In the upper right corner, several of the invaders with booty.

This tapestry is of supreme excellence in design and weave, especially as regards the faces, of which there are 34 developed to show extraordinary individuality. The powerful modeling of the faces is due to marvelous skill in the use of open slits, which are the most difficult and the most necessary feature of tapestry weaving. The vivacious and vibrant quality of the hair, the draperies, and the architecture, is due to the same skilful use of open slits. The three horses are masterpieces that show how far beyond painting is tapestry when contrasts are necessary.

THE BERNE CAESAR

The four Story of Caesar tapestries in the Berne museum (Plate V, j) are a little earlier than the Trojan War group. An excellent book on these Caesar tapestries, with text by Dr. Artur Weese, and with large illustrations in color, was published in Berne in 1911. The height of the tapestries is 13½ feet, with lengths ranging from 20½ to 23½ feet. They are probably the four confiscated by Charles the Bold, Duke of Burgundy, from the estate of Louis de Luxemburg, Count of St. Pol, in 1475, and by Charles the Bold presented to his faithful follower Count Guillaume de la Baume, whose coat-of-arms is sewed on the tapestries. Next they passed, by gift or bequest, to the Cathedral of Lausanne, and in 1536 to the city of Berne. They were made about 1450, probably at Tournai, and are based on one of the numerous semi-historical Roman histories that supplemented the ancient authorities with extracts from medieval romantic poems. A fourteenth century manuscript that may have been used by the author of the tapestries is Nos. 9104 and 9105 in the Bibliothèque Royale of Brussels. It has many illustrations and an inventory shows us that it was still in the possession of the Duke of Burgundy in 1467. The subjects of the tapestries are:

I. Departure of Caesar for Gaul. Caesar receives Gallic ambassadors.
II. Victory of Caesar over Ariovistus.   Caesar's Expedition to Britain.
III. Caesar's Passage of the Rubicon. Victory of Caesar at Pharsalus.
IV. Triumph and Assassination of Caesar.

The one I have chosen for illustration (Plate V, j) is the last, picturing, on the left, the Triumph of Caesar; on the right, his Assassination. The French Gothic inscription in rhyme reads:

Then he wishes to return to Rome, where all who loved him and desired to increase his fame, sought to honor his triumph. And then they elected him the first emperor, in order to increase his power, and reveal him completely as a super-glorious prince.

Among nine of the world's greatest and altogether valiant Heroes, said

Julius Caesar is one as proved by universal agreement. The memory of his heroism and his glory will last forever, and the robust valor of which his heart was full, and of his deeds noble and chivalrous as of a Hero among Heroes, so that the brilliance of his reputation will never be extinguished. As long as the world shall last, his fame and valor will not fall. So be it granted by Him who gives glory and mercy to all.

In the Triumph scene, *cesar* sits on a curule chair in a canopied litter, borne by two damask-draped horses in front and two others behind, and by two lackeys on each side. Costumes, faces, architecture, verdure, are all of the Court of Philip the Good from 1440 to 1450. Caesar wears a long damask robe belted tight at the waist. His brocaded and ermine-lined cloak, which also reaches to his feet, is held at the neck by a broad collar rich with huge jewels. His crown of gold and laurel rests upon a felt hat with ermine brim. He carries neither sceptre nor arms. His hands are bare and rest on his hips. The procession is preceded by two trumpeters who swell their faces furiously in the effort to make an amount of noise worthy of the dignity of Caesar. The two mounted nobles, just behind Caesar, wear short jackets trimmed with fur, and large hats with wide rolled brims. Judging by the richness of costume of himself and horse, the youth in red at the left end of the tapestry, with golden collar of rare magnificence, and with chain of gold for hat band, should be Augustus. Knights in armor bring up the rear. In the distance are seen mountains and castles, and a fox crossing an open field. All this glory had to have a foil. In the middle foreground of the tapestry men and women come to meet Caesar. At their head are the prophet Spurinna, and Caesar's wife, Calpurnia. Spurinna, with arms lifted high, appeals to Caesar earnestly, while Calpurnia on her knees implores him. Spurinna, without hat, wears a green robe, brocaded and trimmed with fur. A heavy gold chain with pendant adorns his neck, and a cutlass hangs from his belt. Calpurnia, with rich jewelry hiding her decolleté, with wide green belt compressing her waist, and with rosary wound around her left arm, wears an enormous two-horned *hennin* with transparent veil. Her attendant lady has a *hennin* even more monumental, but made of heavy material. Inside the wall and gate is pictured the Assassination of Caesar, but without action. The only sign of the approaching tragedy are the daggers held by *caton* and *bruteus*, who stand on each side of the magnificent Gothic throne where *chesar* sits, sceptre in hand and crowned. In the street outside, a horseman and citizens, and across the street, the faces of beautiful ladies framed by the windows through which they look, none of them apprehensive of what is about to happen.

THE REIMS CLOVIS

The two Clovis tapestries at the Cathedral of Reims, which during the war were removed for safe keeping, are probably part of the set of six displayed on the occasion of the marriage of Margaret of York to Charles the Bold in 1468 (Consult *Sartor Reims*). Inherited by the Emperor Charles V, the tapestries were found in his captured baggage after he raised the unsuccessful siege of Metz, and became the property of Duke Francis of Guise. In 1573 they were presented to the Cathedral of Reims by Charles de Guise, Cardinal of Lorraine. In 1840 there were still four of them in existence, illustrated in *Paris Reims*, beside fragments of another. Now there remain only two of them, each with four French Gothic prose inscriptions at the top. The first (Plate 299 of *Hunter 1912*) which was the first of the set, is 15½ feet high by 29 feet long and shows the Coronation of Clovis, and the Siege and Capture of the City of Soissons. The banner of Clovis bears three frogs, the traditional ancient arms of France. The second of the two tapestries, 15½ feet high by 31 feet long shows: the Foundation in Paris of the Church of Saints Peter and Paul, later Sainte Geneviève, now Saint Etiennne du Mont; the Defeat of King Gondebaud of Burgundy; the Preparation for Battle against Alaric; the Stag guiding Clovis to a safe Ford across the River. The story of each tapestry is told in four French Gothic prose stanzas at the top.

The stanzas of the first tapestry read in translation:

In the present story is shown the life of King Clovis, King of France, and the first chapter treats of how said Clovis, son of King Childeric and his wife Queen Baronne, after the death of his father was crowned King with great magnificence.

After which coronation, celebrated with abundance of honour and nobility, this King Clovis summoned the warriors of all the country, and assembled them with the intention of going to besiege the city of Soissons.

And with a multitude of warriors and the war equipment necessary for the undertaking, the said Clovis sets forth, and pushed his siege of the said city of Soissons, and on his side were performed many heroic deeds before the place aforesaid.

And finally as the result of prowess and valor, he conquered and brought to obedience this city, and drove out of it Soages [Syagirius], commander of the said place, who was the son of Gillon the Roman.

CHANSON DE GESTE TAPESTRIES

We now come to tapestries based ultimately on twelfth and thirteenth century French *chansons de geste*—historical novels in verse portraying the romantic deeds of Charlemagne and his followers. I say ultimately because the direct sources were usually fifteenth century French prose compilations with stories that often differ much from any *chansons de geste* that have survived, and that sometimes are closely related to versions in Latin verse or prose. For example, the large incomplete tapestry in the Brussels Cinquentenaire Museum (Plate 61 of *Hunter 1912*) which pictures " Roland at Roncevaux," does not follow the Chanson de Roland, the *chanson de geste* that is regarded as the great national epic of France. It follows instead a Latin prose version of the Spanish campaigns of Charlemagne, the Chronicle of Turpin (Consult *Bédier Epiques*) dating from the middle of the twelfth century. The presence of this important tapestry in a Brussels museum is a perpetual reminder to the Belgians that during the Middle Ages and until the end of the fifteenth century, the art and the literature of the Netherlands were gloriously French in form and inspiration.

In the middle of the left half of the tapestry *rolant* seated on Veillantif splits the head of the Saracen king *marsille* with his good sword *durendal*. In the right half of the tapestry *rolant* appears four times: (1) Fights mounted, his horn hanging behind him, and his sword swung back over his head to the left; (2) Above, to the right, blows his horn to recall Charlemagne; (3) Below, looks at the rock on which he tried to render *durendal* useless; but *durendal* splits the rock without being dulled; (4) In the lower right corner, reclines against a tree, while brother *bauduin* rides away with Roland's horse, horn, and sword. Just above *bauduin*, in an adjacent valley, is *baligant*, brother of *marsille*.

The two complete French Gothic stanzas at the top of the Cinquentenaire Roland read in translation:

"Two pieces he made of the stone of marble, without dulling the sword of fine steel. Then half dead he lay down against a tree, giving thanks to Jesus, the king divine. There he was found by his brother Baudouin, to whom he complained of thirst. But Baudouin could find neither water nor wine to relieve the strong and terrible burning. Baudouin takes horse, horn, and sword, and rides away fearing the Saracens. Now comes Thierry and sees all cut to pieces the flesh of Roland who groans heavily, calling on God who knows all and conquers all; and Thierry weeps at the piteous cries. Thus this good Roland, martyr of Jesus Christ, gave up his spirit like a saint."

The last words of the fragment of a stanza at the left, "he has cut," refer to the head of *marsille*.

APPARITION OF SAINT JAMES

How Charlemagne first came to go to Spain is pictured in a precious tapestry fragment in bad condition, lent by Major J. J. Astor to the Franco-British Exhibition of Textiles in the Victoria and Albert Museum, 1921, No. 59 of the catalogue. Part of the almost illegible French Gothic inscription at the top says: "The king had forty knights watching at the foot of his bed," and "Then came Saint James who told him to go to Spain." The left two-thirds of the tapestry shows *carle* in bed, surrounded by knights with swords and huge lighted candles. The figure above the bed is *s. iaque*. The right third of the tapestry shows Charlemagne setting forth for Spain as instructed by Saint James. Among Charlemagne's companions are *rolant* and *ogier*. Charlemagne's shield, largely restoration, shows the fleurs-de-lis of France.

THE SWAN KNIGHT

A later *geste* is that of Jourdain de Blaye, the beginning of which is pictured on a tapestry illustrated and described in Chapter III (Plate III, h). Still later is the Swan Knight (*Chevalier au Cygne*) one of three *gestes* that glorify the family of Godfrey de Bouillon, grandson of the Swan Knight. Philip the Good in 1462 bought a set of three tapestries picturing the Story of the Swan Knight, from Pasquier Grenier of Tournai. Possibly the piece in the Katherinenkirche at Cracow, 12 by 18 feet, as well as the smaller piece in the Vienna Museum of Art and Industry (Plates VII and VIII of *Kurt Tournai*) are part of this set. The first of the four scenes of the first tapestry shows Elias feeding his swans. In the last of the four scenes Elias appears before King Oriens and Queen Beatrice. One of the two inscriptions reads: "Afterwards the child Elias came before the king in judgment and said that he would champion his mother in the field without assistance." The first of the two scenes of the Vienna tapestry shows the marriage of Elias to a princess. Later, of different design, and made at Brussels, is the Marriage of Oriens and Beatrice, formerly in the collection of Sir Richard Wallace, and now in the Stieglitz Museum at Leningrad. (Illustrated in colour in the *Histoire Générale*.)

PLATE V, b.—MR. MACKAY'S HECTOR AND ANDROMACHE, ONE OF THE GOTHIC TROJAN WAR SERIES, WITH FRENCH INSCRIPTION ABOVE AND LATIN INSCRIPTION BELOW, AND PERSONAGES LABELED WITH THEIR NAMES. FORMERLY IN THE DOLLFUS COLLECTION

PLATES V, c, ca.—CAPTURE OF TROY, ONE OF THE FOUR TROJAN WAR TAPESTRIES AT THE CATHEDRAL OF ZAMORA. CONSPICUOUS IN THIS TAPESTRY ARE THE TROJAN HORSE OF BRONZE, AND PYRRHUS WHO SLAYS PRIAM AND POLYXENA, AND AT THE EXTREME RIGHT OF THE TAPESTRY THE AUTHOR AND HIS ASSISTANTS

PLATE V, d.—THE FUNERAL OF HECTOR, ONE OF MR. KAHN'S THREE GOTHIC TROJAN WAR
TAPESTRIES, FORMERLY AT THE CHATEAU DE SULLY

PLATE V, e.—DETAIL OF PLATE V, d. MOURNERS AT THE FUNERAL OF HECTOR. DEIPHOBUS
IN THE FOREGROUND

PLATE V, g.—DETAIL OF PLATE V, d. TWO OF THE CHOIR AT THE FUNERAL OF HECTOR

PLATE V, h.—MR. EDSON BRADLEY'S "ULYSSES AND DIOMEDES AT THE COURT OF PRIAM," ONE OF THE FAMOUS TROJAN WAR SERIES, FORMERLY IN THE COLLECTION OF LORD HOWARD DE WALDEN

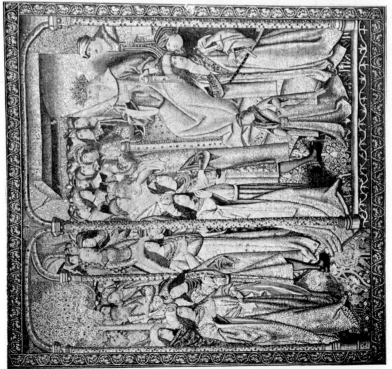

PLATES V, i, ii.—ON THE LEFT, ULYSSES AND DIOMEDES AT THE COURT OF PRIAM. ON THE RIGHT, MARRIAGE OF PARIS AND HELEN. TWO OUT OF A SET OF FOUR FASCINATING LATE GOTHIC TAPESTRIES THAT PICTURE THE STORY OF PARIS AND HELEN. DUVEEN BROS.

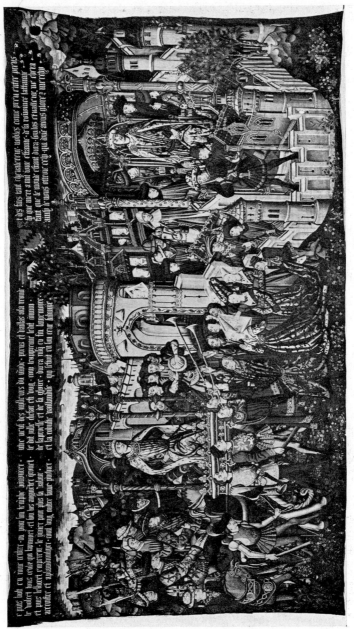

PLATE V, j.—CORONATION AND ASSASSINATION OF CAESAR, ONE OF THE FAMOUS STORY OF CAESAR TAPESTRIES IN THE MUSEUM OF BERNE, SWITZERLAND

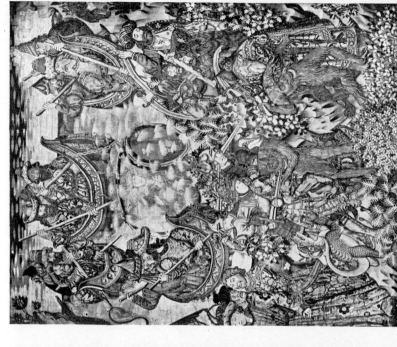

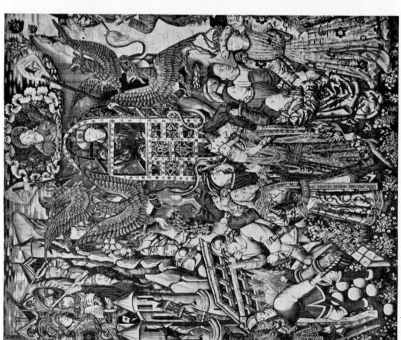

PLATES v, k, ka.—ON THE LEFT, ALEXANDER THE GREAT IN AN AIRSHIP. ON THE RIGHT, ALEXANDER THE GREAT IN A SUBMARINE. DETAILS FROM THE FAMOUS STORY OF ALEXANDER TAPESTRIES IN THE PALAZZO DORIA, ROME

PLATE VI, a.—THE ROSE GARDEN, ONE OF THE THREE LARGE AND BRILLIANT GOTHIC "ROSE
GARDEN" TAPESTRIES IN THE METROPOLITAN MUSEUM OF ART

CHAPTER VI

GOTHIC COUNTRY LIFE TAPESTRIES

UNICORN TAPESTRIES, MARRIAGE TAPESTRIES, HUNTING TAPESTRIES
VISIT OF THE GYPSIES, FLIRTATION, MUSIC, HEROINES, VINTAGE AND
WOOD CUTTERS, ROSE GARDEN, VERDURES WITH AND WITHOUT
PERSONAGES, ARMORIALS, THE TOURNAI INDIES

THE great families of the fourteenth and fifteenth centuries lived largely out-of-doors. Their castles were a refuge from enemies and from bad weather, but when the sun shone and nature smiled, they picnicked perpetually in garden and field and wood. Even when indoors they liked to have the walls hung with out-of-doors tapestries, of which wonderful examples have come to America in the last ten years.

Mr. Rockefeller's Hunt of the Unicorn is the finest of all sets of Country Life tapestries (Plates VI, b, c, d, e, and Colour Plates S, a, b, of the *Subscribers' Edition*). It consists of six tapestries, four of which date from about 1480, and were made by weavers with Tournai training. The other two, that supplement the orginal set, were made later, in France, from designs that show the influence of the Florentine Renaissance. The weave of the later two is inferior, and the figures spot against the background, paint-fashion. The set hung for centuries in the Château de Verteuil of the La Rochefoucauld family, in western France between Poitiers and Angoulême.

The subjects of the tapestries are:

(1) The Start
(2) The Fountain
(3) Crossing the Charente
(4) Wounding a Dog
(5) Death of the Unicorn
(6) The Unicorn in Captivity

8

Nos. 2, 3, 4, 5, are the four older tapestries; Nos. 1, 6, the later two. The unicorn appears in all of the tapestries except No. 1, and appears twice in No. 5. The costumes of several of the principal personages are rich with gold that is still fresh and bright.

The letters A and E (the latter reversed) that are seen tied together with a tasseled cord in the corners and centre of most of the tapestries (Plate VI, b) and on the collars of several of the dogs, should be the initials of the lord and lady for whom the tapestries were made, probably those who are the centre of attention in Tapestry 5.

While these are primarily hunting tapestries, that give a faithful and spirited picture of the life of the period, they are not merely hunting tapestries. The unicorn introduces just the element that would appeal to a lord and lady of the period who wished to emphasize the sanctity of their marriage. The unicorn, which in medieval tradition runs to put its head in the lap of a snow-white maiden, only, is symbolic of Christ, who through the Virgin Mary was brought down from Heaven for the Salvation of Man. Tapestry 2, the Fountain, recalls one of the traditions associated with the unicorn in the Bestiaries that explained to the people of the Middle Ages the habits and peculiar properties of animals, especially of the unfamiliar ones. This tradition was that the horn of the unicorn possessed remarkable powers of purification, and that the other animals of the forest, as seen in the Fountain tapestry (Plate VI, b) would not drink until he had first purified the pool by plunging his horn into it. Belief in the efficacy of the horn of the unicorn was carried so far that one of the most precious possessions of medieval nobles and princes was a piece of the horn mounted like a jewel, with which to test for poison the food and drink offered them. An inventory of 1391 includes: "A piece of unicorn with golden handle to test the food of Monseigneur the Dauphin"; and one in an inventory of the Duke of Burgundy dated 1408: "A piece of unicorn, with silver tip, for testing."

In Tapestry 5 we see the Death of the Unicorn, but in Tapestry 6, one of the later two, he has been resurrected, and is a Captive, chained to a tree, inside a round fence. The tree, it should be noted, is a pomegranate, the fruit of which is symbolic of Life, and of the perpetuation of a family through numerous children. Consequently we find it associated with portraits of the Emperor Maximilian, and of his grandson, the Emperor Charles V, members of the Habsburg family which *by marriage* was said to gain what others had to fight for.

The religious tone of the tapestries is accentuated by the AVE.REGINA.C. (Hail, Queen of Heaven) on a sword-scabbard in one of them.

Possibly the F.R. applied on the canvas at the top of one of this set may be the initials of Francois de La Rochefoucauld, godfather of the French King Francis I. If the four older tapestries came to him by inheritance or gift, it would be natural for him to have his initials added in this manner. He died in 1516.

I find it difficult to express in words my full admiration for these tapestries. The drawing is extraordinary. The personages are real living beings with character expressed in every face. The numerous dogs and other animals and birds are incomparably superior to any we find portrayed by modern tapestry artists or weavers, and equal to the finest of any period. No position was too difficult and no action too elusive to be caught by the eye and pencil of him who composed these tapestries. At trees and flowers and costumes he was equally strong. He understood what to stress and what to slur, and best of all he made cartoons that enabled great weavers to utilize all the possibilities of their marvelous art. Especially would I call attention to Plate VI, c, a detail of the Fountain tapestry. The birds that stand on the marble rim are studies from life, quick and warm, developed by manipulation of bobbins to express what the painter sought but could not in his own medium make obvious. The water stirred by the falling columns has the motion of real water, and reflects the image of the bird's head just as real water would reflect it. The two letters attached to the fountain and the lion mask through which the water escapes, show how effectively gold and silver can be used in tapestry weaving. Perhaps the greatest scene of all is the one illustrated in colour on Plate S, b, of the *Subscribers' Edition*. Plate VI, b, illustrates the strength of faces and hands in both design and weave, marking clearly the position of the diagonal series of stepped slits that effect the modeling. The laciness of the hair and vibrant texture of the hat and pomegranate-patterned jacket of the young man in the foreground are due mainly to cunningly placed slits. The way the horizontal ribs of plain surfaces in high light are forced forward by perpendicular contrast with the vertical hatchings in middle light, which themselves stand upon the horizontal ribs in shadow, is demonstrated on the jacket of the young man at the left, as well as on the cape and wand of the young man in the foreground, and by the leaves of the foliage.

THE CLUNY UNICORN

The most famous Unicorn tapestries in the world are those at the Cluny Museum (Plates CLXIV to CLXVIII, in colour, of *Demotte Gothic*). Made in France near the end of the fifteenth century, with two feet of restoration at the bottom and in a weave much superior to the weave of the later two of the Rockefeller set, but much inferior to that of the earlier four of the Rockefeller set, they have for two generations been fascinating those who visit the Museum, and have won for themselves a permanent position in the world's esteem. Even painters often attempt the hopeless task of copying them on canvas, and then hang the *counterfeit arras* on walls as a

substitute for tapestry, as has been done in the Ladies Dining
Room of the University Club of Chicago.   From the weakness
of the painted copies no one would suspect the strength of
the originals.   Almost as good as the painted copies are those
block-printed on rep, that can be bought by the yard in the
shops of many decorators.

The tapestries were evidently made to celebrate the virtues
of the richly gowned and richly jeweled lady who in all six
is the central figure, supported by the Lion for Strength and
the Unicorn for Purity.   In four of the tapestries she is
attended by her maid, and in two by her little pet dog.   The
coat-of-arms so often repeated, red with three silver cres-
cents on diagonal band of blue, is that of the Le Viste family,
lords of Fresne who gave a president to the French Parle-
ment.   The tapestries formerly hung in the Château de Boussac near Aubusson, and were sold to the Cluny Museum in 1882
by the municipal authorities of Boussac, who had in 1837
acquired them with the Château, still well preserved, that
from a lofty rock dominates the valley of the Little Creuse.

The subjects of the six tapestries are:

I. SIGHT, where the bust of the unicorn is reflected in a mirror held by
the Lady.
II. HEARING, where the Lady plays a small organ that stands on a richly
covered table, and is pumped by her maid (Plate 49 of *Hunter 1912*).
III. TASTE, where the Lady feeds the parrot, and the monkey eats in the
foreground.
IV. SMELL, where the Lady weaves garlands of flowers and the monkey
inhales the fragrance of a rose.
V. TOUCH, where the Lady touches and holds in one hand the standard
carrying the family flag, and feels the horn of the unicorn with
the other.
VI. MON SEVL DESIR, (which in this tapestry appears on the frieze of the
pomegranate-patterned flame-spotted round tent behind the Lady,
with A at the left and I at the right, which may be the initials of
the Lady and her Lover) suggests that "the one desire" is to make
a home.

These tapestries are just as much medallion tapestries as
the Gobelin Don Quixotes and the Gobelin Bouchers of the
eighteenth century, but handled in a Gothic instead of a Louis
XV manner.   While the ground is a brilliant red, strong blue
is the colour of the oval medallion that carries the Lady and
her supporting Lion and Unicorn, with one or more trees at
each end—palm, oak, or pomegranate.   Both medallion and
ground are polychromed with flowering plants that not only
make the two surfaces vibrant with hue, but also gray them
together into harmony.   I should like to have seen these tapestries before the repairer got in his deadly work.   While
they are commonly called *millefleurs,* I prefer to confine that
term to the Gothic verdures of *patternized* floriation that
covers all the ground without introducing long stems, and that
is distinguished by long slits that mark the bending of leaves
to the front.   (Plate VI, ka.)

GOTHIC MARRIAGE TAPESTRIES

Marriage tapestries of much earlier design and weave
are those illustrated on Plates VI, k, l.   The first, belonging
to Mr. Kahn, bears the coats-of-arms of both husband and
wife, and shows the wife training a falcon.   She wears a
lofty *hennin.*   The ground of the tapestry is patterned with
detached flowers, and with the phrase *A mue* inside compasses.
The Musée des Arts Décoratifs has two fragments like the
ground.   The second of these two marriage tapestries was
presented to the Musée by Count Valencia, to whom we are
indebted for the Valencia Museum in Madrid, as well as for
the two large volumes illustrating the finest tapestries of the
Royal Spanish collection.   In it, the lady, who has the initials
A L on her belt, is watering flowers.   Two angels hold open
the curtains of the tent behind the couple.   It is interesting
to compare the scene with that of Tapestry VI of the Cluny
Unicorn set.

GOTHIC HUNTING TAPESTRIES

Brilliant Early Gothic Hunting tapestries are the two illustrated on Plates III, j, k, ka. A little later than these, but still in the second quarter of the fifteenth century, is the Duke of Devonshire's set of four great Hunting Tapestries, for several years on exhibition at the Victoria and Albert Museum (Plate 57 of *Hunter 1912*). While these have been much repaired, and have consequently lost much of their strength of texture, they are of eloquent design. One of them is 14 by 37 feet, the others a little smaller. The M on the trappings of the horse of the lady in one of the tapestries, whose robe is figured with marguerites, is thought by Thomson to associate the tapestries with Margaret of Anjou, wife of King Henry VI of England. Two of the tapestries are illustrated in colour and described in detail in *Thomson History*. Part of a closely related tapestry is the exquisite fragment 11 feet 2 by 10 feet 9 in the Charles Jairus Martin Memorial Collection of the Minneapolis Institute of Fine Arts.

In Mr. Blumenthal's adorable tapestry from the end of the fifteenth century, illustrated on Plate VI, na, the social side of hunting is emphasized. One of the ladies is mounted and holds a falcon on her fist, while her cavalier holds up for her inspection the bird that has just met its fate. The second horse has a double burden. The lady sits sidewise behind her swain, holding his shoulder with her right hand and gazing into his eyes. He has a dog on leash. Cruder in style and weave, and as white as the whitest Louis XVI Aubussons but full of life and vigor, is the Metropolitan Museum's Late Gothic "Stag Hunt," made about 1515. The action in this tapestry is intense. There are three stags, eight horses, and many dogs. The stags are swimming the river, hard pushed by the dogs, with the horses and their riders close after. Several of the huntsmen carry crossbows.

Mrs. Brady's Visit of the Gypsies (Plate VI, m) is the finest of a group of Shepherd and Hunting tapestries made at Tournai near the end of the fifteenth century. It bears the arms of the Effiat family in whose Château near Clermont-Ferrand it formerly hung. The member of the Effiat family who attached the arms was Antoine Coiffier de Ruzé (1581–1632), Marquis d'Effiat, one of the most distinguished men in France during the reign of Louis XIII, who inherited the estate from his maternal grandfather and was planning to make it the most beautiful property in the kingdom when death cut short his triumphal career of diplomat, administrator, and soldier. As Ambassador to England he arranged the marriage of Henriette with Charles I; as French minister of finance he brought order out of chaos; for his conduct in the siege of La Rochelle and in the Italian wars he was made Marshal of France, and appointed Governor of the Bourbonnais, Auvergne, Anjou, etc.

Of his three sons, Henri, the second, was the Marquis de Cinq-Mars, whose tragic story was told so brilliantly by Alfred de Vigny in his romantic historical novel, the first scene of which is located in the dining room of the Château d'Effiat, next the drawing room where the tapestries were.

In the middle of the nineteenth century, the tapestries came into the possession of M. Achille Jubinal, whose *Anciennes Tapisseries Historiées* (Paris 1838) was the first great illustrated book ever published on tapestries. It was M. Jubinal who contributed the illustration of the left third of Mrs. Brady's Fortune Teller to Lacroix's *Manners and Customs of the Middle Ages,* Fig. 369, with the title "Gipsies on the March."

In the middle ground of this tapestry, just to the right of centre, one of the gypsy women is telling the fortune of one of the ladies of the castle. From the left, arrives the gypsy caravan, partly on horseback, with nine children, five of the babies depicted nude, as was then common. The gypsy king with club and sword is certainly a rough looking customer. The gypsy queen at his right is feeding the baby with a wooden spoon from the bowl held by the child beside her. The purse of the lady in the middle foreground is being filched by one of the gypsy children. This lady and her youthful husband are even more richly clad than the older lord and lady who stand at the castle entrance, welcoming the head huntsman who brings a quarter of deer, and the youthful noble who displays a rabbit after which the dog below reaches longingly. Proudly perched on the wall of the castle is a peacock with tail long and luxuriant.

The background of the tapestry is filled with hills and castles and hunting scenes. In the middle, a huntsman is just impaling the deer seized from behind by one of the numerous dogs.   On the left, a fox, another deer, and a huntsman blowing a huge horn.

There are others of this group of Shepherd and Hunting tapestries in Mrs. Brady's collection, and in the collections of the late Senator Clark, Mr. J. E. Aldred, the Brussels Cinquentenaire Museum, the Victoria and Albert Museum, and the Musée des Arts Décoratifs.

FLIRTATION, MUSIC, AND HEROINES

Altogether delightful and probably woven in France, certainly designed there, is the set of six Country Life tapestries in the Cluny Museum (Plate VI, j). All of them are illustrated in colour on Plates CLXXIV to CLXXIX of *Demotte Gothic*. Against a richly floriated background they show gentlemen and ladies out-of-doors, hunting, walking, reading, talking, flirting, spinning, embroidering, and even taking a bath (Plate VI, j).

Even more brilliant than these are the Youth, Sunshine, and Music, of the Duveen collection. In Youth (Plate XXI, e), rich costumes, jewelry, music, flowers, trees, landscape, make a merry party of four young men and four maidens. In the foreground three little folk give scale to the main scene. One of the little folk blows bubbles, another chases butterflies, while the tiny maiden sits holding an apple emblematic of Love. In the background on the right, a castle and personages. In the background on the left, a peasant with beast of burden. The inscription reads:

> Youth plays while ruddy health remains,
> And thinks all lies within its grasp,
> But this triumph is not endless.
> Here you see the example quite plainly.
> Even he is happy with death at his breast.
> This by youth should be noted.

Music, which is the main subject of the third of the set of tapestries just spoken of, is the subject of a number of individual Gothic pieces, among them Pierre de Rohan singing to his Wife's Playing (Plate XXI, f) at the Cathedral of Angers; the Concert (Plate 327 of *Hunter 1912*), at the Gobelins, which it is interesting to compare with the organ tapestry of the Cluny Unicorn Set; the Duet, a tapestry acquired by the Louvre in 1920, in which the man plays the clarinet while the lady plays the zither, both of them gorgeously clad in red; the *Musicque* of the Boston Museum of Fine Arts, which introduces a whole orchestra, while a Latin Gothic inscription explains:

> *Invenere locum per me modulamina vocum*
> *Dat notula scire, musica docta lire.*

The modulations of the voice found their place through me.
The music learned from the lyre enables one to read by note.

Some Gothic historical, religious, and allegorical tapestries are so dominated by verdure as to call for association with the out-of-door group. For example, the two Heroines (*Preuses*): Penthesilea at Angers, and the Semiramis of

Duveen Bros. (Plate VI, ja). The Angers piece shows on the left, part of the same coat-of-arms that Penthesilea displays in the famous Trojan War group (three Queens' heads) and has a French Gothic inscription telling her story. The inscription over Semiramis (Plate VI, ja) who with mirror on one side, and military messenger on the other, seems to hesitate between devotion to beauty and devotion to duty, reads:

Je fus semiramis royne de babilone.
barbariens conquis, indoys, et syriens.
jusques en septentrion ale, et mis mon trosne.
et si occi le roy des ethiopiens.

I was Semiramis, queen of Babylon.
Barbarians I conquered, Indians and Syrians.
Far up in the north I went and set my throne,
And also killed the king of the Ethiopians.

The inscription over the head of Penthesilea reads:

Au grant siege de troie diomedes requis
a terre l'abatiz tant qu'il cy est memoire
avec mon armee tant d'honneur ay acquit
que entre les princes suis en bruit triumphatoire

At the great siege of Troy I hunted Diomedes,
threw him to earth so that it is here remembered.
With my army I won so much honor
that among princes I am triumphantly famous.

Semiramis and Penthesilea were the best known of the Nine Heroines (*Preuses*) developed by feminists of the Middle Ages to match the Nine Heroes (*Les neuf Preux*). (See Chapters III and XVIII.)

PEACE AND LOVE ALLEGORY

A delightful allegorical tapestry, with the out-of-door feature emphasized, is the Marriage of Peace and Love presented by Mr. W. G. Mather to the Cleveland Museum. There are mountains and castles in the distance, and in the foreground a wide expanse of dogs, rabbits, and birds, playing among bright-coloured flowers. The composition and the 13 personages show Florentine influence. Upon the chariot of *mariage* sit *paix* and *amour,* drawn by two sheep, and escorted by *Oeneus* and *hymeneus.* Ahead and behind, marshalled by *fame immortelle,* come the eight Sisters of Happiness: *Amenite, dilleccion, doulceur, concorde, fidellite, Loyaute, Liesse,* and—*elheite.* The inscription reads:

> *Paix et amour en loyal mariage font triompher par immortelle fame,*
> *Les soeurs VIII, dechassant blasine infame, de chastete et pudique couraige.*

> Peace and love in loyal marriage make triumph through immortal fame,
> The eight sisters, driving away infamous slander, with chastity and modest courage.

VINTAGE AND WOOD CUTTERS

Gothic tapestries that give wonderful portrayal of men in action are the incomparable Vintage, details of which I illustrate on Plates f, h, i, from the middle of the fifteenth century; and the two large Wood Cutters in the Musée des Arts Décoratifs, one of the two with the coat-of-arms of Rolin, Chancellor of Philip the Good, (Plate XXI, h) and thirty years earlier than the other, which is illustrated on Plate 345 of *Hunter 1912.* The finer a tapestry is, the better it stands the illustration of details. Each of the Vintage details is a striking picture in itself. The difference between the middle of the century and forty years later can be seen by comparing the original on Plate VI, g, with the copy on Plate VI, h.

THE ROSE GARDEN TAPESTRIES

At the head of garden tapestries (Plate VI, a, in colour) stand the three large pieces from the middle of the fifteenth century that were so much admired at the Exposition des Primitifs, 1904, to which they were lent by Monsieur L. Bardac, and that are now the property of the Metropolitan Museum. These three tapestries are a liberal education in

Gothic composition, texture, colour, and costume; as will testify the many ladies who have studied them with me. The wide vertical floriated bands of red, white, green, suggest those on the walls of the court room in Jean Foucquet's miniature of the trial in 1458 of Jean, Duke of Alençon, at which the French king, Charles VII presided. Miss Rubinstein has pointed out that the colours of Charles VII were red, white, and green. Possibly the tapestries were made for him either in Tournai, or in France by Tournai weavers.

As far as tapestries are concerned, Gothic conventions are much preferable to those of the Renaissance. The introduction of photographic perspective and heavy shadow may have helped painting, but it hurt tapestry. Plate VI, a, shows a composition that is ideal for the tapestry loom. The ladies and gentlemen, in costumes of the middle of the fifteenth century, all laced and belted to make them look slender, with pointed shoes, and with quaintly luxurious hats, are having a party in a garden of roses. The bushes and stocks and birds and flowers are drawn vividly and vigorously. The dominant convention is the one that does most for tapestries. Personages and bushes have been bent back into the plane of the ground and then the whole ground tipped forward to perpendicular. The result is the happy elimination of one dimension. The personages, and bushes of the background are just as large and just as important and just as clearly detailed as the personages and bushes of the foreground. Moreover, the personages and bushes of the background continue the vertical lines of the personages and bushes of the foreground, and give an upward Gothic movement that is accentuated by the vertical Gothic folds of the robes. The result is a composition that while silhouetted, and in paint comparatively flat, has by the powerful line-contrasts of tapestry texture been forced into bold relief. Admittedly this is an artificial convention, but so are all methods of attempting to depict the round against the flat. It is an artificial convention that, like the conventions of all the arts, gains by what it eliminates in conforming to material and process. It is this convention that makes unnecessary a central point of view, or even a central point of interest, and that prevents large Gothic tapestries from seeming "spotty," and hollow in effect, like most large paintings. It is this convention that makes so many tapestries of the century before 1480 superior in life and vigor, though not in idealism, even to the superfine gold tapestries of the end of the fifteenth century.

WITH AND WITHOUT PERSONAGES

The HERCVLES tapestry of the Musée des Arts Décoratifs shows Hercules in armor and with huge spiked club, in a Gothic field of trees, flowers, birds and rabbits, standing between the Lion that represents Heroism and the Cupid that represents Love.

Other Gothic verdure tapestries with personages, are: two in the Martin Le Roy collection (Plates III and IV of the catalogue, Paris, 1908); Mr. Philip Lehman's Falcon tapestry; the two formerly in the collection of Mrs. Chauncey Blair; and the large piece in the Musée des Arts Décoratifs, with peacock in the centre and with tiny cherubs playing here and there among the flowers.

Gothic verdures with animals, but without personages, are the large piece with border, in the collection of Mr. C. Ledyard Blair, the two in Mrs. Harriman's collection, the two in the Duveen collection, the one formerly in the collection of the late Alexander W. Drake, the one from the Robb collection in the Metropolitan Museum, and the one with unicorn illustrated on Plate VI, ka.

GOTHIC VERDURE ARMORIALS

The finest verdure armorial tapestries in the world are the two in the Berne Museum with the blazon of the Duke of Burgundy. The flowering plants, though detached, are closer together and more nearly continuous than is common until twenty years later. The ground is dark blue, against which stand out boldly the creams and golden yellows, light blues and greens, and bricky reds of the ornament. These tapestries were captured from the camp equipment of Charles the Bold, when the Swiss defeated him at Granson in 1476, and testify to the magnificent draping of the tent of that choleric and rash monarch. The larger of the two tapestries shows the Burgundian arms three times, displayed on rectangular field. The smaller of the two tapestries (Plate XVIII, c) shows the Burgundian arms in the lower middle; in the upper middle and the lower corners, Charles' monogram (Plate XVIII, d) two *c*'s facing each other and tied together with tasseled cord like the A and E of Mr. Rockefeller's Unicorn set; in the upper corners, the Burgundian flint and steel striking fire.

Later in date, with patternized millefleur ground, is the armorial at Haddon Hall, with the Royal Arms of England, (the three French fleur-de-lis quartered with the three English lions inside the belt of the Order of the Garter with its *Hony soit qui mal y pense*), in the centre and four corners. The central blazon is surmounted by a helmet, with cap of Maintenance above, and with human-headed crowned lion above that.

Distinguished by a narrow Renaissance border of Italian design, is the long rectangular tapestry in the Victoria and Albert Museum, bearing thrice the arms of the Rezzonico family set in a landscape over which floats a ribbon carrying the motto, FATO. PRUDENTIA. MINOR (Wisdom is less than Fate).

Several important Gothic verdure armorials, some square, and some espalier or frieze shape, have come to America in the last decade. Perhaps most attractive and in the best condition was the one belonging to French & Co., 9½ by 20 feet, with narrow flower and fruit border, and blazoned twice with the Medici arms inside a large flower and fruit wreath.

TOURNAI INDIES

In the accounts of Philip the Handsome, Duke of Burgundy and King of Castile, we read:

To Jehan Grenier, tapissier, resident of Tournai, the sum of 784 livres, 16 sols, for 346 ells of rich tapestry, very richly made, in the style of Portugal and India, which Monseigneur on June 14, 1504, had taken and bought from him to send into France, to Monseigneur de Ville, who was then ambassador there, as a present to a lord of France whom it is not necessary to name here.

Part of this set of six or of a duplicate set are three tapestries in the Château de Brezé, in Anjou—the Lion Hunt, the Giraffe Parade, Shipping the Animals (Part III, Volume VI, of *Les Arts Anciens de la Flandre*). They are interesting to us because they identify and associate together three tapestries now in America: (1) The Lion Hunt (which was No. 1 of M. Seymour de Ricci's catalogue of the J. Pierpont Morgan Collection of Tapestries, Paris, 1913) while not a duplicate of the Brezé Lion Hunt, is clearly part of a companion piece of the same set; (2) The Triumph of the Innocents, No. 114 of the Lydig sale catalogue, New York, 1913, while not duplicating any part of the Brezé Giraffe Parade, is clearly part of a companion piece of the same set; (3) Mrs. Harold I. Pratt's "Ship Tapestry" duplicates one-third of the Brezé "Shipping the Animals." The animal that swings in midair about to join the three camels already in the ship, is a unicorn. All of these except the Lydig piece still retain the top border, which is of the bell-and-pomegranate type that appears also on Mr. Guggenheim's Hercules set (See Chapter V). The three Brezé pieces and the Morgan piece also retain the narrow floral, side and bottom borders.

PLATE VI, b.—THE FOUNTAIN, ONE OF MR. ROCKEFELLER'S GOTHIC UNICORN TAPESTRIES

PLATE VI, C.—DETAIL OF PLATE VI, b

PLATE VI, d.—ANOTHER DETAIL OF PLATE VI, b

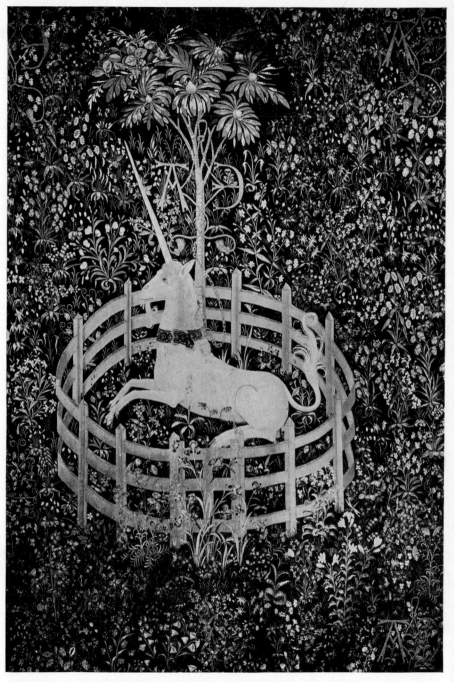

PLATE VI. e.—THE UNICORN IN CAPTIVITY, ONE OF THE TWO LATER PIECES OF MR. ROCKEFELLER'S GOTHIC UNICORN SET

PLATE VI, f.—DETAIL OF GOTHIC VINTAGE TAPESTRY OF THE MIDDLE OF THE FIFTEENTH CENTURY. JACQUES SELIGMANN AND SON

PLATE VI, h.—FORTY YEARS LATER. A LATE GOTHIC VERSION IN THE MUSÉE DES ARTS
DÉCORATIFS, OF THE DETAIL ILLUSTRATED OPPOSITE

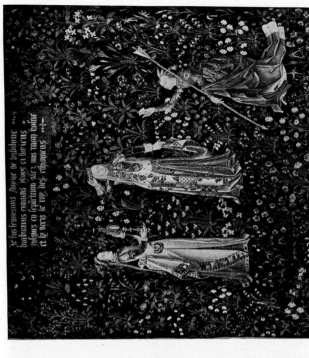

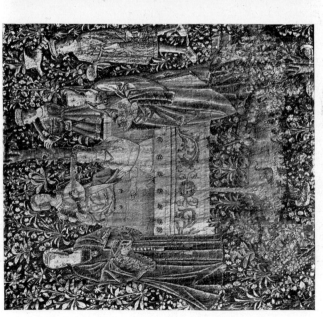

PLATES VI, j, ja.—ON THE LEFT, BATH IN THE OPEN, ONE OF THE SIX BRILLIANTLY BEAUTIFUL COUNTRY LIFE TAPES-
TRIES IN THE CLUNY MUSEUM. ON THE RIGHT, SEMIRAMIS IN ARMOR COMBING HER HAIR, AN EXTRAORDINARY MILLE-FLEUR
TAPESTRY WITH THREE PERSONAGES, AND WITH INSCRIPTION ABOVE. DUVEEN BROS.

PLATES VI, k, ka.—ABOVE, MR. KAHN'S MARRIAGE TAPESTRY, "TRAINING THE FALCON," ONE OF THE MOST ATTRACTIVE SMALL TAPESTRIES IN EXISTENCE (6′ 2″ X 12′ 5″). MADE IN THE SECOND QUARTER OF THE FIFTEENTH CENTURY. BELOW, MISS MILLETT'S LATE GOTHIC MILLE–FLEUR TAPESTRY, WITH UNICORN AND BIRDS

PLATE VI, 1.—MARRIAGE TAPESTRY IN THE MUSÉE DES ARTS DÉCORATIFS, PARIS. MADE IN THE SECOND QUARTER OF THE FIFTEENTH CENTURY. GIFT OF THE LATE COUNT VALENCIA, TO WHOM WE OWE THE VALENCIA MUSEUM IN MADRID AS WELL AS THE TWO LARGE VOLUMES THAT DESCRIBE AND ILLUSTRATE THE SPANISH ROYAL TAPESTRY COLLECTION

PLATE VI, III.—VISIT OF THE GYPSIES, ONE OF MRS. NICHOLAS F. BRADY'S LATE GOTHIC COUNTRY LIFE TAPESTRIES FORMERLY
IN THE CHATEAU D'EFFIAT—NEAR CLERMONT—FERRAND

PLATES VI, n, na.—ABOVE, ONE OF A SERIES OF LATE GOTHIC ALLE—
GORICAL TAPESTRIES PICTURING MAN AS A FRAGILE DEER.   WILDENSTEIN & CO.
BELOW, MR. BLUMENTHAL'S ADORABLE EQUESTRIAN HUNTING TAPESTRY, WITH
TWO LADIES AND THEIR ATTENDANT PAGES, TWO HORSES, A DOG, A FALCON
ON FIST, AND OTHER BIRDS

PLATE VII, a.—ANNUNCIATION, ONE OF THE ROYAL SPANISH SET OF SIX VIRGIN TAPESTRIES RI◌
WITH GOLD, THE FINEST SET IN THE WORLD

CHAPTER VII

GOTHIC TAPESTRIES RICH WITH GOLD

MAZARIN TRIUMPH OF CHRIST, SPANISH VIRGIN TAPESTRIES, CHRIST
AND THE WOMAN, VERONICA, SAINT CLAUDIUS, DAVID AND BATHSHEBA
SAINT JOHN THE BAPTIST, MASS OF SAINT GREGORY, SAINT LUKE
PAINTING THE VIRGIN, DAVILLIER TRIUMPH OF THE VIRGIN,
APPARTAMENTO BORGIA, CATHEDRAL OF SENS

THE finest tapestry in the world is the Mazarin, formerly
in the Morgan collection, exhibited for several years at the
Victoria and Albert Museum, and afterwards at the Metropolitan Museum. It is now in the collection of Mr. Joseph E.
Widener. It is rich with gold that has been marvelously
employed to heighten the effect of a cloth that without gold
would still rank near the top.

The finest *set* of tapestries in the world is the Virgin series,
also rich with gold, and as fresh as the day it left the loom, of
the Royal Spanish collection. I shall never cease to be grate-
ful to the King of Spain for allowing me to study it alone at
leisure, and for permitting me to have splendidly large photographs made that I expect to publish later, in large format.

I wish I knew who was the Author of the Mazarin tapestry.
He comes first in my consideration. Upon his scenario principally depends the greatness of the five pictures that make
the composition, one in the middle, two on each side. (The
same arrangement as in the Spanish Virgin tapestry on
Plate VII, a.) Filled and thrilled with the Story of Salvation as told in the magnificent Credo and Salvation tapestries
(Chapter IV), he locked it all into one single tapestry, in
perfect form. It is the most dramatic story ever told. God

111

let his only Son sacrifice himself for the Salvation of Man. Then the New Law took the place of the Old Law, the New Dispensation of the Old Dispensation, the Christian Church of the Jewish Church, the Roman Empire of the Persian Empire. This was the Triumph of Christ.

Christ sits high in the middle of the tapestry, crowned and richly robed, on a rich Gothic throne (Plate S, n, of the *Subscribers' Edition,* and Plate 369 of *Hunter 1912*), his right hand making the sign of benediction, his left hand holding open towards us an illuminated copy of the Gospels. Two angels hold the rich drapery behind him. Two angels stand beside him, one with the Sword of Justice, the other with the Lily of Mercy. A delightful landscape separates the throne in Heaven from the Earth below, where the Emperor and his Court and the Pope and his Court, bow in Adoration. The Emperor's sword is on the ground beside him, in token of humility. Standing on the column at the right (the spectator's right I mean), is a woman blindfolded, symbolic of the Synagogue, with the Mosaic tables of the Law, and with broken lance. Standing on the column at the left, is a Bishop with Chalice and Crozier, symbolic of the Christian Church. Thus Sargent portrayed Synagogue and Church in the Boston Public Library.

On the right of the tapestry, next the Synagogue, are two scenes picturing the Persian Empire of the Old Dispensation. The lower scene shows Ahasuerus putting the marriage ring on the hand of Esther. The upper scene shows Esther making preparation for the banquet she gave to the King and to Haman. A subordinate group, in the upper left corner of the lower scene, shows Esther kneeling before Ahasuerus, when she came before him unsummoned, at the risk of death, in the effort to save the people of her race, the Jews, whom Ahasuerus at the instigation of Haman had condemned to death.   A Latin Gothic inscription on the arch over the lower scene, reads:

> *cum osculatum fuerat*
> *sceptrum assueri*
> *hester scipho utitur*
> *regis pleno meri*

which is to say:

> When Esther had kissed the sceptre of Ahasuerus, she uses the King's cup full of wine.

If the marriage of Ahasuerus and Esther has reference to any contemporary marriage, it is that of Philip the Handsome, ruler of the Netherlands, to Joanna of Spain, daughter of Ferdinand and Isabella.

On the left of the tapestry, next to the Christian Church, are two scenes picturing the Roman Empire of the New Dispensation.   Below, the Sibyl of Tibur kneels before the Emperor Augustus (whose name *octavianus* is woven at the bottom of the scene), summoned by him to declare whether he should yield to the desire of the Roman Senators to worship him as God.   Tradition is that the Sibyl replied:

> Token of doom. The Earth shall drip with sweat.
> From Heaven shall come the King forevermore,
> And present in the flesh, shall judge the World.

Forthwith, as shown in the subordinate group in the upper right corner of the scene, where the Emperor kneels beside the Sibyl: The Heavens were opened, and a great brightness lighted upon him.   He saw in the Heavens a Virgin, passing fair, standing upon an altar, and holding a man-child in her arms, whereat he marveled exceedingly.   And he heard a voice from the Heavens saying, ''This is the Altar of the Son of God.''   The Emperor straightway fell to the ground, and worshipped the Christ that should come.   The Vision took place where now is the Church of Santa Maria on the Capitol. Therefore it is now called Santa Maria in Aracoeli (Altar of Heaven).   Because of the Vision, Augustus did not suffer himself to be worshipped, but said, "Mortal I am, and will not call me Lord." Afterwards he built a high altar on the spot where he had seen the Vision, and wrote thereon in Latin saying: "This is the Altar of the Son of God." The upper scene on the left of the tapestry shows the breaking of ground for the construction of the altar.

The story of the lower scene is told in Latin Gothic inscription on the arch:

> *regem regum adoravit*
> *augustus imparator*
> *cum sibilla demonstrarat*
> *quo patuit salvator*

In English:

The Emperor Augustus adored the King of Kings, when the Sibyl pointed out where the Saviour was visible.

The church of Santa Maria in Aracoeli is still rich with traditions of ancient Rome. While the present building dates from the fourteenth century and later, the 22 columns of the nave are ancient. The third on the left bears the inscription, A CVBICVLO AVGVSTORVM. The left transept contains an octagonal canopy supported on columns of alabaster, known as the CAPELLA DI S. ELENA (Chapel of Saint Helena, mother of Constantine). Inside this altar is an ancient altar inscribed ARA PRIMOGENITI DEI, said to have been erected by Augustus. It was in this church, that Gibbon, October 15, 1764, first conceived the idea of writing his history of the *Decline and Fall of the Roman Empire*. Yearly, in one of the chapels on the left of the nave of Santa Maria in Aracoeli, the ancient legend is acted out for the faithful and the curious. The Virgin Mary with the Firstborn of God in her lap, sits in a grotto in the foreground. Saint Joseph stands beside her. Behind them are the ass and the ox. Above, God the Father, surrounded by clouds of cherubs and angels. In the background, a pastoral landscape on which the painter has lavished his skill. In the middle-ground, Augustus and the Sibyl, whose presence has here the same supreme significance as in the Mazarin tapestry.

The Mazarin tapestry was made in Brussels about the middle of the reign of Philip and Joanna (1486–1506). There are inferior copies of it, without gold, and with modifications of the design, in the Brussels Cinquentenaire Museum and in the collection of the Cathedrals of Saragossa. Whoever planned the copies, thought to increase the grandeur of the idea by extending the story back to the Creation, and by continuing it into the Christian Middle Ages. In narrow panels on each side of the throne group (which has been increased in numbers, with Christ holding the Globe and Cross of Empire instead of the Gospels), appear Adam and Eve, nude, she holding the fatal apple. In narrow panels in the upper corners of the tapestry appear the three Christian Heroes (*Preux*); on the left, Charlemagne in armour, and with shield, and sword, standing over a prostrate Saracen; on the right, King Arthur and Godfrey de Bouillon, each with his proper coat-of-arms. Both of the Latin Gothic inscriptions have been omitted, and the small scene, Esther kneeling before Ahasuerus has been expanded to fill the whole panel, crowding out the marriage scene. Wherever these two tapestries differ from the Mazarin, it is for the worse. The marvelous scenario of the orginal has been perverted; draftsmanship and weave have been weakened. Even the columns and arches that frame the whole into separate scenes have lost their dignity. The Engel-Gros collection contained a copy of the middle third of the Brussels and Saragossa Triumphs of Christ.

Rich with gold, and brilliant as a whole and in detail, is the Esther and Augustus tapestry (Plate VII, c), the right wing of which reproduces the left wing of the Brussels and Saragossa pieces, which is nearly the same as that of the Mazarin, except that in the Mazarin, Augustus holds a sceptre, while in the others he holds a sword. In the Esther and Augustus tapestry, letters of gold identify OCTAVIANUS, SEBILLA, and

KAROLUS. The middle and left wings of the tapestry are devoted to the Story of Esther. So we have represented in the tapestry the Persian Empire of the Old Dispensation, the Roman Empire of the New Dispensation, and the Christian Hero (*Preux*) Charlemagne. The main scene, in the middle of the tapestry, shows Esther beseeching Ahasuerus to rescind the law destroying her people. The first scene, in the upper left corner, shows Mordecai, uncle of Esther, already established in Court favour, kneeling before Ahasuerus (the Persian King known to the Greeks and us as Xerxes). The second scene, in the lower left corner, pictures a great service rendered by Mordecai to King Ahasuerus. Learning that two of the royal chamberlains, of those who kept the door, sought to lay hands of violence on the King, Mordecai told Esther, who then told the King. In this scene, the two criminals are brought under arrest into the presence of Queen Esther and King Ahasuerus. Note the two sheriffs, one with slashed hat, and one with spiked helmet, both of whom appear also in the main scene. The third scene, at the right of the first scene, shows Esther by command of Ahasuerus dictating the decree that saved the Jews. In the Middle Ages this triumph of Esther's was held to foreshadow the later Triumph of the Virgin and of Christianity.

Mr. Blumenthal's Charlemagne reproduces on the left, not the left but the right wing of the Brussels and Saragossa pieces— Esther kneeling before Ahasuerus; Esther making Preparations for the Banquet; the two Christian Heroes, King Arthur and Godfrey de Bouillon, with their coats-of-arms. The rest of the tapestry is taken up with the Story of Charlemagne, the iconoclast (Plate 371 of *Hunter 1912*).

SPANISH VIRGIN TAPESTRIES

Close to the Mazarin tapestry in design and weave, with less powerful story but in far better condition, is the set of six tapestries rich with gold, picturing the Story of the Virgin, in the Royal Spanish collection, with the same triptych division by Gothic columns and arches into five scenes. All the tapestries but one have a floral border (Plate VII, a) instead of the jeweled moulding of the Mazarin tapestry. (Plate VII, b). I class these six tapestries as a set, although one has a different border (Plate VII, b), and the last two have a floral foreground, and greater height than the first four—11½ feet as compared with 10½ feet.

The set was made for Philip and Joanna, brought to Spain by Philip and Joanna, and for half a century hung close to Joanna. Her son Charles V and her grandson Philip II were equally fond of it. It has been suggested that some of the scenes introduce Philip and Joanna, Juan and Margaret, and other members of the family, picturing scenes connected with Habsburg betrothals and marriages. This is not at all improbable, even when the likenesses are not apparent, and even when the scenes are primarily sacred. With this in mind I hope soon to study the tapestries closely again. The subjects are:

     I. Annunciation (Plate VII, a).
     II. Nativity A (Plate VII, b).
     III. Triumph of the Virgin.
     IV. The Virgin as Intercessor (Plate VII, ba).
     V. Presentation of Jesus.
     VI. Nativity B.

There is a duplicate of No. VI in the collection of the Saragossa Cathedrals (Plate VII, ha); and of No. V in the Martin Le Roy collection, formerly in the Saragossa collection. Other similar tapestries at Saragossa, with different borders, are: (1) Marriage of David and Bathsheba, with Nathan standing reproachful in the foreground; (2) Solomon and the Queen of Sheba; (3) Resurrection of Lazarus, with Gothic inscriptions over each of the seven scenes, there being two scenes in each of the upper corners.

These tapestries represent the art of weaving perfected to

its highest point. While the faces have not the strength of earlier Gothic tapestry faces, and have in imitation of the early Florentine painters been made angelic at the expense of individuality, the simplicity and richness of composition are what we should expect from full-size cartoons that might have been painted by Gerard David (Consult *Bodenhausen David*) for Philip and Joanna, and that were woven in tapestries by the most skilful masters of the period. Without attempting to establish David definitely as the designer, I wish to suggest the possibility.

CHRIST AND THE WOMAN

Another tapestry suggesting Gerard David is Mr. Widener's Christ and the Woman, with more silver and less gold, all in perfect condition, and consequently with a mysterious and unique quality that suggests the lustre of ancient Spanish pottery. The dramatic force of the picture is extraordinary (Plate VII, g). On the right and on the left separated by Gothic columns from the main scene, are the Four Evangelists with their Symbols: Matthew, with winged cherub; Mark, with lion; Luke, with ox; John, with eagle; all busy with their books. The main scene is located in the Temple at Jerusalem, pictured as a Gothic church, with distance given by a strip of landscape seen through the open door. A Latin inscription gives the subject:

"He that is without sin, let him first cast stones at her."

In the foreground, kneels the Woman, with the inscription just below her, on the inside edge of the border. Facing her, on the right, under a noble canopy, stands Jesus, in the act of uttering the phrase that dumbfounds the accusers. Behind the Woman, on the left, two of the accusers hold in their hands the stones that they have lost the desire to cast at her. In the middle-ground are other accusers and spectators.

The story is based on the eighth chapter of the Gospel according to Saint John:

Early in the morning, Jesus came again into the temple, and all the people came unto him; and he sat down, and taught them. And the Scribes and Pharisees brought in to him a woman taken in adultery; and when they had set her in the midst, they said unto him, Master, this Woman was taken in adultery, in the very act. Now Moses in the Law commanded us that such should be stoned; but what sayest thou? This they said, tempting him, that they might have to accuse him. But Jesus stooped down, and with his finger wrote on the ground, as though he heard them not. So when they continued asking him, he lifted up himself, and said unto them, He that is without sin among you, let him first cast a stone at her.

The Scribes and Pharisees were anxious to apprehend Jesus in some violation of the Law. If He said that the Woman should be stoned, his judgment would be contrary to the Roman Law, which was the supreme Law of the country. If He said that she should *not* be stoned, his judgment would be contrary to the Jewish Law, that was the Law of his people. Whatever his answer, they counted on being able to show that He was wrong. With genius has the critical moment of the story been portrayed. Astonishment and dismay reveal themselves equally in the faces of the accusers. Evidently they have been caught in the trap set for another. By the words of Jesus the accusers have become the accused. Their faces and eyes are masterpieces of artistic accomplishment. Here again woven cloth has surpassed painted canvas in portraiture (Cf. Plates III, a; V, a). Christ and the Woman excels not only in the qualities that make a great tapestry, but also in the qualities that make a great painting. The weaver has understood with his wool and his silk how to get paint effects without losing tapestry effects, and how to employ silver and gold lavishly, skilfully, wisely.

VERONICA AND SAINT CLAUDIUS

Tapestries brilliant with gold in the Knole-Morgan collection were the Veronica, and the Miracles of Saint Claudius, the former now in the collection of Mr. Philip Lehman (Plates VII, e, f), the latter in the collection of Mrs. F. T. Bradbury

(Plate VII, a). The Veronica is a scene from the Vengeance of Jesus Christ (Chapter IV). Vespasian, sick with leprosy is cured by looking at the picture of Christ imprinted on the handkerchief with which his face was wiped on the Road to Calvary. Here we have another strong and effective composition, with many personages richly gowned. The gold has been used wisely. Its effect can be detected even in my half-tone (Plate VII, e). Prominent in this tapestry is the pomegranate pattern (For example, on the robe of Titus, son of Vespasian, who stands behind his father, with his left arm thrown affectionately around him), which was the favorite drapery pattern of Gothic tapestries during the last half of the fifteenth century and at the beginning of the sixteenth.

Brilliant also is the Miracles of Saint Claudius (Plate VII, h), with the beautiful dog in the foreground, and the two rescued children with protecting angel, both on the right. I went to the Bollandist *Acta Sanctorum* for the story, that was identified by Monsieur Roger-Miles (Consult the description of Plate V in *Ricci Morgan*). This tapestry is a little later in date than those we have been discussing. The scenes are laid in the Free County of Burgundy (Franche Comté), which was the personal domain of Margaret of Austria. Here in the seventh century lived Claudius, who was Archbishop of Besançon for seven years and Abbot of the Monastery of Saint Oyand for fifty-five. Today, as in the time of Caesar, the principal city is Besançon (Latin *Vesontio*), 330 miles south-east of Paris.

The monastery of Saint Oyand was in the extreme south of Franche Comté. The name of the village was changed to Saint Claude in the twelfth century, upon the discovery of the body of Saint Claudius, which had been hidden at the time of the Saracen invasions. Among famous personages who made pilgrimages to Saint Claude, were Philip the Good in 1422, 1442, 1443; Charles the Bold in 1461; Louis XI in 1456, 1482; Anne of Brittany, wife of Louis XII in 1500, to give thanks for the birth of her daughter Claudia. The Miracles of Saint Claudius pictured in the tapestry are two: the Restoration of Two Drowned Boys, in the foreground; the Resuscitation of a Drowned Boy, in the background; Saint Claudius being the especial patron of drowned persons. In both scenes, the central figure is God, by whom the miracles were accomplished, *through the intercession* of Saint Claudius who stands near him. On the left of the first miracle the boys are seen falling into the stream; on the right, saved from it. In the foreground the father and mother kneel before God, who wears crown and sceptre. In the scene of the second miracle, we see the rescued boy in the arms of the traveler who had pulled his body out of the water, and on the extreme right the mother with the nun who advised her to appeal to Saint Claudius to resuscitate her dead child. Other interesting tapestries with gold follow:

OTHER TAPESTRIES RICH WITH GOLD

I. Deposition in the Brussels Cinquentenaire Museum, with foreground figures borrowed from a Pietá by Perugino, and with one of the personages showing the name PHILIEP on the edge of his cape.

II. Road to Calvary, with Crucifixion in the background; and Deposition, both 10 feet in height, in the Royal Spanish collection (Plates, 18 and 19, of *Valencia*). The Spanish collection also contains another version of the same Deposition, with Gothic columns, which I date at 1510, the first two at 1515.

III. Birth and Passion of Christ, in seven pieces, 8 feet in height, at the Cathedral of Trent. The Road to Calvary duplicates the design of the Road to Calvary in No. II. One of the tapestries of this set bears letters that have been read PEETER DE ARSETTL. I cannot see it as the signature of Peter van Aelst.

IV. Nativity, in the Budapest Kunstgewerbe Museum, which duplicates the design of the Trent Nativity.

V. Passion of Christ, in four small pieces, described and illustrated by Joseph Destrée in *La Revue d'Art,* in 1922. It bears the arms of Pietro Soderini who was *Gonfaliero* of Florence from 1502 to 1512, when the Medici returned with a Spanish army and sent him into exile. Though this set has no gold, I have introduced it here because of the character of the designs.

VI. Splendid and ranking high among tapestries rich with gold are the David set in three pieces and the John the Baptist set in four pieces, 11½ feet high, in the Royal Spanish collection. Both sets have short Latin Gothic inscriptions in the top border. Brilliant also is the David-Turnus tapestry that in true medieval fashion associates the stories of David and Æneas.

VII. Made about 1515, with Latin Gothic inscription in the top border and names in Roman lettering, are the Virtues and Vices (Faith, Fame, Infamy, Fortune, etc.) in nine pieces (Plates 32 to 40 of *Valencia*); and the Honors in three pieces (Plates 20 to 22 of *Valencia*); all with Latin Gothic inscriptions in the top border and with names in Roman lettering, and all in the Royal Spanish collection.

VIII. The earliest tapestry in the Royal Spanish collection is the Nativity, with gold, made about 1470. The faces are strongly individualized in the early Gothic manner. God with angels, and with Latin Gothic inscriptions, appears in Heaven above. The architecture that forms the framework is vigorously designed and boldly employed. On each side of the Nativity scene are the prophets Isaiah and Micah, with their Latin Gothic placards.

IX. Much later, about 1500, is the Mass of Saint Gregory, rich with gold and suggestive, with its two prophets and scrolls bearing Latin Gothic inscriptions, of the great Salvation group (Chapter IV). Before the altar kneels Saint Gregory, with numerous letters on the hem of his garment, among them BRVXEL. Behind the altar is the Resurrection of Christ, with the Veronica. In the upper corners are the Kiss of Judas, and the Road to Calvary. This tapestry was presented by Joanna to her mother Isabella.

X. Saint Luke painting the Virgin, in the Louvre, (Plate 257 of *Hunter 1912*) after the picture by Roger van der Weyden at the Munich Museum, of which there is a duplicate in the Boston Museum of Fine Arts. The landscape background is effective. Saint Luke's identity is made certain by the s. LUCAS on the scroll behind him.

XI. Davillier Triumph of the Virgin, in the Louvre (6 feet by 9 feet 4). Dated 1485. Architecturally framed into a triptych, with niches for four prophets above. The central idea is of the Virgin as the Fountain of Life. In Heaven above, beneath a Gothic dome, is God with crown and sceptre. Two angels place on the head of the Virgin a crown bearing the Holy Spirit in the form of a dove. The Child in the Virgin's lap holds a pomegranate. In the foreground, a fountain. On the left of the tapestry, Moses and the Fall of Manna; on the right, the Piscina Probatica, with the angel stirring the pool, and Christ in the background. The four prophets have Latin Gothic scrolls. The two long lines of Latin on the frame at the bottom are in Roman lettering. The upper of the two lines reads (*Song of Solomon IV*, 15): A FOUNTAIN OF GARDENS, A WELL OF LIVING WATERS, AND STREAMS FROM LEBANON. MADE IN THE YEAR 1485. Other inscriptions are quotations from the Bible about water and thirst.

XII. The Eucharist, as symbolized by the action of the Child pressing the juice out of a bunch of grapes (Plate VII, ga): Annunciation and Crucifixion; Road to Calvary; Holy Family: all small tapestries rich with gold in the Appartamento Borgia at the Vatican.

XIII. Christ and Mary Magdalen, and the Entombment, two small tapestries rich with gold at the Louvre.

XIV. Adoration of the Magi, Pietá, and Triumph of the Virgin, at the Cathedral of Sens. All small. The last of the three is the longest, and has the central scene flanked with the Coronation of Bathsheba by her son Solomon, on the left; and with Esther welcomed by Ahasuerus, on the right. The last is one of the finest small tapestries in the world.

XV. Annunciation, and Adoration of the Magi, at the Gobelins.

XVI. Other interesting small tapestries with gold are: the Life of the Virgin, in the Altman collection at the Metropolitan Museum; the Crucifixion, with other scenes, made about 1515, in the Dreicer collection at the same museum, previously in the Hainauer collection; Mr. Kahn's *Noli me tangere* formerly in the Lydig collection; Mr. Mackay's Adoration of the Magi; Mr. Severance's Childhood of Jesus, in three scenes (Plate VII, fa); Mr. George Blumenthal's Veronica, and Pietá, the latter of especial importance; Mr. Ryan's Pietá; Mr. Arthur Lehman's Holy Family; Virgin and Child, in the Madrid Archeological Museum; Deposition, Entombment, and Resurrection, a tapestry in three scenes in the Murray collection, at the Victoria and Albert Museum.

PLATES VII, b, ba.—ABOVE, NATIVITY; BELOW, INTERCESSION WITH
THE VIRGIN. FROM THE ROYAL SPANISH VIRGIN SET

PLATES VII, d, da.—ABOVE, DETAIL FROM MR. BLUMENTHAL'S CHARLE-
MAGNE TAPESTRY, SHOWING KING ARTHUR AND GODFREY DE BOUILLON WITH
THEIR COATS-OF-ARMS. BELOW, DETAIL OF MR. PHILIP LEHMAN'S VERONICA
TAPESTRY, FORMERLY IN THE KNOLE AND LATER IN THE MORGAN COLLECTION

PLATE VII, e.—VESPASIAN KNEELING BEFORE VERONICA, DETAIL FROM MR. PHILIP LEHMAN'S
VERONICA TAPESTRY

PLATES VII, f, fa.—ABOVE, MR. PHILIP LEHMAN'S VERONICA, THE MOST BEAUTIFUL TAPESTRY OF THE KNOLE-MORGAN COLLECTION. BELOW, MR. SEVERANCE'S "CHILDHOOD OF JESUS" IN THREE SCENES

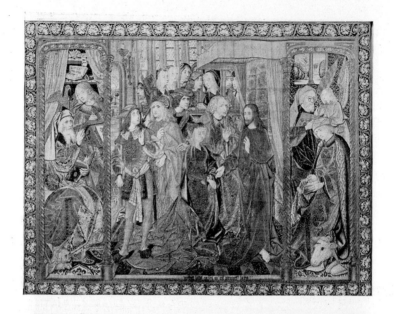

PLATES VII, g, ga.—ABOVE, MR. WIDENER'S CHRIST AND THE WOMAN,
A TAPESTRY INTENSELY DRAMATIC, WITH WEAVE OF SUPREME EXCELLENCE.
BELOW, THE EUCHARIST, A SMALL TAPESTRY IN THE BORGIA APARTMENTS
OF THE VATICAN

PLATES VII, h, ha.—ABOVE, MRS. F. T. BRADBURY'S SAINT CLAUDE
TAPESTRY, FORMERLY IN THE KNOLE–MORGAN COLLECTION. BELOW,
NATIVITY, ONE OF A GROUP OF FOUR TAPESTRIES RICH WITH GOLD
IN THE COLLECTION OF THE SARAGOSSA CATHEDRALS

CHAPTER VIII

FLEMISH AND FRENCH RENAISSANCE TAPESTRIES

BERNARD VAN ORLEY, LUCAS VAN LEYDEN, RAPHAEL, GIULIO ROMANO
FONTAINEBLEAU

RENAISSANCE tapestries have many virtues. The borders are wide and interesting. The texture, though inferior. to that of Gothic tapestries, still possesses power. The compositions are clear and picturesque, though less suitable for tapestry technique, because of the lowering of the horizon and the consequent increase of uninteresting sky; because of the introduction of photographic perspective and the consequent centralizing of the attention, and weakening of the background; because of the introduction of too many horizontals, and the consequent complication and confusion of lines. The colours are harmonious and pleasing, though the reds are weak as compared with Gothic, and the golden yellows and cream whites occupy too much of the surface.

The only Renaissance tapestries that equal the great Gothics are those picturing the Passion of Christ, designed by Bernard van Orley, court painter to Margaret of Austria (Regent of the Netherlands and aunt of the Emperor Charles V), and made in Brussels between 1515 and 1530. Their greatness is due to their having retained so many of the virtues of Gothic design and texture, and being Renaissance principally as regards details of costume and architecture. In some respects they are even superior to most of the Late Gothics rich with gold. They are much more dramatic, and fasten the attention more quickly and more forcefully. Like them, they are square in shape, so that the centralizing of the interest does not harm. As in them, gold has been employed with marvelous skill, and lavishly. Most important of all, the full-size cartoons were executed by the master painter himself, and the tapestries were woven under his direct supervision, so that the perfection of detail is extraordinary. There are six in the Royal Spanish collection:

    I. Last Supper (Plate 66 of Valencia Spanish).
    II. Gethsemane (Plate 28 of Valencia Spanish).
    III. Road to Calvary (Plate 29 of Valencia Spanish).
    IV. Crucifixion (Plate 26 of Valencia Spanish).
    V. Crucifixion (Plate 30 of Valencia Spanish).
    VI. Deposition (Plate 31 of Valencia Spanish).

Nos. II, III, V, VI, have the same border and were made as a set for Margaret of Austria, who bequeathed them to her nephew the Emperor Charles V. They were woven at Brussels, by Pierre van Pannamaker. On Sept. 1, 1520, Bernard van Orley witnessed a contract made between Margaret of Austria and Pierre van Pannamaker for the weaving of two Passion tapestries. No. I was purchased by Charles V from Pierre van Panamaker, at the price of 38 florins a square ell. These five tapestries are 11 feet 4 inches high and nearly square. No. IV is considerably smaller. It is one of the three tapestries constituting the Dais of Charles V. It is in Van Orley's early style, while he was still under the influence of his predecessors, and before he had completely developed his own individuality. Also from Van Orley's early period are the Baptism of Christ in the Brussels Cinquentenaire Museum, (Plate 21 of *Destrée Cinquentenaire*), and Mr. George Blumenthal's Crucifixion (Plate VII, c).

The finest set of Van Orley Passion tapestries is in America, three-fourths of it:

  I. Last Supper, in the collection of Mr. Philip Lehman (Plate VIII, ca).
  II. Gethsemane, in the collection of Mr. Joseph Widener.
  III. Road to Calvary, in the Jacquemart-André Museum, Paris.
  IV. Crucifixion, formerly in the Morgan-Dollfus collection, now in the collection of Mr. Joseph Widener.

This set excels in weave, and the border is much better than that of the Spanish set. Nos. II, III, and IV were once in the Berwick and Alba collections (Nos. 5, 6, 7 of the catalogue, Paris 1877). No. I duplicates the panel but not the border of No. I in the Royal Spanish collection. Nos. II and III duplicate Nos. II and III of the same collection. No. IV is altogether different from, and vastly superior to No. V of the Spanish collection. Mr. Lehman's Last Supper (Plate VIII, ca) I cannot sufficiently praise. For me it is the finest of all the Van Orley tapestries that have survived (Plate VIII, b). Mr. Widener is fortunate to have the small Pietá from the Berwick and Alba collection. The design duplicates that of one of Van Orley's paintings in the Brussels Museum of Painting—the middle section of the Hanneton Triptych—but the tapestry is more fully developed and incomparably superior as a work of art. The border is exquisitely rich. The Metropolitan Museum has the small Adoration of the Magi formerly in the Altman-Hainauer collection (Plate VIII, a).

Interesting, but not all comparable with the Passion tapestries, are Van Orley's:

I. Notre Dame de Sablon, a set of four large tapestries formerly in the Spitzer collection, two of them divided, each into three fragments. The most important of the four is now in the Brussels Cinquentenaire Museum (Plate 79 of *Hunter 1912*).

II. Romulus and Remus, in six pieces, in the Royal Spanish collection (Plates 41 to 46 of *Valencia*).

III. Battle of Pavia, a set of seven large tapestries in the Naples Museum (Plate 309 of *Hunter 1912*).

IV. Hunts of Maximilian, a set of twelve large tapestries in the Louvre (Plate VIII, d, da).

V. Mr. Albright's two Story of Isaac tapestries shown at the Buffalo Tapestry Exhibition, 1914.

VI. The Homage Scene listed by Schmidt as belonging to the German State Secretary von Kuhlmann (Plate No. 114 of *Schmidt Bildteppiche*).

VII. The large David and Goliath tapestry of the Ffoulke collection, shown at the Avery Library Tapestry Exhibition, 1914, and at the Brussels Tapestry Exhibition, 1905. (Plate 43 of *Ffoulke* in colour.)

10

VIII. Months, of which there are two in the Metropolitan Museum, and two of a different set in the Palazzo Doria.

Count Tiele-Winckler's Story of Jacob in ten pieces is also by Van Orley, but the Story of Abraham, at Hampton Court, with duplicate sets in Madrid and Vienna, is by Giulio Romano.

The Notre Dame de Sablon set listed (Plate 79 of *Hunter 1912*) is on the border line that separates Renaissance from Gothic. The columns and borders are Renaissance, but the background architecture is still Gothic and the inscriptions that fill half the border are in Gothic lettering. The tapestries were presented to a church in Brussels, Notre Dame de Sablon, that is still in existence, by Francis de Taxis, Imperial Postmaster of Charles V, who inscribed in Latin in the right border of the tapestry that is in the Brussels Museum:

The worthy Francis de Taxis of pious memory, master of the posts, had this made in 1518.

The tapestry is divided by columns into three panels, and Francis de Taxis appears in each scene. The youthful Charles V and his brother Ferdinand appear in the middle panel; their father Philip the Handsome, and grandfather Maximilian, in the scene on the left; and Ferdinand with his four sisters and his aunt, Margaret of Austria, in the panel on the right. The coat-of-arms in the top border is that of Margaret of Austria. The story of the tapestry is told in the Latin inscriptions and on pages 78–80 of *Hunter 1912*.

The Romulus and Remus set listed above is one of the most delightful products of Brussels Renaissance looms. It has a rich Van Orley border, and at the top long narrow panels carrying a Latin inscription in Roman letters.

The Battle of Pavia, commemorating the victory of the Imperial troops over the French, in 1525, is less agreeable. Four of the borders are missing and have been replaced by strips of painted canvas. The height of this set is 13 feet 9 inches, with lengths from 25½ to 29 feet. There are numerous portraits, among them one of the French king Francis I being taken prisoner. The set was presented to the Emperor Charles V by the States General of the Netherlands, in 1531. Van Orley's original small sketches are in the Louvre.

The Hunts of Maximilian, (Plate VIII, da) which introduce, long after his death, portraits of the Emperor Maximilian, grandfather of the Emperor Charles V, and also portraits of Charles V and his brother Ferdinand, are exceedingly interesting and are a vivid picture of the life and conditions of the period. The Hunts take place in the Forest of Soigne in the neighborhood of Brussels. Many of the landscapes and much of the architecture have been identified (Consult *Migeon Maximilian*). Each of the tapestries bears the appropriate sign of the Zodiac in the top border. The original small sketches are in the Louvre (Plate VIII, d). The tapestries were probably woven after 1530 and bear a monogram not yet identified. They were captured in the baggage of the Emperor Charles V after his unsuccessful siege of Metz, and thus came into the possession of the victorious general the Duke of Guise. Hence the name often applied to them, Les Belles Chasses de Guise.

MONTHS OF LUCAS

The Months of Lucas, (Plate VIII, e) have by some been assigned to Van Orley, but I prefer to accept the traditional attribution to Lucas van Leyden. They naturally show the influence of Van Orley and of the period. Mrs. E. H. Harriman has five of them—April, May, September, October, December—10½ feet high and nearly square, the longest being 13 feet 9 inches. All have the appropiate sign of the Zodiac in the top border, and in the upper corners medallion portraits of the Emperor Charles and his wife Isabella of Portugal pictured as ancient Romans, besides medallions of cherubs in the lower corners. The designs must have been made shortly after the marriage of Charles V in 1526. Both Charles and Isabella appear several times in the set, notably three times in January, which as shown in my illustration of the Gobelin reproduction (Plate XXII, b) has floor tiles patterned with the Imperial double eagle.

ITALIAN VS. FLEMISH-ITALIAN DESIGNS

Flemish Renaissance tapestries of the early period divide themselves into two groups of designs—Italian, and Flemish-Italian. We have already regarded the Flemish-Italian designs of which Bernard van Orley was the chief exponent. We now come to the purely Italian designs of Raphael and Giulio Romano. As a rule the tapestries of Flemish-Italian design had borders with flower and fruit motifs (Plates VIII, c, d, e) which while wider than Late Gothic borders were narrower than the compartment borders introduced by the Italians (Plate VIII, g). But sometimes we find Flemish borders framing Italian designs (Plate VIII, ga).

RAPHAEL'S ACTS OF THE APOSTLES

The most famous set of tapestries in the world is the Acts of the Apostles, with gold, designed by Raphael for Pope Leo X. They were first shown, seven of them, the others not being yet completed, in the Sistine Chapel on the day after Christmas, 1519. According to one of the guests: ''They were considered by everybody the most beautiful specimens of the weaver's art ever executed.'' They were made in Brussels by Peter van Aelst, tapestry merchant and manufacturer, who had been Philip the Handsome's tapestry chamberlain, under the supervision of Bernard van Orley. The weaving is said to have cost 1,500 ducats apiece (about $4,500). The painting of the cartoons cost 100 ducats apiece, making the total cost of the set 16,000 ducats (about $48,000), although rumor had it that the total cost of the set was 20,000 ducats. These tapestries are still one of the greatest glories of the Vatican, where they are always to be seen in the long narrow tapestry gallery that does not display them to advantage, the light being unfavorable. They were removed from the Sistine Chapel by the imperial troops under the Constable Bourbon, who sacked Rome in 1527, and sold as booty. Of one of the tapestries "Elymas Struck Blind," only half ever came back, and that in fragments in bad condition. Two of the tapestries wandered to Constantinople where they were bought by the Constable Montmorency, and by him returned to the Vatican, as commemorated in the Latin inscription at the bottom of one of the woven pilasters. In 1798 this famous set again left the Vatican. It was sold at auction, with the rest of the Vatican furnishings, by the French Army under Berthier for 1,250 piastres each. It was taken to Paris by the dealers who bought it and offered for sale to the French Government. For a time it hung in the Louvre. Finally in 1808 it returned to the Vatican where it has since remained.

THE RAPHAEL CARTOONS

In the Photograph Room of the Library of the Metropolitan Museum are large photographs picturing the Vatican set *as it is now,* made for Mr. Morgan and by him presented to the museum. The subjects of the tapestries are:

    I. The Miraculous Draught of Fish.
   II. The Charge to Saint Peter.
  III. The Cure of the Paralytic.
   IV. The Death of Ananias.
    V. The Stoning of Saint Stephen.
   VI. The Conversion of Saint Paul.
  VII. Elymas Struck Blind.
 VIII. The Sacrifice at Lystra.
   IX. Saint Paul on the Areopagus.
    X. Saint Paul in Prison.

Seven of the full-size cartoons are in the Victoria and Albert Museum (Plate VII, f). They are left-handed because planned for low-warp looms, that in weaving reverse the pattern, the tapestry that faces down reproducing the cartoon that faces up (Plate XIX, c). I admit frankly that I like the Raphael Cartoons better than the Raphael tapestries. The compositions are better suited to paint technique than to tapestry technique. But while admitting this, I place the Vatican Acts of the Apostles next to the Van Orley Passion, among Renaissance tapestries, which shows how extreme is my admiration of the Cartoons.

Oddly enough the Vatican Acts of the Apostles never really had any borders, merely a woven band between each pair of tapestries, a narrow woven moulding at the top, and at the bottom a woven base simulating marble bas-relief. This was due to the architectural conditions of the Sistine Chapel for which the tapestries were designed. The large frescoes beneath which the tapestries formerly hung are separated by painted pilasters. The tapestries, being spaced to the size of the paintings above, had a woven pilaster designed to go between each pair of tapestries, continuing the line of the pilaster above. These pilasters were woven separately and are now attached sometimes to one tapestry, sometimes to another. For subsequent sets of the Acts of the Apostles, the woven pilasters were developed into full sets of compartment borders, (i.e., with compartments containing allegorical figures) on three sides (Plate VIII, g).

The popularity of this set of tapestries can best be judged by the number of reproductions made not only at Brussels in the sixteenth century but also at Brussels and other places in the sixteenth, seventeenth, eighteenth and nineteenth centuries, some good and many bad. The best of those made at Brussels in the sixteenth century are now in the Royal Spanish collection, in the Berlin Museum, at Mantua in Italy, in the National Austrian collection. From these reproductions "St. Paul in Prison" was uniformly omitted because of its small size and lack of interest. One of the finest Brussels sets of the sixteenth century was burned at Paris in 1797, by order of the Directory, for the gold it contained. The small Life of Christ tapestries in the Vatican woven after Raphael's death, with several duplicates at the Castle in Mantua, are detestable. Raphael would be ashamed of them. Whoever painted the large cartoons made a mess of it. Also, the weave is bad, though rich with gold and attributed to Peter van Aelst.

GIULIO ROMANO

As a designer of tapestries, Giulio Romano was the most prolific Italian. After he left Rome for Mantua, his reputation as Raphael's favorite assistant brought him many orders for sketches to be expanded into tapestry. Some of these orders came from Ferrara, where some of the tapestries from Giulio's sketches were probably woven, or at least woven *first*. Ferrara tapestries look so much like Flemish that it is hard to distinguish them, which is perhaps not strange, inasmuch as the master weavers were Flemings fresh from the Netherlands. Among famous Flemish sets rightly attributed to Giulio Romano, are:

I. Story of Scipio, of which there are four in Mr. Hearst's collection (Plate VIII, ga).

II. Fruits of War, of which there are two Late Renaissance sets in the National Austrian collection, signed with the monogram of Martin Reymbouts.

III. Triumphs of the Gods, of which there are three signed with the monogram of François Geubels, in the French National collection.

IV. Grotesque Mouths, for illustrations of which I refer the reader to the Gobelin reproductions (See *Fenaille Gobelins,* volume II).

V. Children Playing, of which there is a set of six in the Royal Spanish collection, and another set of six in the collection of Count Doná delle Rose, Venice, signed with the monogram of William van Pannamaker.

VI. Story of Abraham, of which there is a set rich with gold at Hampton Court (Plate VIII, g), and sets without gold in the Royal Spanish and National Austrian collections.

VII. Story of Mercury and Herse, of which two rich with gold are in the George Blumenthal collection, and the others still in Madrid in the possession of the heirs of the Duchess of Denia—the Duke of Medinaceli (3), the Count of Gavia, the Duchess of Aliaga, the Duke of Tarifa.

For illustration and description of Scipio sets made in the sixteenth, seventeenth and eighteenth centuries, I refer the reader to Colonel d'Astier's *Belle Tapisserie du Roy* (Paris, 1907). The designs were inspired by Petrarch's Latin poem, *Africa,* an epic on Scipio Africanus. Fifteen out of twenty-two of the original small sketches are in the Louvre. The sketches appear to have been brought to France by Giulio Romano's assistant Primaticcio, who was commissioned to take them to Brussels to have them developed into tapestries by Marc Crétif. This set was purchased by Francis I for the Château of Madrid, and burned in 1797 for the gold it contained. Mr. Hearst's four pieces (Plate VIII, ga) belong to a set made about 1550 for the Marshal de Saint-André, of the Albon family the arms of which they carry in the border. The set passed later into the collection of Cardinal Mazarin, and after that into the Royal French collection. It escaped into private possession during the French Revolution. The set of seven, with narrow border, in the Royal Spanish collection, was bought from an Antwerp dealer in 1544 by Mary of Hungary, sister of Charles V, who succeeded Margaret of Austria as Regent of the Netherlands. The Royal Spanish collection also contains two Late Renaissance sets, each in six pieces and both with gold, made at the beginning of the seventeenth century: one with narrow border, signed with the monogram of Martin Reymbouts; the other with wide allegorical compartment border. There are duplicates of five of the last named set in America.

In the Salting collection at the Victoria and Albert Museum, there is one of the original small sketches for Children Playing, as well as a tapestry attributed by the museum tapestry catalogue to Ferrara or Florence. It may be Ferrara; it cannot be Florence. For the Moses set of the Cathedral of Milan, see Chapter XV.

OTHER FLEMISH RENAISSANCE TAPESTRIES

Monumental Flemish Renaissance sets in the Royal Spanish collection, a large proportion of them bearing the Brussels mark and the monogram of the maker, are: the Apocalypse, Saint Anthony, Seven Deadly Sins, Conquest of Tunis by Charles V, Vertumnus and Pomona, all rich with gold; Triumphs of Petrarch, Story of Tobias, Saint Paul, Venus, Cyrus the Great, without gold. The Vertumnus and Pomona sets, three with gold and one without gold, are especially attractive. Two of them hang in the large dining-room of the Royal Palace in Madrid. In the Conquest of Tunis, which is too military and too crowded with soldiers to be interesting, appear portraits of Charles V and of the designer, Jean Vermeyen. There are long Spanish inscriptions in the top border, and long Latin inscriptions in the bottom border. The set consists of ten large pieces, and was made by William van Pannamaker.

Flemish Renaissance sets in the National Austrian collection are: (1) Joshua, Moses, Saint Paul, Tobias, Romulus and Remus; (2) Months, Virtues, Vertumnus and Pomona, Deadly Sins, Ages of the World, Diana, David, Hercules. Most of these bear the monogram of the maker and the Brussels mark. Four of an Early Renaissance set of Vertumnus and Pomona, with Latin Gothic inscriptions and of different design from the four sets in the Royal Spanish collection are now in America. These were formerly in the Berwick and Alba collection. Five of an Early Renaissance set introducing Charles V and his intimates, are in the Gardner collection at Fenway Court, Boston. Five pieces of a Renaissance Story of Vulcan, with gold were sold in Paris at the Hotel Drouot on May 23, 1887, and are illustrated in the catalogue.

I hope some one of my readers will be able to locate them for me. This is the set that was copied so successfully at Mortlake.

In the last half of the sixteenth century the Netherlands suffered greatly from religious troubles, and from the campaigns of the Duke of Alba. Industry generally came to a standstill. Many of the Protestant tapestry weavers sought refuge in other countries. Among them was Francis Spiering who went to Delft, and whose Story of Diana, formerly in the Barney collection, and formerly exhibited at the Metropolitan Museum is one of the best sets of the Late Renaissance (Plate VIII, ea). The frieze-shaped David tapestry, narrow and long, at Williams College, bears Spiering's signature. I am indebted to Mrs. E. Parmelee Prentice for a photograph of it. Mrs. Ray Atherton of Chicago also has a tapestry signed by Spiering and dated 1602. Spiering made the famous Defeat of the Spanish Armada set, that hung in the British House of Lords until burned with the Houses of Parliament in 1834. Much inferior were the tapestries made by Spiering's designer, Karl van Mander, who somewhat trickily set up for himself as a manufacturer in Delft, and several of whose signed tapestries formerly in the Prince Demidoff collection sold at San Donato in 1880 are now in America. The half of one in the Chicago Art Institute is signed IKVMANDER FECIT. AN. 1619, at top of the bottom border, except that the KVM are combined into a monogram. The I stands for *invenit*—designed.

Flemish Late Renaissance tapestry borders (from 1560 to 1615), are a combination of the Early Renaissance "Italian" and "Flemish-Italian," retaining the width and often the allegorical figures of the Italian, but covering the ground richly with flat Flemish verdure (Plate VIII ea). The substitution of wide sculptural borders for these wide, flat verdure borders, marks the transition, about 1615, from Renaissance to Baroque. Most Flemish Late Renaissance tapestries are obviously a continuation of the traditions of the middle of the sixteenth century, and sometimes are close but inferior copies. As a rule they lessen the story interest, so that their stories are difficult to identify except by reference to the earlier tapestries that inspired them.

ENGHIEN LARGE LEAF VERDURES

Distinctively Enghien of the middle of the sixteenth century are the "large leaf verdures," with reds usually gone, which was once called Gothic because of the spiky edges of the huge curling leaves. The borders when preserved are always full Renaissance. There are two, with borders, in the collection of Mrs. Harold I. Pratt; three fragments in the Metropolitan Museum; and a set of seven in the National Austrian collection, some of which bear the mark of Grammont, a suburb of Enghien; besides many elsewhere.

FRENCH RENAISSANCE TAPESTRIES

France was a poor second at tapestry weaving in the sixteenth century. The religious sets of the first half of the century were archaic and crude. One of the best of these sets made at Tours in 1527 is Saint Saturnin, 8½ feet high, of which there is one long piece in three scenes at Angers, and one scene in the Château de Langeais. The French inscriptions in the bottom border and the Latin inscription on the scroll of the Langeais piece are in Gothic lettering. On the third scene of the Angers piece there are portraits of the donors, Jacques de Beaune, Baron de Semblençay and his wife, Jeanne Ruzé. The whites are dominant in most of these Touraine tapestries. Touraine tapestries from the last half of the century are the Gombaut and Macée set, with five or six French quatrains on each, in Roman lettering, of which many examples have survived, the best known being the set at Saint Lô. The set was copied at the Early Gobelins, with new borders. Felletin Renaissance tapestries were still cruder than those of Touraine. The Nine Preux at the Château de Langeais, of which there are several examples in America, seem to me typical.

FONTAINEBLEAU RENAISSANCE TAPESTRIES

At Fontainebleau, the story is different. Every effort was made by Francis I and Henri II to rival Brussels. Oddly enough the most important set that survives is not in France, but in the National Austrian collection (Plates VIII, h, ha). The designs were copied from the stuccoes and paintings of the Francis I gallery of the Château at Fontainebleau, executed by Il Rosso; with exception of the Dance, that was by Primaticcio, who had worked under Giulio Romano at Mantua. The cartoons were painted by Claude Baudouin, and among the weavers were Jean and Pierre Lebries. (L. Dimier in *La Renaissance de l'Art Français*, April, 1921.) The set consists of six pieces, each 11 feet high by 20 feet long. It is rich with gold, and well woven, but the architectural frame work is too heavy. In the middle of the piece illustrated (Plate VIII), Francis I appears as a Roman Emperor. The other scenes are mythological, picturing the Story of Jupiter and Danae, Centaurs and Lapithae, Cleobis and Biton, the Death of Adonis, etc. The draftsmanship is splendid.

Also important is the Story of Diana in eight pieces, seven of which are known to survive—four at the Château d'Anet, one in the Rouen Museum, and two in the Harry Payne Whitney collection. The story is told in long French inscriptions, in Roman lettering, at the top. The subjects of the two in the Whitney collection are: (1) Niobe urging her People not to worship Latona; (2) Death of Britomart.

Of a third Fontainebleau set, with oval picture medallions in the centre, and with grotesque *alentour*, there is one complete tapestry at the Gobelins, (Page 176 of *Guiffrey Seizième*), and two fragments. There are also two fragments in the Lyons Museum, and several small fragments elsewhere.

PLATE VIII, b.—CHRIST AND SAINT JOHN, DETAIL FROM MR. PHILIP LEHMAN'S "LAST SUPPER"
See Plate VIII, ca

PLATES VIII, C, C3.—ON THE LEFT, MR. BLUMENTHAL'S "CRUCIFIXION" RICH WITH GOLD, DESIGN OF BERNARD VAN ORLEY. ON THE RIGHT, MR. PHILIP LEHMAN'S "LAST SUPPER" RICH WITH GOLD, DESIGN OF BERNARD VAN ORLEY

PLATES VIII, d, da.—ABOVE, BERNARD VAN ORLEY'S ORIGINAL SKETCH NOW IN THE LOUVRE, FOR FEBRUARY, ONE OF THE TWELVE "HUNTS OF MAXIMILIAN." BELOW, THE TAPESTRY, MADE AT BRUSSELS WITH GOLD IN THE SIXTEENTH CENTURY

PLATES VIII, e, ea.—ABOVE, APRIL, ONE OF MRS. E. H. HARRI-
MAN'S "MONTHS OF LUCAS," MADE AT BRUSSELS IN THE SIXTEENTH
CENTURY. BELOW, "DIANA AND EGERIA," ONE OF MRS. E. F.
HUTTON'S LATE RENAISSANCE "STORY OF DIANA," MADE IN DELFT
AT THE BEGINNING OF THE SEVENTEENTH CENTURY

PLATES VIII, f, fa.—ABOVE, CHRIST'S CHARGE TO PETER, ONE OF THE SEVEN LARGE CARTOONS NOW IN THE VICTORIA AND ALBERT MUSEUM, DESIGN OF RAPHAEL. BELOW, THE FIRST TAPESTRY WOVEN FROM THIS CARTOON, ONE OF THE SET MADE AT BRUSSELS IN THE FIRST QUARTER OF THE SIXTEENTH CENTURY FOR POPE LEO X

PLATES VIII, g, ga.—ABOVE, SACRIFICE OF ISAAC, ONE OF THE "STORY OF ABRAHAM" TAPESTRIES AT HAMPTON COURT, DESIGN OF GIULIO ROMANO. BELOW, CARTHAGINIAN SUPPLIANTS, ONE OF MR. HEARST'S FOUR RENAISSANCE "SCIPIO" TAPESTRIES, DESIGN OF GIULIO ROMANO

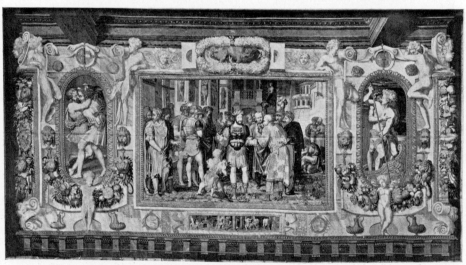

PLATES VIII, h, ha.—ABOVE, DANAE, DETAIL OF ONE OF SIX FRENCH RENAISSANCE
TAPESTRIES RICH WITH GOLD MADE AT FONTAINEBLEAU IN THE MIDDLE OF THE SIXTEENTH
CENTURY. BELOW, FRANCIS I AS ROMAN EMPEROR, ANOTHER TAPESTRY OF THE SAME SET.
IN THE NATIONAL AUSTRIAN COLLECTION

PLATE IX, 3.—TRIUMPHAL ENTRY OF LOUIS XIV INTO DUNKIRK, ONE OF THE FAMOUS "STORY OF THE KING" GOBELIN

CHAPTER IX

GOBELIN TAPESTRIES OF THE SEVENTEENTH CENTURY

EARLY GOBELINS, DUBREUIL'S DIANA, ARTEMISIA, RINALDO AND
ARMIDA, PSYCHE, THE GREAT CONDÉ, LOUIS XIV GOBELINS, RENAIS-
SANCE DESIGNS COPIED, GIULIO ROMANO AND RAPHAEL, MONTHS
OF LUCAS

IN THE seventeenth century, supremacy in tapestry weaving passed from Flanders to France, from Brussels to Paris.
The finest tapestries of this century were woven at the Gobelins. The tapestries of the Early Gobelins (1601–1662) are
equal to those of Brussels in weave, and are superior in design,
while the Louis XIV Gobelins excel greatly both in design and
weave. This artistic supremacy was made possible by the
political and commercial supremacy of France. It was
directly due to the encouragement of the tapestry industry
in France by the French kings Henri IV and Louis XIV. It
began with the establishment of the Gobelin Tapestry Works
in Paris, on the left side of the Seine, at the end of the long
Avenue des Gobelins, by two tapestry manufacturers whom
Henri IV persuaded to immigrate from Flanders.

The story is told briefly in the two tablets on each side of
the entrance gate of the Gobelins. The name Gobelins is that
of the dye plant taken over. As the tablet on the left says:
"Jean and Philibert Gobelin, merchant dyers of scarlet, who
have left their name to this quarter of Paris and to the tapestry factory, had their works here at the end of the fifteenth
century." The tablet on the right says: "April, 1601, Marc
de Comans and François de la Planche, Flemish tapestry
weavers, install their workrooms on the banks of the Bièvre."
Marc de Comans came from Brussels, Frans van der Planken

(the Flemish form of the name) from Oudenarde. They were not laborers, but capitalists and merchants whose success was due to their business sagacity. While they received large subventions and important privileges, there were also burdens like the training of apprentices and the establishing of tapestry factories in the provinces. This in accordance with the edict of Henri IV incorporating the enterprise in 1607. Not long after the death of François de la Planche in 1627, his son Raphael drew out his interest and founded a rival factory in the Faubourg St. Germain on the Rue de la Chaise. The tapestries made at these two plants, as well as at the other plants amalgamated with the Gobelins in 1662 (those of the Louvre and la Trinité, in Paris, and the one established by Fouquet at Maincy near his palace Vaux-le-Vicomte) I call *Early Gobelins,* which seems to me less misleading than the Vieux Paris common in auction catalogues.

There are two contrasting groups of Early Gobelins, those with wide and heavy Baroque borders, like the great Diana and Artemisia sets; and the later Classic ones, with narrower borders of Italian inspiration, like those on the Metropolitan Museum's Foundation of Rome which was woven at the Louvre by Pierre Lefebre, head of the Medici Tapestry Works in Florence but called back to his native France by Mazarin in 1647 (Consult Page 293, Vol. I, of *Fenaille Gobelins*).

DUBREUIL'S DIANA

At the head of the Baroque group of Early Gobelins, stands the Diana set of eight tapestries rich with gold and silver, designed by Toussaint Dubreuil. There are sets in the National French, Royal Spanish, and National Austrian collections, and five of the set in the Morgan Memorial at Hartford. Mr. Albright's "Diana rejecting Otus" was No. 60 in the catalogue of the Buffalo Tapestry Exhibition, 1914.

Formerly there were five of this Diana set, without gold,

in the Wanamaker collection. The story of Diana (Consult *Ovid's Metamorphoses* and *Gayley Classic Myths*) lends itself to tapestry illustration. There is a splendid example of "Diana before Jupiter" in the Hartford set. The gods are assembled in solemn council, Mars, Venus, and Cupid, and Mercury, on the right; Juno, Minerva, Cybele, Bacchus, Pan, and Ceres, on the left, all magnificently clothed and with their distinctive attributes. Diana, marked by lunette in her hair, kneels before the throne of Jupiter, beseeching him for perpetual virginity.

Another powerful tapestry of the set, is Niobe's Children, one of which is at Hartford, and another of which was No. 19 in the catalogue of the Cleveland Tapestry Exhibition, lent by Jacques Seligmann. Niobe was the wife of Jupiter's son Amphion, and the mother of seven strong sons and seven beautiful daughters. She boastfully compared her fourteen children to Latona's two, and urged her people to worship her instead of Latona. Latona appealed to her two children Apollo and Diana, who, as shown in the tapestry, fired their fatal arrows from the sky and slew all of the fourteen children, one after another.

There is now a "Diana shooting Orion" in the Wildenstein collection. In this tapestry Diana appears twice, once in the foreground, seated, with her maidens and dogs, once high on the left in the act of shooting at a mark indicated by her brother Apollo. Orion was a mighty hunter favored by Diana. Apollo disapproved but his chidings were in vain. One day seeing Orion in the distance wading in deep water with his head just exposed, Apollo pointed out the tiny black object as something Diana could not hit. She shot and hit. The waves rolled to land the body of Orion dead. Diana sorrowfully placed him as a constellation among the stars, a giant with girdle, sword, lion's skin and club. Sirius, his dog follows him. The Pleiads, once nymphs of Diana, fly before him.

ARTEMISIA

Another famous set of Early Gobelins is the Story of Artemisia of which there are five (two of them entrefenetres) in the Metropolitan Museum, lent by Mrs. H. N. Slater; ten in the collection of Mr. Edward B. McLean, formerly in the Ffoulke collection; and twenty-eight in the National French collection, from four different sets. Artemisia was Queen of Caria in Asia Minor in the fourth century B. C. Mourning her husband Mausolus, she built him such a magnificent monument that similar monuments have ever since been called *mausoleums*. The statues of Mausolus and Artemisia from the monument are now in the British Museum. Some of the many designs, executed by Antoine Caron and others in the sixteenth century to celebrate the widowhood of Catherine de Medici, appear to have first gone on the looms in the reign of Louis XIII to celebrate the widowhood of Marie de Medici, and to have been repeated later to celebrate the widowhood of Anne of Austria, mother of Louis XIV. Mrs. Slater's three larger panels are: (1) Artemisia rewarding the Orator who delivered the best funeral oration over Mausolus; (2) Artemisia and the young prince at table listen to the Architect; (3) The Prince consecrated to the arts of Peace and War.

Other important sets of Early Gobelins from the Ffoulke collection (Consult *Ffoulke Tapestries*) are Mr. Hearst's Coriolanus; and Mrs. Twombly's Amintas and Sylvia, and Rinaldo and Armida.

RINALDO AND ARMIDA

Rinaldo and Armida was cartooned after paintings by Simon Vouet illustrating Tasso's "Jerusalem Delivered," and is signed with the monogram of Raphael de la Planche. Armida, daughter of the King of Damascus, and niece of a famous magician, goes at the suggestion of her uncle to the camp of the Crusaders, and asks Godfrey de Bouillon for ten of his knights to help her organize her still faithful subjects against

a usurper.   Many of the youthful Crusaders are so enchanted
by her beauty that they follow her, even without Godfrey's
consent.   Rinaldo remains insensible to her charms, but having quarreled with the Prince of Norway, leaves camp to
avoid Godfrey's reproof.   Accidentally he encounters all the
knights who had followed Armida, being taken by her to
Damascus as prisoners. He releases them, whereupon Armida
puts him to sleep with a siren song, intending to kill him before
he wakes. Instead she falls in love with him, and bears
him magically away through the air to one of the Isles of
Fortune in the Atlantic.   He wakes loving her as she loves
him.   The most attractive of Mrs. Twombly's set, of which
there is a duplicate in the Hampton Shops collection, also made
in the shop of Raphael de la Planche, pictures "Rinaldo in the
arms of Armida."   On the extreme left, partly hidden in the
trees, are Carlo and Ubaldo come to recall Rinaldo to duty.
On the right, attended by cupids, reclines Rinaldo holding a
mirror into which Armida gazes, kneeling beside him and
adorning her hair with a string of pearls.   In the words
of Tasso:

> She, with glad looks, he with inflamed, alas,
> Beauty and love beheld, both in one seat,
> She in the glass; he saw them in her eyes.

In 1639 was published the *Ariane* of Desmarets de Saint-
Sorlin, illustrated with seventeen engravings by Abraham
Bosse, after Claude Vignon.   Tapestries based on two of these
engravings are in the collection of French & Co.   Duplicates
of them without borders were in the second Stanford White
sale, 1907.   The subjects are "Ariane kills two Scythians,"
and "Melinte escapes on horseback carrying Ariane."   There
are three others of the set in Madame Guiffrey's collection
(Page 370, Vol. I of *Fenaille Gobelins*).
   Early Gobelin Tapestries in the Metropolitan Museum are
the "Diana with her Maidens" (*Plate IX, ca*); and the three

"Foundation of Rome" panels, after Giulio Romano. This Diana tapestry has nothing to do with the Diana set after Dubreuil, named above, but suggests the style of Nicolas Poussin.

STORY OF PSYCHE

Most attractive among Early Gobelins from the point of view of both design and story interest, is the Story of Psyche (Plates IX, d, e) based on the designs of Raphael, or one of his pupils, as reproduced in the engravings of Agostino Veneziano (Plate IX, ea, and Chapter XVIII). It is perhaps needless to say that for tapestry reproduction at the Early Gobelins, the nudities of the original designs were elaborately suppressed. For the story, see the description of Boucher's Psyche set in Chapter XI. There are two Early Gobelin Psyche sets in the National French collection, one of them at Pau. There are five of the Early Gobelin Psyche set in the collection of Mrs. W. K. Vanderbilt, Jr., among them Psyche's Toilet and Psyche at Dinner. A brilliant example of Psyche carried to the Mountain was No. 21 in the catalogue of the Cleveland Tapestry Exhibition, 1918, lent by Jacques Seligmann.

THE GREAT CONDÉ

One of the most interesting of the Early Gobelins with which I am acquainted is the "Submission to Louis XIV of the Great Condé," No. 20 in the catalogue of the Cleveland Tapestry Exhibition, lent by Mr. Howard P. Eells. It bears the two dates 1659 and 1664, years of beginning and completion. Condé was called Great because of his success as leader of the armies of France. Becoming dissatisfied with the government of his native country, he went over to the Spanish. It was one of the provisions of the Peace of the Pyrenees made in 1659 between France and Spain that Condé should be pardoned. Condé was himself a Bourbon and consequently has his robe adorned with fleurs-de-lis, and three fleurs-de-lis on his coat-of-arms at the top of the tapestry. The bar sinister shows that he belonged to the younger branch of the family. Condé kneels in the foreground, his diadem on the ground beside him, taking the oath of loyalty to the youthful Louis XIV, whose long flowing hair is beautifully rendered. Other Early Gobelin tapestries connected with the youth of Louis XIV are the two formerly in the Mercy d'Argentan collection of Belgium, sold at the American Art Galleries on January 21, 1921, and illustrated in the catalogue. One of the tapestries shows Mazarin's niece Marie Mancini masquerading as the Royal Hunter; the other, Louis XIV as Diana. It was Marie Mancini who said to Louis XIV when her uncle insisted on parting the sweethearts: "You are King, you weep, and yet I go."

LOUIS XIV GOBELINS

Since the reorganization in 1662 of the Gobelins as a State institution, the world's finest tapestries have been woven in France. The reorganization vastly increased the size and financial resources of the establishment, and made it the constant recipient of heavy government orders, while leaving the shop proprietors free to take private orders. It also brought to the Gobelins as Director, from the service of Fouquet at Vaux-le-Vicomte, Charles Lebrun who for twenty-eight years was to be decorative dictator of France. Lebrun was a syndicate rather than an individual. He understood how to get the best out of many different painters, each at his specialty better than himself. Monumental sets created by him are the Story of the King, in 14 pieces, the Story of Alexander, in 11, the Royal Residences, in 12. The Story of the King (Plate IX, a) is the most important set ever made at the Gobelins. Here we find an official and solemn glorification of important events during the first twenty-five of the seventy-two years of the reign of Louis XIV (1643–1715). The complete set was woven once on high-warp looms, three times

on low-warp looms, all with gold.   The high-warp set was 17
feet high with a united length of 354 feet, and cost 166,698
livres.   It is still preserved in the National French Collection, together with two of the low-warp sets.   The low-warp
sets were only 13 feet high.   Vandermeulen, who had a salary
of 6000 livres a year and apartments at the Gobelins, was
given the landscapes and views of cities to prepare, accom-
panying the King on his campaigns.   The original small
sketches were. by Lebrun.   The full-size cartoons for the high-
warp were painted by the elder Ivart, Testelin, the elder
Mathieu, and the junior Sève.   The left-handed full-size cartoons for the low warp were painted by Bonnemer, Saint-
Andre, Ballin, and De Melun.   The first two sets went on the
looms in 1665 and were completed in 1680.   The third set was
completed in 1715, and the fourth set in 1735.   The subjects are:

    I. Coronation of Louis XIV in the Cathedral of Reims, June 7, 1654.
   II. Interview of Louis XIV and Philip IV of Spain at the Isle des
        Faisans, June 7, 1660.
  III. Marriage of Louis XIV with Marie-Therèse of Austria, eldest daughter
        of Philip IV, June 9, 1660.
  IV. Satisfaction given to the King by the Spanish Ambassador, March
        24, 1662.
   V. Entry of the King into Dunkirk after having recovered it from the
        English, December 2, 1662.
  VI. Reduction of the city of Marsal in Lorraine, September 1, 1663.
 VII. Renewal of the Alliance between France and the Swiss, at the Cathe-
        dral of Notre Dame in Paris, November 18, 1663.
VIII. Audience given by the King at Fontainebleau to the Pope's Legate,
        Cardinal Chigi, July 29, 1664.
  IX. Siege of Tournai where Louis XIV exposed himself to the enemy's
        fire, June 21, 1667.
   X. Siege of Douai in July, 1667.   The King in danger.
  XI. Capture of Lille in August, 1667.
 XII. Defeat of the Spanish under Count Marsin near Bruges, August 31,
        1667.
XIII. Visit of Louis XIV to the Gobelins with Colbert, October 15, 1667.
XIV. Capture of Dôle, February 16, 1668, the King commanding in person.

One of the high-warp set, the Entry of Louis XIV into Dunkirk is illustrated on Plate IX, a. In the middle of the bottom border is the inscription:

ENTRY OF KING LOUIS XIV INTO
DUNKIRK THE SECOND OF DECEMBER
MDCLXII AFTER HAVING RECOVERED
THIS CITY FROM THE HANDS OF THE ENGLISH

The King on horseback, baton in hand, rides towards Dunkirk, preceded and accompanied by a large escort. The inscriptions over the sphinxes in the side borders, on the left, LOUIS XIIII, 1668, and on the right, LOUIS XIIII, 1671, show that the tapestry was begun in 1668 and completed in 1671. The Royal coat-of-arms is in the middle of the top border, with the Royal sun-burst and NEC PLURIBUS IMPAR, in each corner. In the lower corners of the tapestry, the King's monogram with crown.

The Story of Alexander was in special favour at the French Court because it seemed to reflect the victories of Louis XIV in those of Alexander. By 1686 it had been produced five times in high warp, and three times in low warp, all with gold except the last. There is a complete high-warp set in the National Austrian collection. Four of one of the sets were exhibited by the French Government at San Francisco in 1915 and at the Brooklyn Museum in 1918. The set was copied over and over again at Brussels, Oudenarde, and Aubusson.

The Royal Residences—Versailles, Madrid, Louvre, Tuileries, Chambord, etc., one for each month of the year, with hunting scenes, promenades, cavalcades, balls—scenes appropriate to the season—was woven over and over again between 1668 and 1680.

Other sets created by Lebrun were: Verdures, Meleager, Muses, Elements and Seasons, Child Gardeners. The best examples of Child Gardeners are in the National French collection, the Florence Tapestry collection, and the collection of Lord Iveagh.

Of the Story of Moses, eight were by Poussin; (Plate IX, c), two by Lebrun.

An attractive set of six, woven three times in the seventeenth century and three times in the eighteenth was based on the paintings of Mignard at St. Cloud. The subjects are: Spring, Summer, Autumn, Winter, Parnassus, Latona. There is a Winter at the Hotel Commodore, formerly at Sherry's.

The Indies (Plate 333, *Hunter 1912*), was based on paintings presented to the King by the Prince of Nassau. They pictured in rich profusion the men, animals, plants, and fruits of the Indies "painted on the spot." The subjects are: Zebra, Two Bulls, Elephant, Indian Hunter, Animals Fighting, King carried by Moors, Indian on Horseback, Fishermen.

RENAISSANCE DESIGNS COPIED

Sets of tapestries copied from sixteenth century tapestries, paintings, or engravings are:

    I. Acts of the Apostles, after Raphael.
    II. Constantine, after Raphael and Giulio Romano.
    III. Chambers of the Vatican, after Raphael.
    IV. Triumphs of the Gods, after Giulio Romano.
    V. Mythological Subjects, after Giulio Romano.
    VI. Mythological Subjects, after Raphael.
    VII. Fruits of War, after Giulio Romano.
    VIII. Story of Scipio, after Giulio Romano.
    IX. Hunts of Maximilian, after Bernard Van Orley.
    X. Grotesque Months, after Giulio Romano.
    XI. Months of Lucas, after Lucas van Leyden.

Nearly all of these are richly represented in the National French collection, with numerous repetitions. Many of these are always on exhibition at the Louvre, the Gobelins, Versailles, and other French museums.

The set of Raphael's Acts of the Apostles, copied by the junior Jans from a Brussels Renaissance set, has disappeared.

It was in ten pieces, and rich with gold. The tenth piece showed God the Father in a blaze of glory, supported by the symbols of the Four Evangelists.

The Early Gobelins had woven the story of Constantine after designs by Rubens. Of these there are seven in the National Austrian collection, and many in the National French collection.

The Constantine set of the Louis XIV Gobelins is a different one begun at Maincy for Fouquet. Four of these were based on the Vatican paintings of Raphael and Giulio Romano, while the others were original compositions of Lebrun. Part of this Constantine set is duplicated in the later Chambers of the Vatican, in ten pieces, based on copies of Raphael's frescoes, made by pupils of the French School at Rome. The first three picture the battle of Constantine against Maxentius. The others are: Vision of the Cross by Constantine, School of Athens, Mass of Bolsena, Attila chased from Rome, Parnassus, Heliodorus expelled from the Temple, Burning of Rome. The Parnassus is especially effective in tapestry. There are four of the set in the National Austrian collection.

The Triumphs of the Gods, in eight pieces, after Giulio Romano, reflect the mural paintings of ancient Rome, with compartments framed in fanciful architecture like that of the Boscoreale Frescoes of the Metropolitan Museum, and are full of nudities. They are closely related to the pilasters of the Loggie of the Vatican, to the Psyche paintings in the Palazzo del Te at Mantua, and to certain friezes in the Castel St. Angelo that suggest the erotic pictures of Giulio Romano around which Aretin wrote verses. The cartoons for these Gobelin tapestries were based by Noel Coypel on a set of Brussels tapestries, with gold, three of which are still in the National French collection. Of the Gobelin Triumphs of the Gods (Bacchus, Venus, Apollo, Minerva, Mars, Hercules, Religion, Philosophy), there are many in the Garde Meuble at Paris, and others at Fontainebleau, in the French Academy at Rome, in the collection of the city of Paris, in the Florence Tapestry collection, besides the Minerva at the Gobelins, and the Hercules at the Louvre.

GIULIO ROMANO AND RAPHAEL

Fascinating and with fascinating borders are the Mythological Subjects, one set of eight after Giulio Romano, the other set of eight after Raphael. The Giulio Romano set is based largely on his Psyche Room in the Palazzo del Te at Mantua, but expurgated and with fewer nudities (Compare Plate IX, f, with Plate IX, fa). It will be noticed that in the Bath tapestry as drawn by Giulio Romano, the personages are Mars and Venus attended by Cupid, while in the Gobelin adaptation by Person, Mars and Venus have been transformed to Cupid and Psyche. There are Louis XVI Gobelin reproductions, without borders, of this tapestry and of the Left Dance of the Nymphs, in the collection of the Duke of Alba. There are Louis XIV sets of these Giulio Romano Mythological Subjects in the Louvre, in the Palais de l'Elysée, and at Compiègne. The Raphael Mythological Subjects are: Judgment of Paris, Elopement of Helen, Marriage of Alexander and Roxane, Wedding of Cupid and Psyche, Venus and Adonis, Venus in her Chariot, Right Dance of Nymphs and Satyr, Left Dance of Nymphs and Satyr. There are fewer nudities than in the original designs, but even at that, in order to please Madame de Maintenon, fleshly portions of a completed Marriage of Alexander and Roxane had to be cut out and replaced with draperies. The Raphael set as a whole is not nearly as attractive as the one after Giulio Romano. There are two of the Raphael sets in the National French collection, all high warp and with gold.

The Fruits of War, after Giulio Romano, was copied from a Brussels Renaissance set presented to Mazarin by the King of Spain after the ratification of the Peace of the Pyrenees.

It is closely related to a cannon-firing fresco by Giulio Romano in the Castel Sant'Angelo.

The Scipio set after Giulio Romano, was copied from a Brussels Renaissance set of ten, also from the Mazarin collection. The subjects are: (1) Roman Navy, (2) Scipio receives the Carthaginian Envoys, (3) Attack on Carthagena, (4) Banquet, (5) Continence of Scipio, (6) Battle of Zama, (7) Scipio saves his Father, (8) Scipio and Hannibal, (9) Another Battle, (10) Burning the Numidian Camp.

The Grotesque Months, after Giulio Romano, incorrectly called the Arabesque Months, was copied from a Brussels Renaissance set, rich with gold, that in 1797 was one of seventeen ancient sets burned for the gold they contained. Each month has the life-size figure of its tutelary god under a canopy in the middle, with the proper sign of the Zodiac inside a frame held in the right hand of the god, and a Latin inscription in the top border. On each side of the panel are small landscapes appropriate to the season. There are pieces from different low-warp sets without gold at Pau, in the Louvre, and at the Garde Meuble.

The Hunts of Maximilian after Van Orley was copied from a Brussels Renaissance set, with gold, now on exhibition at the Louvre (See Chapter VIII). There are sets at Chantilly, Fontainebleau, at the Garde Meuble, and in the collection of the city of Paris.

MONTHS OF LUCAS

The Months of Lucas, after Lucas van Leyden, was copied from a Brussels Renaissance set rich with gold, also burned in 1797. The first set was made for Colbert before 1682. Ten pieces of the second set are at Pau, the other two at Leningrad. These were low-warp sets. The finest set of the Months of Lucas ever woven was by Audran at the Gobelins in the second quarter of the eighteenth century for the Count of Toulouse (See Chapter XII and Plates XII, b, c, d; XVII, e, f).

The nine Months in the National Austrian collection (Set No. XXXVIII), made at Bruges in the last half of the seventeenth century, are greatly inferior to any of the Gobelin sets, and only in small part from the same designs.

The Balloch Castle Seasons of Lucas, rich with gold, in the collection of Mr. Frank H. Ginn, appears to have been copied from sixteenth century tapestries of the same designer, and made privately by Gobelin weavers in the last half of the reign of Louis XIV. Several sets of these Seasons some earlier and some later, some Gobelin and some not Gobelin, have passed through European auction rooms in the last fifteen years. There are duplicates, with some of the panels extended, of three of these Seasons in the collection of Mrs. Wm. Bayard Cutting, and in that of Mrs. John T. Morse, Jr. Mrs. Morse's were purchased by her father at the Louis Philippe sale in 1852. The finest set in the United States is the four, each 13 by 19 feet that enrich the walls of the Brookline Trust Co. (Plate XXI, g). They were formerly in the collection of Viscount Wimbourne, and were made in one of the Gobelin shops about 1690.

PLATE IX, b.—TRIUMPHAL ENTRY OF ALEXANDER THE GREAT INTO BABYLON, ONE OF THE FAMOUS "STORY OF ALEXANDER" TAPESTRIES, DESIGNED BY CHARLES LEBRUN, SHOWN WITH OTHER GOBELIN TAPESTRIES IN THE EXHIBITION OF THE FRENCH GOVERNMENT AT THE PANAMA–PACIFIC EXPOSITION, SAN FRANCISCO, 1915, AND AT THE BROOKLYN MUSEUM IN 1918

PLATES IX, c, ca.—ABOVE, FINDING OF MOSES, LOUIS XIV GOBELIN TAPESTRY, DESIGN OF POUSSIN. BELOW, DIANA BATHING, AN EARLY GOBELIN TAPESTRY WITH SOME METAL, IN THE METROPOLITAN MUSEUM OF ART, PROBABLY DESIGN OF POUSSIN

PLATES IX, e, ea.—ABOVE, OLD WOMAN TELLING THE
STORY OF PSYCHE, ONE OF A SERIES OF PSYCHE DESIGNS
FROM THE STUDIO OF RAPHAEL, AS ENGRAVED BY
AGOSTINO VENEZIANO, IN THE FRENCH BIBLIOTHÈQUE
NATIONALE. BELOW, EARLY GOBELIN TAPESTRY IN THE
FRENCH NATIONAL COLLECTION

PLATES IX, f, fa.—ABOVE, GIULIO ROMANO'S FRESCO OF MARS AND
VENUS, IN THE PSYCHE ROOM OF THE PALAZZO DEL TE, MANTUA. BELOW,
LOUIS XIV GOBELIN TAPESTRY IN THE LOUVRE BASED ON THIS DESIGN,
BUT WITH MARS AND VENUS CHANGED INTO CUPID AND PSYCHE.

PLATES X, a, aa.—THE STORY OF DECIUS. ABOVE, ORIGINAL LARGE CAR-
TOON BY RUBENS, IN THE GALLERY OF PRINCE LIECHTENSTEIN, VIENNA. BELOW,
TAPESTRY WOVEN IN BRUSSELS FROM THIS CARTOON, IN THE SECOND QUARTER
OF THE SEVENTEENTH CENTURY. NATIONAL AUSTRIAN COLLECTION

CHAPTER X

FLEMISH TAPESTRIES OF THE SEVENTEENTH AND EIGHTEENTH CENTURIES

RUBENS, JORDAENS, TENIERS, LOUIS XIV BRUSSELS
JEAN VAN ORLEY, LOUIS VAN SCHOOR

DURING the seventeenth century, the leadership in tapestry weaving passed from Flanders to France, from Brussels to the Gobelins in Paris, in spite of the efforts of the Archdukes, Albert and Isabella, the latter the daughter of Philip II, son of Charles V, to restore prosperity to the industries of their wasted provinces. Many of the best weavers emigrated to Paris and to Mortlake (See Chapters IX and XVI). Nevertheless, there was a revival of tapestry weaving in the Southern Netherlands, especially after the world-famous Rubens and his followers began to supply new and spectacular designs. Sets created by Rubens are:

     I. Story of Constantine (See Chapter IX).
    II. Story of Decius (Plates X, a, aa).
   III. Triumph of Religion.
   IV. Story of Achilles.

Of the story of Decius there is a full set in the Palace of Prince Liechtenstein in Vienna, where the tapestries can be compared with the full-size cartoons executed in Rubens' studio, which hang in the next room (Plate X, a). It will be noticed that the cartoons were painted left-handed, for execution on low-warp looms that in weaving reverses the direction of the design. There are five of the set in the National Austrian collection (Plate X, aa) and a complete set in the Royal Spanish collection. The triumph of Religion was designed by Rubens about 1625 for the Archduchess Isabella, who presented the first set to a convent in Madrid where it still hangs. There was a set of eleven in the Berwick and Alba collection (Nos. 50 to 60 of the catalogue, Paris, 1877). In recent years several pieces have passed through the auction rooms of Paris and New York. There are five of the Story of Achilles in the Brussels Cinquentenaire Museum, and three in the Boston Museum of Fine Arts.

Typical examples of seventeenth century Baroque weaving are:

I. Mrs. C. Wheaton Vaughan's Samson and Delilah, 13 feet 6 inches high, in four pieces: One 22 feet long; one 15 feet 4 inches; the other two, narrow entrefenetres; signed by Jan Raes with monogram in right selvage and full name in bottom selvage. Nos. 11, 12, 13 of the catalogue of the Philadelphia Tapestry Exhibition, 1915. (Plate X, c).

II. Story of Judith, in 8 pieces, lent by Mr. W. Hinckle Smith to the Metropolitan Museum. Exhibited at Brussels in 1910, and at the Buffalo Tapestry Exhibition in 1914. They are signed in the bottom selvage, some H. REYDAMS; the others, E. LEYNIERS (Plate X, b).

III. Story of Cleopatra, of which there are five in the Metropolitan Museum (Plate X, ca), some signed G. V. D. STRECKEN, the others I. V. LEEDAEL or I. V. L. There are also five in the Royal Italian collection at Florence; and several with colours fresher than is usual in the collection of the Tiffany Studios.

IV. Story of Solomon, of which there are five in the Hotel St. Regis, signed I. V. ZEVNEN.

V. Story of Belisarius, of which there are seven in the Park Lane Hotel, signed GILLAME BOLECIR.

VI. Story of Augustus, of which there were three in the Morgan collection. There are others in the Royal Swedish and Royal Italian collections and a full set of eight in the National Austrian collection.

VII. Story of Hadrian, of which there were five in the collection of Mr. W. A. Read.

VIII. Story of Cyrus, of which seven were exhibited in 1916 at the Harvard Club of New York. (Now in the Benjamin Franklin Hotel, Philadelphia.)

IX. Story of Phaethon, of which there are five at the Morgan Memorial in Hartford.

Most of these tapestries are signed in the bottom selvage with the Brussels mark, as well as with the name of the manufacturer. The borders are uniformly wide, with details large and in bold relief. The reds have usually faded.

Renaissance sets often reproduced at Brussels in the seventeenth century, usually with new borders, are: (1) Raphael's Acts of the Apostles, of which there is a set by IAN RAES and Jacques Geubels, at Hampton Court, formerly in the Berwick and Alba collection, presented to the British Nation by Baron d'Erlanger; (2) Giulio Romano's Scipio; (3) Fruits of War. There were four of the Scipio set in the Salomon sale, New York, 1923.

LOUIS XIV BRUSSELS TAPESTRIES

In the last third of the seventeenth century there was a marked change of style. Borders became narrower, personages smaller, and the designs less sculptural and better suited for interpretation in tapestry. Towards the end of the century gilt-frame borders became common and continued through the eighteenth century, when borders were not omitted altogether. Verdures, of the type now most commonly known by that name, became popular; and verdure backgrounds were developed with small personages in the foreground. The influence of the Gobelins was so great that sets such as Lebrun's Story of Alexander were frequently copied, and the style of the Gobelins and of Beauvais was imitated to such an extent that many Brussels tapestries of the Louis XIV period have been sold as Gobelins, and are still called *Louis XIV Brussels*. Flemish in design are the *tenières* cartooned from the peasant painting of Teniers, by his son and others. Typical examples are shown on Plates X, d, da, e, ea. The weave is uniformly good. As indicated above, eighteenth century tapestries were often made without borders. In the last third of the century, in Flanders as in France, designs, colours, and weave lost their strength.

Two popular designers of Brussels tapestries were Louis van Schoor at the end of the seventeenth century, and Jean van Orley in the first third of the eighteenth. Van Schoor's name often appears woven on the panel, with the weaver's name in the bottom selvage. The Abundance that was No. 42 of the Philadelphia Tapestry Exhibition, 1915, was signed L. VAN. SCHOOR. INVT. PINXT and A. AVWERC. The border is a rich floral, of the width common from 1680 to 1690, narrower than the wide borders of the sixteenth and seventeenth centuries, but wider than the narrow borders of the fifteenth and eighteenth, and with few of the architectural and sculptural exaggerations of the Baroque style. Other tapestries by Van Schoor are the Four Seasons and Abundance formerly in the Baumgarten collection, with borders missing. Of these there are numerous duplicates. The National Austrian collection has a set of eight tapestries signed by Van Schoor and Auwercx, with allegorical presentation of the Powers that rule the World—Monarchia, Fortitudo, Magnificentia, Fidelitas, Simplicitas, Abundantia, Sapientia, Mandatum; a brilliant set of eight signed by Gerard Peemans picturing Apollo, Minerva and the Muses; another brilliant set of eight signed by Van Schoor and Jan van der Borght (I. V. D. B.) picturing, Sacrifice of the Four Seasons to Apollo, Minerva welcomed by the Muses, Flora crowned by Cupid and Zephyrus, Bacchus brought by Mercury to the Nymphs, Venus and Adonis, Bacchus and Ariadne, Eurydice.

Jean van Orley's tapestries have slenderer personages, and narrow gilt frame borders. A typical example is the New York Public Library's Parnassus, 13½ by 21½ feet, signed I.DE.VOS. The subordinate banquet scene on the right Van Orley borrowed from Raphael's Story of Psyche in the Farnesina. The chariot of the Sun in the sky is reminiscent of Raphael's Judgment of Paris, while the group of Apollo and the Muses is a development from Van Schoor. For further details see the Library's pamphlet entitled the "Parnassus Tapestry." Another attractive Van Orley tapestry is the Feast of Bacchus belonging to Mrs. Frederic Pratt of Buffalo. The Cathedral of Bruges has a set of eight Van Orley tapestries picturing the Life of Christ. It also has the full-size cartoons from which they were woven. A Brussels reproduction of the principal panel, 12½ by 19 feet, of the Atalanta and Meleager series designed by Lebrun for Fouquet, was No. 53 in the catalogue of the Philadelphia Tapestry Exhibition, 1915. It is signed G. PEIMANS. A Meleager set of nine tapestries, 10 feet high, with heavy Baroque borders, of Flemish design, hangs in the drawing room of Mr. Cyrus McCormick. It came from the Island of Mallorca, from the collection of Don Raimon d'Allones. It was bought in Antwerp in 1679 for Don Ramon Forton, Count of Montenegro and Mantua, a resident of Mallorca. The correspondence connected with placing and delivering the order has been preserved. Exact sizes of each panel, and the various expenses—for lining, packing, export duties at Antwerp, and import duties into Holland, freight from Antwerp to Amsterdam, export papers from Amsterdam, insurance to Mallorca, brokerage, and commission are all given in detail. Part payment was made with the proceeds of oil sold for Don Ramon in Amsterdam. I found on measurement that the tapestries are narrower, but 3 inches higher now than when they were new. This is a change of shape to be expected, due to the weight of tapestries stretching them vertically.

Other Louis XIV Brussels tapestries in America are the Commerce belonging to Mr. Robert Goelet, previously in the Stanford White collection; the four large Story of Cyrus tapestries, formerly in the collection of the Archduke Franz Ferdinand of Austria-Este, with his arms in modern tapestry attached at the top, now in New York in the White-Allom collection. The four are signed by the Van der Borghts, Jacob and François.

Mrs. H. N. Slater has five eighteenth century Brussels tapestries picturing the Story of Telemachus. There is one of the set in the Brussels Cinquentenaire Museum (Plate 36 of the catalogue). The Brussels Museum has several fine tenières, and the Victoria and Albert Museum has one. The two large tenières in the Musée des Arts Décoratifs were made not in Brussels, but in Beauvais, which followed Brussels as soon as the new style became popular.

The largest and finest groups of tenières and other Brussels tapestries of the seventeenth and eighteenth centuries are those of the National Austrian collection.

PLATE X. b.—TRIUMPH OF JUDITH, ONE OF MR. HINCKLE SMITH'S IMPOSING SET OF EIGHT BRUSSELS SEVENTEENTH

PLATES X, c, ca.—ABOVE, BETRAYAL OF SAMSON, ONE OF MRS. C. WHEATON
VAUGHAN'S "SAMSON AND DELILAH" TAPESTRIES, WOVEN AT BRUSSELS EARLY IN
THE SEVENTEENTH CENTURY BY IAN RAES. BELOW, BATTLE OF ACTIUM, ONE OF
THE METROPOLITAN MUSEUM'S "ANTONY AND CLEOPATRA" TAPESTRIES, WOVEN AT
BRUSSELS IN THE MIDDLE OF THE SEVENTEENTH CENTURY BY IAN VAN LEEFDAEL

PLATES X, d, da.—ABOVE, TENIÈRE, WOVEN IN BRUSSELS EARLY IN THE EIGHTEENTH
CENTURY BY D. LEYNIERS. BELOW, A TYPICAL OUDENARDE VERDURE

PLATES X, e, ea.—ABOVE, SANCHO PANZA TOSSED IN A BLANKET, EIGHTEENTH
CENTURY BRUSSELS TAPESTRY, SIGNED BY U. LEYNIERS, IN THE CLEVELAND MUSEUM.
BELOW, THE NEW YORK PUBLIC LIBRARY'S "PARNASSUS," MADE AT BRUSSELS EARLY IN
THE EIGHTEENTH CENTURY, SIGNED BY I. DE VOS

PLATE XI, a.—JUPITER AND ANTIOPE, ONE OF MRS. E. F. HUTTON'S PAIR OF EXQUISITELY BEAUTIFUL BEAUVAIS–BOUCHERS. THE TITLE LISTED ON THE RECORDS OF THE BEAUVAIS WORKS IS JUPITER EN RAISIN, THUS BLENDING TWO ANCIENT STORIES, JUPITER EN SATYR AND BACCHUS EN RAISIN

CHAPTER XI

BEAUVAIS TAPESTRIES

BÉHAGLE AND BÉRAIN, TELEMACHUS, OUDRY, BOUCHER, PSYCHE
CHINESE SET, LOVES OF THE GODS, NOBLE PASTORALE, HUET-BOUCHER
PASTORALS, CONQUEST OF THE INDIES

THE famous tapestry factory at Beauvais, fifty miles north of Paris, was founded in 1664. This was an important step in the seventeenth century campaign that transferred supremacy in the tapestry industry from Flanders to France. Colbert wanted not only a State factory producing mainly for the State, but also a private factory producing for the general public and for export. Having decided to take over and organize the Gobelins as the State factory, he encouraged Louis Hinart a Paris tapestry dealer born in Beauvais, and with looms in Flanders, to establish a private factory in Beauvais which already had a reputation for weaving "small, cheap and common" tapestries.

Hinart had no reason to complain of the generosity with which he was treated by the French Crown. He received on loan 30,000 livres towards the acquisition of the necessary real estate and buildings, and another 30,000 livres for the purchase of supplies. He also received 20 livres for every foreign workman attracted to France, a bonus of 20 livres for every set of tapestries over 45 feet long exported abroad, and 30 livres a year toward the maintenance of each of 50 apprentices. During the twenty years 1664 to 1684, he drew from the royal treasury over 250,000 livres of which 94,666 livres paid for 254 tapestries, the rest being subventions of one kind or another.

Most of these tapestries were *verdures*, some of them based on the designs of Rubens' assistant Jacques Fouquières

(1580–1659). Compared with the tapestries then being made at the Gobelins they were inexpensive, costing only from one-half to one-fourth as much per foot. Many of them were very coarse, but some were enriched with gold, notable a set of Children Playing.

Either there was no money to be made weaving verdures in France at this period, or Hinart was a bad manager. In 1684 his financial difficulties were such that he was obliged to retire, and his place as proprietor of the Beauvais Tapestry Works was taken by his competitor Philip Béhagle, a native of Tournai established in Paris, whose success had been marked by the order received from Madame de Montespan to make a set of tapestries after designs by Bérain for her little son, the Count of Toulouse.

BÉHAGLE AND BÉRAIN

Naturally the favor of Montespan meant the favor of the King. An inscription engraved on the garden wall of the Beauvais Tapestry Works says: "King Louis XIV rested under this shade in 1686. Sieur Béhagle was then director of the factory." The twenty years of Béhagle's proprietorship (1684–1705) was a period of great activity. When the Gobelins shut down in 1693 for lack of money in the royal treasury, Béhagle was able to give employment to many of the weavers.

Béhagle was ambitious. He was not content to confine himself to verdures like Hinart. He employed Jean Bérain and other painters to originate important figure pieces.

The most noteworthy example of Béhagle's work in America is the set of six Italian Grotesques after Bérain, in the collection of Mr. Clarence H. Mackay (Plate XI, c). The seventh of this original set of eight is in the Victoria and Albert Museum, given by Mrs. John Mackay in 1909. Six of a similar set, but with different border and two subjects different, woven after Bérain's death, are in the Museum at Aix-en-

Provence. Two of the set with a wider border are illustrated in *Badin Beauvais* (opposite pages 12 and 16). One of these two is in the Musée des Arts Décoratifs.

The most elaborate single Beauvais-Béhagle tapestry in America is the armorial, 12 feet 9 by 14 feet 6, of the Duke of Boufflers, Marshal of France, with portrait medallions of himself and wife, lent by Mrs. Archibald Thomson to the Philadelphia Tapestry Exhibition of 1915 (No. 70 in the catalogue). Like several of the Mackay set it bears the signature BÉHAGLE.

A famous set of four tapestries signed by both Bérain and Béhagle, formerly in the Hirsch collection and recently in America, is the Marine Divinities rich with silver and gold, bearing in the lower corners the coat-of-arms of the Count of Toulouse, son of Louis XIV and Madame de Montespan, and High Admiral of France, for whom they were woven. The central figures are:(1) Amphitrite, (2) Venus, (3) Eurus, (4) Thetis. In the fourth tapestry the youthful Admiral is seen receiving helmet, cuirass and shield, from Thetis.

The Martin Le Roy collection (See Plates XII and XIII of v. 4 of the catalogue, Paris 1908) has Apollo and Mars, two out of an original set of twelve designed by Bérain and originated by Béhagle, picturing the Twelve Great Gods. There are four of a similar set in the Château d'Alaincourt, and four others in the Château de Vantoux.

The Beauvais Cathedral has a set of eight of Raphael's Acts of the Apostles made and signed by Béhagle (Plate 91 of *Hunter 1912*).

Of the Conquests of Louis the Great designed by Vandermeulen's pupil Jean Baptiste Martin, commonly known as "Martin of the Battles," there is an inferior piece at Versailles (the Battle of Cassel), while *Badin Beauvais* locates two pieces rich with gold in Florence. In the Royal Swedish collection (See *Boettiger Swedish*) there are four large tapestries rich with silver and gold picturing battles of the Swedish King Charles XI against Denmark, cartooned by Martin after sketches of the paintings by Lembke, with borders by Vernansal after Bérain.

This same Vernansal was also the principal designer of the first Beauvais *chinoiserie* set of tapestries. I found his woven signature on one. Also, one of those in the Gargan sale of 1904 was signed BÉHAGLE, which makes it certain that the set was originated by Béhagle. The signature BEAUVAIS, without maker's signature, on a panel now in America (Plate XI, b) would indicate completion after Béhagle's death. There are two of the set in the Museum of Compiègne.

STORY OF TELEMACHUS

Still another set originated by Béhagle is the Story of Telemachus (Plate XI, g) designed by Arnault, of Brussels. It is much superior both in design and weave to the Brussels Telemachus set of the National Austrian collection woven by the Leyniers, as well as to the Telemachus tapestries of the Royal Spanish collection, some of them belonging to the Leyniers group, the others made in Spain after the cartoons of Houasse.

All of these tapestries were inspired by the "Adventures of Telemachus" the famous story created by Fénelon, Archbishop of Cambrai, for the political instruction of his pupil the Duke of Burgundy, grandson of Louis XIV and heir to the throne. What made everybody anxious to read the book as soon as published was that in one of the characters Fénelon seemed to satirize Louis XIV.

The tapestry before us (Plate XI, g) shows Telemachus, the son of Ulysses, with the features of the youthful Duke of Burgundy, saved from the temptations of the Temple of Venus. The scene is Cythera on the Island of Cyprus, whither Telemachus had been brought by fate, after being a captive in Sicily and a slave in Egypt. At first Telemachus had been struck with horror at the dissolute practices of the beautiful youths and maidens who served the Goddess of Love. But as time passed, vice became familiar and no longer alarmed him. His innocence was universally derided and his modesty was treated as a joke. Every art was used to excite his passions. Daily he felt himself less capable of resistance. At this critical period arrived Mentor, beloved tutor of Telemachus (personifying Fénelon as well as Minerva the Goddess of Wisdom). In the tapestry Telemachus kneels before Hazael the rich Syrian of whom Mentor is slave.

Despite Béhagle's great ability and energy, and success in selling tapestries abroad and at home, he got into financial difficulties towards the end of his career and left to his wife and son Philip a business that was liability rather than asset, especially under the unfavorable industrial conditions that prevailed in France during the latter part of the reign of Louis XIV. They gave up the proprietorship in 1711.

JEAN BAPTISTE OUDRY

In 1726 a designer was hired for the Beauvais Tapestry Works, destined to regenerate the whole establishment, and make it envied by the Gobelins. This designer was the animal painter Jean Baptiste Oudry, whose illustrations of Lafontaine's Fables inspired a majority of the tapestry furniture coverings of the eighteenth century and since, as well as many landscape-verdure wall panels with birds and small animals. It is interesting to note here that one of Oudry's descendants, also a painter, came to America and settled in Pittsburgh, leaving a daughter who is now in Europe studying the work of her illustrious ancestor.

Among sets of tapestries designed by Oudry for Beauvais are: (1) *New Hunts* in six pieces, Wolf, Stag, Fox, Wild Boar, Limer, Buck; (2) *Country Games* in 8 pieces, Leapfrog, Blind Man's Buff, Shepherdess, Pied de Boeuf, Knuckle Bones, Seesaw, Joueur de Broche, Bagpipe; (3) *Comedies of Molière* in 4 pieces; (4) *Ovid's Metamorphoses* in 8 pieces;

(5) *Fine Verdures in* 10 pieces, Pheasant, Oiseau Royal, Fox, Wild Duck, Bittern, Clarinette, Bustard, Charmille, Dog and Pheasant, Lion and Wild Boar; (6) *Lafontaine's Fables,* Lice et Compagne, Deux Chèvres, Renard et Buste, Lion et Sanglier, Renard, Raisins, Poissons et Cormoran, Loup et Renard. It will be noticed that many of these are *verdures,* thus continuing the Beauvais tradition established by Hinart, and not neglected by Béhagle or his successors.

The subjects of the Comedies of Molière, which appears to have been woven only twice, are: (1) Médecin malgré lui, (2) Dépit Amoureux, (3) Ecole des Maris, (4) Malade Imaginaire. The last three of these, formerly in the Kann and Morgan collections, now adorn the residence of Mrs. William Hayward. The one illustrated on Plate XI, ca is the Malade Imaginaire. It is signed on the lower left of the panel, *J. B. Oudry, 1732* and in the bottom selvage with a round shield carrying three fleurs-de-lis. The other two of Mrs. Hayward's Oudry tapestries have not only this shield but also N. BESNIER A BEAUVAIS, Besnier being the proprietor of the Works.

The Malade Imaginaire is a comedy in three acts interspersed with music and dancing, produced in Paris for the first time February 10, 1673 and for the fourth time on February 17. At the last performance Molière who himself played the part of *Argan* is reported to have said as he left the stage: "Gentlemen, I have played the part of an imaginary invalid, but I am really an invalid whose illness is serious." He died that night.

Argan, the principal character of the Malade Imaginaire, though really in the best of health, spends all his time doctoring himself, and attempts to compel his older daughter to marry a physician in order to have one in the family for quick and free consultation. In the tapestry before us (Plate XI, ca) he is trying to make his younger daughter further his plan. She, seeing on the chair the switch with which he intends to coerce her, exclaims: "Oh, Papa!"

One of Ovid's Metamorphoses by Oudry, the Palace of Circe, as reproduced later at Aubusson, is shown on Plate XIII, c.

An important factor in Oudry's continued success at Beauvais was Nicolas Besnier, who in 1734 became proprietor of the Beauvais Tapestry Works, De Mérou the former proprietor having got into serious financial difficulties. Besnier was a splendid manager under whom the Beauvais Tapestry Works became so prosperous as to arouse the bitter jealousy of the shop proprietors at the Gobelins. Even more important than Besnier was François Boucher, the greatest tapestry designer of the eighteenth century. Oudry had the good sense or good luck to give him a trial, and for forty years cartoons by Boucher kept the looms of Beauvais busy.

FRANÇOIS BOUCHER

Of Beauvais-Bouchers there are six sets in forty-five pieces: (1) *Italian Set* in 14 pieces, (Plate XI, d); (2) *Story of Psyche* in 5 pieces (Plates XI, ca and XXI, c); (3) *Chinese Set* in 6 pieces (Plate XI, da); (4) *Loves of the Gods* in 9 pieces, (Plates XI, a, e, f); (5) *Opera Fragments* in 5 pieces (Frontispiece in colour of *Hunter 1912*); (6) *Noble Pastorale* in 6 pieces.

The first three of the Italian set went on the looms in 1736, the fourth in 1738, the fifth and sixth in 1739, the seventh in 1744, the eighth and ninth in 1745, the tenth in 1746, the eleventh in 1751, the twelfth in 1754, the thirteenth and fourteenth in 1762, and there were constant reorders. They were small tapestries evidently planned for popular consumption, but were often woven two in one piece (Plate XI, d); and at least once, four in one piece. While less pretentious than the later sets, they possess great charm, and show that Boucher during his years spent in Italy must have lived a great deal out of doors. The subjects are: Charlatan (Plate XI, d), Fortune Teller, Hunters, Fishing, Peep Show,

Girls with Grapes, Dancing, Luncheon, Music, Gardening, Shepherdess, Tavern Keeper, Parrot, Egg Merchant. There are four of them in the collection of Mr. Archer Huntington.

BOUCHER'S STORY OF PSYCHE

The Italian set was thrown completely into the shade by the Story of Psyche (Plates XI, ea and XXI, c) that went on the looms in 1741. Psyche established Boucher as first among designers of tapestry. It is a monument not only to his skill but also to the beauty of his wife who was his model for all or nearly all of the female figures. Clearly Boucher listened well to his friend Bachaumont, who advised him when he received the commission: "Read and read again the Psyche of Lafontaine, *and above all things study well Madame Boucher.*" As the quotation indicates, the story of Psyche that Boucher studied was not the ancient Latin narrative of Apuleius from the second century A. D., but the vastly enriched and improved version made at Château Thierry by Lafontaine for his friend and patroness the Duchess of Bouillon, one of the nieces of Mazarin.

Anciently in Greece, writes Lafontaine, there was a king with three marriageable daughters, all beautiful, but most beautiful of all, Psyche the youngest. Indeed, she was so beautiful as to arouse the jealousy even of Venus, the goddess of Love, who complained bitterly to her son Cupid. Presently the two sisters of Psyche married, but because of the enchantment of Venus, no suitor sought the hand of Psyche. Her parents, in distress, questioned the oracle, who responded: "The Husband that destiny reserves for your daughter is a cruel monster who lacerates hearts, destroys families, feeds on sighs, bathes in tears. . . He is a poisoner and an incendiary, a tyrant who loads young and old with chains. Let Psyche be given unto him; let her try to please him. Such is the decree of Fate, of Love, and of the Gods. Conduct her to a rock on top of a mountain, where her monstrous husband is waiting. Celebrate her departure with funereal pomp, since she must die for her sisters and for you."

What the oracle urged was done, and Psyche was duly abandoned in a desolate and terrible part of the mountains, inhabited by dragons, hydras, and other awful beasts. Fainting with fear, she suddenly felt herself raised gently by a god whom she learned to be Zephyr, and conveyed to a wonderful palace, where she was welcomed by a troop of lovely maidens, who complimented her without end, but failed to answer clearly her questions as to the owner of the splendid castle.

This is the part of the story illustrated by the first of the Boucher set, "Psyche Arrives at Cupid's Palace." (Plate XXI, c). In the middle of the scene flies Zephyr, a beautiful youth with butterfly wings, ushering into a Louis XV palace, Psyche, beautiful but timid. On the floor, a savonnerie carpet, loosely laid in large folds. On the right and on the left, welcoming maidens with flowers and music, and on the extreme left an altar of Love, richly garlanded, with cupids flying above.

Having shown Psyche through the magnificently furnished halls and apartments of the palace, the maidens finally usher her into a spacious bathroom and start to assist her to disrobe. At first she made resistance, but finally let them have their way, and all the arts of the boudoir were employed to render her body fresh and fragrant.

After the bath, Psyche Dressing (Plate XI, ea). Boucher has chosen to transfer the scene out of doors. Backgrounded by classic fountain and pool, and by terrace with classic marble steps and balustrade and vase, which are themselves backgrounded by woods and sky, sits Psyche, innocently nude, soon to be attired by the maidens in wonderful wedding garments and adorned with a wreath of diamonds and precious stones. In the foreground, a bowl and pitcher in solid plate, artfully placed. Altogether, one of Boucher's best efforts.

Next came dinner. The table was laden with ambrosia

of every variety, and with divine nectar for beverage. But Psyche ate little. After the meal, music of lute and voice was heard without instrument or singer being visible. Of the songs the one that pleased Psyche most began: "All the universe is obedient to Love. Beautiful Psyche, submit your soul to him. Without Love all these exquisite objects, these gilded frames, woods, gardens, and fountains, have a charm that soon fatigues. Love is of your hearts the happiness supreme. Love, only love, for naught else counts."

The next morning the only thing about Psyche's wedding night that troubled her was that her husband had left before daylight, warning her that she must never try to see him either by the light of day or by lamplight. Nevertheless, the honeymoon passed agreeably and rapidly, until Psyche began to miss her sisters and long to see them again. Against his will, her husband had them brought by Zephyr, god of the softest breeze that blows. Psyche's joy was extreme. She kissed her sisters a thousand times, and her caresses were returned as warmly as their jealous natures permitted. It was bad enough for her to have a palace, each chamber of which was worth ten kingdoms such as their husbands had: but to be a goddess! It was too much! And she the youngest of all!

Eagerly Psyche hastened to show them her treasures, her dresses first—bureaus and cabinets and closets in endless succession, all crowded with the most precious and most delicate materials fashioned into robes by fairies with more than mortal skill. And then vases and bowls of gold and silver, chased in finest relief, and bracelets, and rings, and collars, and jewels, and pearls, and diamonds in ropes and bands— and so on, until her sisters sighed while smiling, and secretly hated Psyche for what she had as well as for what she was.

This is the part of the story illustrated by the third tapestry of the set, "Psyche Displays her Treasures to her Sisters." Again the background is a Louis XV palace, with

columns and pilasters and arches, while Psyche on a bench
that stands on a platform, on the upper step of which is signed,
"F. BOUCHE," displays her treasures to her two sisters on the
left. They almost equal her in beauty, and are also lightly
clad. The furnishings of the apartment are luxurious to a degree possible only for a great decorator, such as Boucher was.

On a subsequent visit, Psyche's sisters questioned her
closely about her husband, and finally compelled her to admit
that she had never seen him. The rest was easy. They
reminded her of the oracle and insisted that her husband was
the dreadful monster meant, shunning the light because of
his ugliness. Ultimately he would destroy her, and her only
hope of escape was to slay him while he slept. So Psyche
took knife and lamp, with intent to do her sisters' bidding, but
no sooner did she see the divine beauty of her sleeping husband than she thrilled with love for him and—but, alas, a
drop of hot oil from her lamp fell on his shoulder, burning
and awakening him. Forthwith he reproached her disobedi-
ence and flew away. The fourth tapestry, "Psyche Abandoned by Cupid," is also a scene transferred by Boucher from
inside to outside. Beside a mountain pool lie Psyche and her
maidens. Psyche with hand upraised appeals in vain to Cupid,
whose childish figure recedes rapidly heavenward.

Deserted and disconsolate, Psyche sets forth in search of
her husband, finally arriving at the home of an aged fisherman,
who also makes baskets. The patriarch, who has two youthful
granddaughters, receives Psyche kindly; and when she has
told her story, treats her as a goddess. This part of the
story is illustrated by the fifth tapestry of the set, "Psyche
at the Fisherman's." On the left, the grandfather gently
assisting the alway lightly clad Psyche across the mountain
stream that separates them from the equally lightly clad
granddaughters with their baskets and withes. Especially
rich and effective are the woods and vegetation of this tapestry. Like most modern love stories, the ancient one of Cupid

and Psyche has a happy ending, and even Venus is finally persuaded to approve of the marriage, and smiles upon her grandchild, Pleasure.

Mrs. Alexander Hamilton Rice has the complete set
(Plate XXI, c). The Mrs. George Gould collection contained
a splendid example of "Psyche displaying her Treasures."
The Royal Swedish collection contains the complete set with-
out borders, and the Royal Italian collection at the Quirinal
has all of the set except the first. Mr. Edward Tuck, an
American, long resident in Paris has "Psyche's Arrival at
Cupid's Palace" and "Psyche displaying her Treasures to
her Sisters" combined in one. He has bequeathed them to the
Petit Palais. They will be the only important Beauvais-
Boucher tapestries in any French museum.

BOUCHER-DUMONS CHINESE SET

In 1743 the Chinese Set went on the looms, originated by
Boucher in the form of small sketches now in the Besançon
Museum, and developed into full-size cartoons by Jean Joseph
Dumons. The subjects are Chinese Banquet, Chinese Fair,
Chinese Dancing, Chinese Fishing, Chinese Hunting, Chinese
Toilet. Mrs. E. T. Stotesbury has the second, third and
fourth of the set, the fourth in two pieces.

The Chinese Fair (Plate XI, da) belonging to Mrs. F. F.
Prentiss, and shown at the Cleveland Tapestry exhibitions in
1918, is as fresh as the day it left the looms. At the top is
the coat-of-arms of the French King. In the centre, a lady
sits in a canopied wheel chair. High on a platform behind
her stand two jugglers, one solemnly reading an announce-
ment to the public, while the other holds a snake whose outstretched mouth grasps the rim of the unsuspecting "bark-
er's" hat. At the left, a bird merchant leans on one of his
cages, while his little boy fingers a flute, and a noble personage
counts out money. On the ground, four birds perch upon a
revolving wheel, beside a covered vase and saucers of exquisite

colour. In the distance, a Chinese gateway with tower. Nearer, a cavalier and a crowd of the curious. Still nearer, an elephant with rider. Over the head of the two jugglers is a triangular banner bearing the Chinese dragon.

The freshness of the tapestry is due to the fact that for most of its existence it was preserved in the metal cylinder that conveyed it from Paris to Pekin. It is one of a Chinese Set presented to the Chinese emperor, Chien-lung. The other five at last accounts were in the Pekin Museum. This is the set listed in the Beauvais records of 1763 as *6 pieces of the Chinese delivered to M. Bertin to send to China.*

M. Bertin the French Minister of Foreign Affairs was anxious to promote artistic relations between France and the Far East. He commissioned two young Chinese Christian priests, Fathers Ko and Tang, to take the tapestries, together with a collection of Sèvres porcelain and twelve mirrors, to China. Under date of December 31, 1766, M. Bertin wrote to the two priests: ''The intention of the King is that you make every effort that the tapestries from His Majesty's factory, of which he made you the bearers, and which have remained in the magazines at Canton, should be presented to the Emperor of China, not as a gift from the King, but only to try to find out in this way what might be the Emperor's taste regarding the productions of our tapestries and our arts.''

Under date of November 10, 1767, Michel Benoist, Jesuit, Superior of the Residence of the French Mission at Pekin, wrote to France: ''The Grand Master of the Palace avows that the Emperor was overwhelmed with admiration at sight of the six tapestries. He told me that His Majesty having had them placed under different points of view, and having admired them more and more as he examined carefully the delicacy of the work, at first thought of adorning with them the temples of his palace in which, here as elsewhere, are placed one's most precious possessions. But having reflected that attached as we are to our holy religion we might be distressed when we learned that objects we had offered to His Majesty, His Majesty had used to decorate the temples of divinities that we do not recognize as such, he gave orders to have his European palaces searched for apartments where one could place these tapestries. But no place being found in the European palaces, His Majesty gave orders for the construction of a new palace in which the proportion of the walls of his apartment should agree with the dimensions of the tapestries.''

BOUCHER'S LOVES OF THE GODS

The reputation established for Boucher by the Psyche set, was more than confirmed by the Loves of the Gods in 9 pieces, which went on the looms in 1749. The earliest record that I find of a tapestry on this subject, is in Ovid's Metamorphoses, where Ovid describes the famous weaving contest between Arachne and Minerva. Arachne pictured the amorous weaknesses of the gods unblushingly (Page 15). Here was a subject made to Boucher's heart and hand. In it he had a marvelous opportunity to revel in the rosy nudities that he made so attractive in tapestry. In it he had a marvelous opportunity to show how much he had learned painting scenery for the Opera. In it he had a marvelous opportunity to work in his sketches of ruined Roman architecture brought back from Italy, and to utilize delicate foliage effects learned from the Chinese. The subjects of Boucher's *Loves of the Gods* are: (1) Bacchus and Ariadne, (2) Pluto and Proserpine, (3) Neptune and Amymone, (4) Jupiter and Antiope, (5) Mars and Venus, (6) Boreas and Orithyia, (7) Jupiter and Europa, (8) Vulcan and Venus, (9) Apollo and Clytie.

Bacchus and Ariadne was the most popular tapestry designed by Boucher. Everybody talked about it and everybody wanted it. According to the Beauvais records, it was woven seventeen times. The finest example in America is that belonging to Mrs. E. F. Hutton. It is fresh and unfaded as it came from the loom. It is if anything finer than the one in the Royal Italian collection, although the latter is impressive because of its extra length, Boucher having extended the design on both sides to make it fit a larger space. Quite equal to the Royal Italian Bacchus and Ariadne is the one belonging to Mr. George F. Baker. Another duplicate of the Italian one, but less fresh, is that in the Metropolitan Museum of Art (Plate XI, e).

Here we have the naturalistic style of Rococo at its best— animal life and plant life and architecture in harmony and melting into one another. The cupids next the columns seem almost to have been born from the marble. The trees seem almost to *breathe* in sympathetic appreciation of the romance. Bacchus and Ariadne and their companions seem so completely children of Nature as to need none of the refinements of man-made civilization to protect them from the elements. The scene is the island of Naxos where Ariadne had been abandoned by Theseus, whom she had assisted in his battle with the Minotaur, giving him the spool of thread that enabled him to retrace his way through the Daedalian labyrinth, and with whom she had eloped from her native Crete. Already the wooing of the wine god has banished from her the despair that impelled her to suicide. Still another brilliant Bacchus and Ariadne tapestry in America is the one belonging to Mr. C. Ledyard Blair, woven in charming combination with Jupiter and Antiope, and hence having a special splendor due to monumental size. Jupiter and Antiope (Plate XI, a) shows the wooing of the latter by Jupiter disguised as satyr. Mr. George F. Baker's Jupiter and Antiope is almost as brilliant as his Ariadne. The Royal Italian collection at the Quirinal has fine examples of Mars and Venus (Plate XI, f), Boreas and Orithyia, and Jupiter and Antiope wrongly described as Psyche Dressing. Mars and Venus pictures the most notorious of ancient flirtations more modestly than does Sodoma in the Metropolitan Museum. Mr. George F. Baker has Boreas and Orithyia. Jupiter and Europa shows the king of the gods disguised as a white bull in order to escape the notice of his jealous wife, and deceive the maiden from whom the continent of Europe got its name. A splendid example was No. 38 in the Cleveland Tapestry Exhibition of 1918, lent by Wildenstein & Co. and now in South America. Vulcan and Venus emphasizes the contrast between the goddess of love and her rough and coarse husband on the occasion when in her dove-drawn chariot she visited him in quest of arms and armour for Æneas, the son she had born to the Trojan Anchises. As a companion piece to Bacchus and Ariadne, the Metropolitan Museum has a Vulcan and Venus of the same extended size. Apollo and Clytie introduces the water nymph whose love for the sun god was unreturned and who from sunrise to sunset kept her eyes fastened on him in his course, until her body took root in the ground, and her face became the sunflower turning (in the words of Thomas Moore) "on her god when he sets the same look that she turned when he rose."

The set of Opera Fragments in five pieces, one of which does not appear to have been woven, went on the looms in 1752. In tapestry it recalls scenes designed by Boucher for the stage, among others the colour sketch for the opera of Issé exposed at the Salon in 1742. Issé was one of Apollo's sweethearts, wooed by him as shepherd. The most popular of the set was Vertumnus and Pomona (Frontispiece in colour of *Hunter 1912*) of which there is an inferior and faded example in the Altman collection at the Metropolitan Museum. Here we have Vertumnus, ancient Italian god of the seasons, transformed into an old woman in order to woo Pomona, ancient Italian goddess of fruit. Thanks to his disguise he is able to talk to her freely and by telling her love stories that turned into tragedies because of the coldness of the fair one, to stir her emotions until when he returns to his own youthful and manly form her avowed lover, she no longer resists but meets kiss with kiss.

BOUCHER'S NOBLE PASTORALE

Boucher hit the bull's eye again with his Noble Pastorale in 6 pieces, which, according to the Beauvais records, went on the looms in 1755. The subjects are: (1) Fountain of Love, (2) Flute Players, (3) Fishing, (4) Bird Catchers, (5) Luncheon, (6) Shepherdess. The last was unimportant and was woven only once. The Fountain of Love and Bird Catching were woven eleven times, Fishing and Luncheon ten times, and Flute Playing twelve times. There is a fine example of Bird Catchers in the Harry Payne Whitney collection. The Fountain of Love is in the collection of the late Senator Clark, as well as in that of Mrs. C. B. Alexander.

Mr. H. E. Huntington has all of the set except the last, acquired from the Kann collection, and illustrated in the Kann catalogue (Paris, 1907). By far the most important pieces, because of the monumental size as well as the attractiveness of the designs and the originality of the compositions are Fountain of Love, and Bird Catchers, the former being 19 feet 5 inches wide, the latter 19 feet 3. Fishing is only 13 feet wide, Flute Players 12 feet 4, Luncheon 11. All are typically Boucher with background of trees and ancient Roman sculpture and architectural ruins, and foreground of sheep and children and youthful lovers. The most prominent features of the different pieces are: (1) *Fountain of Love,* with fountain in the middle, foregrounded by children and a goat and sheep and a pair of lovers, flute-playing couple on the left backgrounded by a round squat tower and other buildings, loving couples on the right backgrounded by woods; (2) *Flute Players,* three loving couples on the right two of which play the flute, on the left a youthful shepherd looking on enviously, in the distance a squat round tower and

13

other buildings; (3) *Fishing,* rods and baskets and scoop net, with a dog playfully biting the bare arm of the lover who is putting a fish into the bucket; (4) *Bird Catchers,* in the foreground youthful bird catchers with wooden cages, on the right what looks like a tennis net but is a net for catching birds, in the left background the Temple of Vesta and other Roman architecture and sculpture; (5) *Luncheon,* grapes.

This was the last set of tapestries designed by Boucher for Beauvais. In accordance with instructions from the government, he devoted himself thereafter to the Gobelins.

Other sets originated at Beauvais in the reign of Louis XV were Natoire's Don Quixote in 1735, Homer's Iliad by Deshayes in 1761, of which there are five in the Royal Spanish collection signed A.C.C. BEAUVAIS, Leprince's Russian Sports in 1769, Casanova's Country Pleasures in 1772. Nine of the Don Quixote set of ten, and four of the Russian Sports set of six, are in the Museum of Aix-en-Provence. Luncheon, one of the Russian Sports, was formerly in New York in the Alavoine collection.

HUET-BOUCHER PASTORALS

Although Boucher died in 1770, his work lived on, and in 1780 the Pastorals of Jean Baptiste Huet, inspired by Boucher and closely related to some of his sketches and paintings, went on the looms at Beauvais. The subjects of the four most important of the ten pieces scheduled are: (1) Cherry Pickers, (Plate XI, fa), (2) Bird Nesters, (3) May Pole, (4) Swing. The late Mrs. George Gould had a set of these four. Mr. George F. Baker has a similar set except that "Kite Flying" takes the place of "Bird Nesters." These are the most attractive tapestries originated at Beauvais in the reign of Louis XVI (1774–1792).

The trouble with most Louis XVI tapestries is that they are weak and stupid. Among sets represented in America are Casanova's Gypsies, and Military Scenes; Lavallée Poussin's

Conquest of the Indies, and Story of Alexander; Desoria's Story of Achilles.

The Conquest of the Indies in three pieces was woven only twice, once in 1785, and once in 1788. Fragments of the later set now serve as overdoor panels at Compiègne. The earlier set is still in perfect condition in the collection of Mr. Clarence H. Mackay. The subjects are: (1) Departure of Vasco da Gama, (2) Return of Vasco da Gama, (3) Vasco da Gama made Admiral of the Indies. Two of the Alexander set and two of the Achilles set (Plate XI, ga) are in the Jacques Seligmann collection.

PLATE XI b.—AUDIENCE OF THE EMPEROR, ONE OF VERNANSAL'S CHINESE SET MADE AT BEAUVAIS IN THE FIRST QUARTER OF

PLATES XI, C, Ca.—ON THE LEFT, MUSICIANS, ONE OF MR. MACKAY'S BEAUVAIS–BÉRAIN ITALIAN GROTESQUE SET. ON THE RIGHT, MALADE IMAGINAIRE, ONE OF MRS. WILLIAM HAYWARD'S COMEDIES OF MOLIÈRE FORMERLY IN THE KANN COLLECTION, SIGNED J. B. OUDRY, 1732

PLATES XI, d, da.—ON THE LEFT, THE CHARLATAN, LEFT HALF OF A TAPESTRY THAT COMBINES TWO OF THE PICTURES OF BOUCHER'S ITALIAN SET, THE CHARLATAN AND THE PEEP SHOW. ON THE RIGHT, CHINESE FAIR, ONE OF BOUCHER'S CHINESE SET PRESENTED BY LOUIS XV TO THE CHINESE EMPEROR, NOW IN THE COLLECTION OF MRS. F. F. PRENTISS

PLATES XI, e, ea.—ABOVE, THE METROPOLITAN MUSEUM'S "BACCHUS AND ARIADNE," ONE OF BOUCHER'S "LOVES OF THE GODS," SIGNED OUDRY AND A. C. C. BEAUVAIS. BELOW, "PSYCHE DRESSING," ONE OF BOUCHER'S FAMOUS PSYCHE SET AT THE QUIRINAL

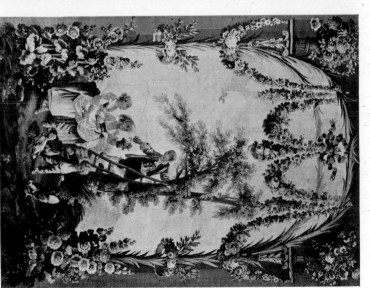

PLATES XI, f, fa.—ON THE LEFT, "MARS AND VENUS," ONE OF BOUCHER'S FAMOUS "LOVES OF THE GODS," AT THE QUIRINAL.
ON THE RIGHT, ONE OF THE HUET-BOUCHER "PASTORALS"; DUVEEN BROS.

PLATES XI, g, ga.—ABOVE, TEMPLE OF VENUS, ONE OF THE TELEMACHUS
SET WOVEN AT BEAUVAIS EARLY IN THE EIGHTEENTH CENTURY; WILLIAM
BAUMGARTEN & CO. BELOW, "ACHILLES DISCOVERED," DESIGN OF DESORIA,
MADE AT BEAUVAIS IN SECTIONS IN 1792 OR 1793. JACQUES SELIGMANN & SON

PLATE XII, a.—COWARDICE OF SANCHO PANZA, ONE OF MR. MACKAY'S FIVE "DON QUIXOTE" TAPESTRIES
DESIGNED BY CHARLES COYPEL AND WOVEN AT THE GOBELINS IN THE MIDDLE OF THE EIGHTEENTH CENTURY

CHAPTER XII

GOBELIN TAPESTRIES OF THE EIGHTEENTH CENTURY

MONTHS OF LUCAS, PORTIÈRES OF THE GODS, DON QUIXOTE, OPERA
FRAGMENTS, HUNTS OF LOUIS XV, ESTHER, GOBELIN-BOUCHERS
PORTRAITS IN TAPESTRY

THE eighteenth century compares with the seventeenth as
Spring does with Winter. Brightness displaces Solemnity,
Individuality upsets Conformity, Grace supplants Dignity,
Rubens and Lebrun yield to Watteau and Boucher.

Eighteenth century reproductions and adaptations of
Renaissance tapestries are usually preferable to those of the
seventeenth. This superiority is marked in the Months of
Lucas. The Louis XIV versions are heavy and awkward and
crude, as compared with those of Louis XV. Those of
Louis XV, especially those woven in. Michel Audran's high-
warp shop, are immeasureably superior not only to Months
of Lucas of the seventeenth century but also to all that have
survived from the sixteenth century. The new borders, and
the remodeling and refining of the designs by eighteenth century Gobelin cartoonists, transformed the spirit of the Months
of Lucas from Flemish Renaissance to French Rococo, and
while obscuring and sometimes confusing some of the original
costume details, uniformly substituted good drawing for bad,
and exquisiteness for rawness of colouration. The finest set
is that made by Audran, for Alexander, Count of Toulouse
(1678–1737), ten of which are now in the collection of Mr.
Rockefeller, (Plates XII, b, c, d); the other two, February
and June, in the French Embassy at Leningrad (Page 365 of
v. II of *Fenaille Gobelins*). This is the same Count of Toulouse for whom tapestries had been made at Beauvais by

Béhagle (Chapter XI).   His initial *A* appears in the four
corners of the tapestries; his coat-of-arms, the three Bourbon
fleurs-de-lis with bar sinister, in the middle of the top borders;
and the zodiacal sign of the month, in the middle of the bottom
border.   The flowers of the border designed by Perrot are
of extraordinary excellence as regards both design and weave.

The couple that appear three times in January (Plate
XII, b) are the Emperor Charles V and his wife Isabella of
Portugal (Consult Chapter VIII).   The two-headed eagle of
the Empire will be noted in the floor tiles.

The subjects of the set are:

> I. March, the Ram.   Fishing and Gardening.
> II. April, the Bull.   Music and Boating.
> III. May, the Twins.   Archery.
> IV. June, the Crab.   Sheepshearing.
> V. July, the Lion.   Hunting with Falcon.
> VI. August, the Virgin.   Reaping.
> VII. September, the Scales.   Stag Hunt.
> VIII. October, the Scorpion.   Vintage.
> IX. November, the Archer.   Sowing.
> X. December, the Goat.   Skating.
> XI. January, the Water Carrier.   Dancing.
> XII. February, the Fish.   Indoor Games.

Other eighteenth century Gobelin Months of Lucas still
in existence are the set by Audran and Monmerqué in the
Royal Palace at Dresden, the set by Monmerqué and Cozette
in the French Ministry of Foreign Affairs, the set by Lefebvre
at Pau and in the Garde Meuble.   Mrs. F. F. Prentiss has
June, one of the three Months of Lucas signed by Audran
which were formerly in the Ffoulke collection.   May and
December, the latter signed cozette, are in the Palazzo Doria
at Rome.   April and June are on exhibition at the Louvre.

The New Indies that went on the looms in 1740, was the
Louis XIV Indies modified and repainted by Desportes, who
introduced many European animals and plants.   There are

sets in the National Austrian collection, and at the Quirinal, both signed NEILSON (Plate XII, e).   The Duke of Alba has four of the set signed COZETTE 1789.

CLAUDE AUDRAN'S PORTIÈRES OF THE GODS

The Portières of the Gods that went on the looms in the year of 1700, marked the beginning of a new era.   Though inspired by the Louis XIV Triumphs of the Gods and Grotesque Months, there is nothing Baroque about them and little that is Italian.   The designer Claude Audran, one of the masters of Watteau, produced compositions that are delightfully original, and thoroughly French.   The subjects are: (1) Venus for Spring, (2) Ceres for Summer, (Plate XII, f) (3) Bacchus for Autumn, (4) Saturn for Winter, (5) Juno for Air, (6) Diana for Earth, (7) Neptune for Water, (8) Jupiter for Fire—the Four Seasons and the Four Elements.   Senator Clark had a splendid set of the Elements, and there are individual pieces in other American collections.   There are many in the National French collection, and others at the Quirinal, at Windsor Castle, and in the collection of the Duke of Richmond.   In the same style, and almost as attractive, are Claude Audran's Twelve Grotesque Months, woven pilasters usually made in groups of three.   There are complete sets in the Bischoffsheim collection, and in the Venetian palace of Prince Giovanelli.   There are nine of the months, each framed separately, at the Palazzo Doria in Rome.   A fascinating eighteenth century tapestry portière is the Diana, with small medallion, designed by Perrot.

COYPEL'S DON QUIXOTE

The most important series of tapestries originated at the Gobelins in the eighteenth century, are the twenty-eight designed by Charles Coypel to illustrate Cervantes' story of Don Quixote (Plate XII, a).   They are so highly prized in Europe that few have been allowed to cross the Atlantic.

Among European collections listed by M. Fenaille as containing tapestries from the series are: Marquis de Venneville, eleven; Royal Italian collection, twenty-one; Count d'Argenson, five; Empress Eugénie, seven; Duke of Richmond, four; Duke of Portland, eight; Anitchkoff Palace at Leningrad, four; Marquis de Vogüé, six; Royal Swedish collection, four; Royal Palace in Berlin, six; Palace of the Archduke Ferdinand in Vienna, four; with most of all, of course, in the National French collection.

The series was never woven as a complete set, but always in small groups selected according to the taste of the purchaser, or the convenience of the giver, who was in almost every case the King of France. To quote the words of the Director of the Gobelins, under date of October 22, 1752: ''One advantage of this series of hangings is that it can be separated into as many or as few pieces as desired, and is consequently more convenient for the King to present to Princes or Ambassadors.''

While the Old Testament and Iliad sets, completed by Charles Coypel but largely the creation of his father Antoine Coypel, were rather old-fashioned, there was nothing old-fashioned about the Don Quixote series. They were eighteenth century Rococo in every detail as well as in general plan and composition, without the slightest suggestion of Renaissance or Baroque. They set the fashion of small-picture-on-large-decorative-background (Plate XII, a) which was imitated later in the Gobelin-Boucher medallion tapestries. The painting of the twenty-eight small pictures occupied much of Coypel's life, the first being completed by him in 1714, the last in 1751. Of the elaborate backgrounds (*alentours*), with double frame, and with two-tone yellow or crimson, mosaic or leafy mat, there was a succession of six designed under the supervision of Coypel by Fontenay, Claude Audran, Desportes and Tessier. The peacock, dogs, monkeys and sheep were by Desportes. The exquisite flowers of the later backgrounds were by Louis Tessier, who has never been surpassed for work of this kind.

The coloured frontispiece of this chapter illustrates one of Mr. Mackay's Don Quixote set of five. The subject as woven on the blue panel at the bottom is the Cowardice of Sancho Panza (POLTRONNERIE DE SANCHO A LA CHASSE). The scene is a lively one. In the foreground Don Quixote, in armor, sustains with his sword the attack of the wild boar whom the dogs worry and two other hunters pierce with spears. On the left the frightened Sancho Panza climbs a tree. In the background the Duke and Duchess with two of their attendants. The mat part of the *alentour* is a two-tone golden mosaic adorned with festoons of richly coloured flowers. Inside and outside the mat, woven gilt frames. In the corners of the outer frame, the monogram of the King. Perched on top of the inner frame a splendid peacock. Below the inner frame, a gladiator in a lunette held by a lion mask. On both sides of the lunette, flowers and flags and books and armor and dogs and sheep. The others of Mr. Mackay's set are: (2) Don Quixote made Knight by the Landlord of the Inn, signed COZETTE, 1764; (3) Entrance of Sancho into the Island of Barataria, signed AUDRAN, 1757; (4) The False Princess Micomicon comes and asks Don Quixote to Restore her to the Throne, no signature; (5) Don Quixote in Barcelona dances at the Ball given him by Don Antonio, signed COZETTE, 1778.

A set of five formerly on exhibition at the Metropolitan Museum as part of the Morgan collection, is that of Mrs. Dixon, with leafy crimson mats. It came to the Morgan collection from the King of Spain's grandfather, Don Francisco de Assisi. Four of the tapestries originally belonged to the Archbishop of Reims, presented to him in 1774 by Louis XVI, who had been baptised by him, confirmed by him, married by him, and in 1775 crowned by him at Reims. Two years after the coronation, the Cardinal died at the age of eighty, and the furnishings of his home were sold in Paris.

The fifth of the set originally belonged to the Duke of Hesse-Darmstadt, presented to him by the Emperor Napoleon in 1810. This is the only one of the five that was woven on a low-warp loom.

DON QUIXOTE'S FIRST EXPEDITION

The first of Mrs. Dixon's set is Don Quixote guided by Folly. It is signed NEILSON EX. 1783. Don Quixote is pictured sallying forth on his first expedition in search of heroic adventure. He is equipped in a full suit of armor, and mounted on his scrawny steed Rozinante. Folly, wearing the barber's basin as helmet, points to a distant windmill, which, to the distempered imagination of the knight, appears a monstrous giant armed with huge club and terrific scimitar. Cupid, the God of Love, directs Don Quixote's attention to Dulcinea del Toboso, a coarse country wench whom Don Quixote's fancy has invested with the attributes of a high-born and beautiful damsel. As Don Quixote phrased it for his future biographer: "Scarcely had ruddy Phoebus spread over the face of the spacious earth the golden tresses of his lovely hair; scarcely had the painted little choristers with forked tongues begun in soft and melodious harmony to hail the approach of the blushing Aurora, who deserting the soft couch of the jealous husband, had just disclosed herself to mortal eyes through the portals of the Manchegan horizon; when the renowned Don Quixote disdaining soft repose, mounted his famous steed Rozinante, and proceeded over the ancient plain of Montiel."

Mrs. Dixon's other Gobelin Don Quixote tapestries are: (2) Don Quixote misled by Sancho, mistakes a Peasant Girl for his Dulcinea, signed COZETTE, 1773; (3) Don Quixote through Sancho asks permission of the Princess to address her, signed COZZETTE, 1773; (4) Don Quixote served by the Ladies, signed COZETTE, 1773; (5) Sancho's Departure for the Island of Barataria, signed AUDRAN, 1773. Don Quixote, not at all discouraged by the mistake in Tapestry 2, proceeds in Tapestry 3 to pay his respects through Sancho to a richly-dressed lady mounted on a milk-white palfrey, whom one evening near sunset as he issued from a forest, he beheld in the distance among a group of ladies and gentlemen engaged in hawking. Oddly enough, the lady this time turned out to be of high rank, in fact a real Duchess, and mistress of the hunting party. The Duchess and the Duke her husband quickly grasped the situation, and planned to make sport of the crazy knight and his simple squire. They conducted them with much ceremony to the Duke's castle, where Don Quixote was treated with extraordinary deference, supplied with rich robes, and waited upon by the Duchess' ladies (Tapestry 4). Finally the Duke and Duchess, delighted with their success in hoodwinking the knight, decided to practice on his squire. They pretended to bestow upon him the governorship of the island Barataria. Wild with joy Sancho took leave of his benefactors and of his former master, and set forth for his government, dressed like a professor of the law, wearing over his other clothes a loose gown of grave-coloured camlet, and a cap of the same material (Tapestry 5).

COYPEL'S OPERA FRAGMENTS

Other sets designed by Charles Coypel are Opera Fragments and Stage Scenes, the former in four pieces, the latter in five. The first of the *Opera Fragments,* Angelica's Marriage, pictures a scene from Quinault's opera Roland, and is charming. Cut on a tree at the right is the inscription: *"Angelica pledges her heart. Médor has conquered it. How happy is Médor. Angelica has crowned his vows."* Through an archway on the left, is seen the wedding feast. In the middle foreground, Roland learns of Angelica's infidelity and flight with Médor. This tapestry can be seen at Compiègne, and there is another in the Royal Swedish collection. There was formerly one in America. The other three subjects of Opera Fragments are all from Quinault's opera Armide. The subjects of *Stage Scenes* are from (1) Molière's ballet Psyche, (2) Racine's Bajazet, (3) Corneille's Rodogune (4) Quinault's Alceste, (5) Racine's Athalie. The title of the first is Psyche abandoned by Cupid. Later, a companion Psyche piece was designed by Belle "in the style of Coypel."

Sets originated near the end of the reign of Louis XIV are Jouvenet and Restout's rather old-fashioned New Testament, and the Metamorphoses by several painters. The most interesting of the Metamorphoses are Louis de Boulogne's Renaud et Armide, Diana's Return from the Hunt by Delafosse, Bacchus and Ariadne, Zephyrus and Flora, Narcissus. Among pieces listed by M. Fenaille were four in the collection of Don Francisco d'Assisi, and four in the Paris collection of Mrs. Louis Stern.

OUDRY'S HUNTS OF LOUIS XV

Oudry's success at Beauvais (Chapter XI) brought him into the limelight. In 1733 he was appointed Head Inspector of the Gobelins, and was commissioned to design the Hunts of Louis XV (Plate XII, ea) to be executed at the Gobelins. Only two sets were woven, one of which is in the Royal Italian collection at Florence, the other in the Garde Meuble. The latter was shown in the French Hunting Exhibition at the Musée des Arts Décoratifs in 1923. The subjects are: (1) The Rendezvous at Puys du Roi. (2) The Death of the Stag in the Ponds of Saint Jean. (3) Hunting the Stag within sight of Compiègne. (4) The Stag turning on the Dogs at the Rocks of Franchart, in the Forest of Fontainebleau. (5) The King holding the Limer. (6) The Relay. (7) The Pack on the way to the Rendezvous. (8) The Curée. (9) The Forhu. The height of the set is 11 feet 6 inches. No. 1 is 19½ feet long; No. 2, 16½ feet; No. 3, 26¼ feet; No. 8, 22 feet; the others, all small. All the tapestries are signed J. B. OUDRY with the year that dates the cartoon. The scene of No. 1 is an open circle where several heavily wooded avenues meet. In the background the pack. In the foreground, that great hunter, the Count of Toulouse, son of Louis XIV, mounted and hat in hand, reports to the King who has just alighted from his six-horse calèche, and is having his boots put on. In No. 3 the stag crosses the Oise within sight of Compiègne, leaving the water just at the right of the horse-drawn water-coach, which is crowded inside and above with spectators. In the high foreground on this side of the river, the King and other noble huntsmen with dogs. In No. 8 the dogs receive their quarry (*curée*). In No. 9 the Hunt ends with the Recall (*forhu*).

This set of nine tapestries, though faded, still pictures vividly stag hunting as practised at Compiègne by the Court of Louis XV. Only one of the scenes is located at Fontainebleau. As might be expected of Oudry, the animals are splendid, the personages passable, the landscapes interesting.

DE TROY'S ESTHER

A Bible story skilfully handled and richly costumed is De Troy's Esther in seven pieces. Another set by De Troy, also in seven pieces, illustrates the Story of Jason as told in Ovid's "Metamorphoses." Of two Turkish sets, one was by Parrocel, the other by Vanloo. Parrocel's Turkish Embassy, which was begun with the title "New Story of the King," by contrast with the "Story of the King" of Louis XIV, consists of only two pieces, the Turkish Ambassador entering the Garden of the Tuileries, and the Turkish Ambassador leaving the Garden of the Tuileries. Vanloo's Turkish Costumes, developed from his paintings for the bedchamber of Madame de Pompadour at Bellevue, shows (1) Sultana at Luncheon, (2) Sultana Dressing (3) Sultana's Sewing Room (4) Odalisques dancing before Sultan. Nos. 2 and 3 are at the Louvre, and the corresponding full-size cartoons are at Compiègne. Of Vanloo's Theseus, planned for seven pieces, the only piece executed was "Theseus conquers the Bull of Marathon," of which there are two examples in Paris and one in

the Royal Swedish collection.   The Story of Daphnis and
Chloe was the subject of two Louis XV sets; the first in four
pieces, after Philip of Orleans, Regent of France; the second,
in seven pieces, after Jeaurat.   Three of the Jeaurat set were
sold at the Havemeyer sale in 1914.   There was formerly one
of Natoire's Antony and Cleopatra set at Sherry's.   One of
Jeaurat's Fêtes de Village, was No. 35 in the catalogue of the
Cleveland Tapestry Exhibition, 1918.   It was 9 feet 4 by 18
feet 9, and showed on the left a recruiting sergeant busy at his
task, and on the right a market with buildings and peddlers,
girls dancing, children at the wheel of fortune, and a quack
doctor holding up a printed placard.

GOBELIN BOUCHERS

François Boucher as the most brilliant and successful tapestry designer of the eighteenth century.   No one appreciated
this more than Audran, Cozette, and Neilson, shop proprietors
at the Gobelins.   In 1754 they submitted a memorial to the
administration stating that "to prevent the decadence of the
Gobelin Factory, it would be necessary to attach to it Sr.
Boucher," and that "for nearly twenty years the Beauvais
Factory has been kept up by the attractive paintings made for
it by Sr. Boucher."   The administration listened, and the next
year when Oudry died, appointed Boucher his successor as
Head Inspector of the Gobelins.   "M. Boucher," wrote the
administration to the three Gobelin shop proprietors, "not
only has refused the inspection of the Beauvais factory with
the intention of giving his attention to the Gobelins, but he has
even refused an interest that the Beauvais directors wished to
give him in their enterprise."

Already Boucher had designed for Madame Pompadour, to
be executed at the Gobelins, the Rising of the Sun and the
Setting of the Sun, the paintings of which are in the Wallace
collection, while the one set of tapestries made from the paint-

ings was sold in England after Madame de Pompadour's death, and cannot be located.

For the Loves of the Gods, a series of twenty-two by different painters, Boucher designed three tapestries: Venus and Vulcan, Cupids, Génies des Arts. There is a Génies des Arts in the Jacques Seligmann collection and a Venus and Vulcan in the Museum of the Gobelins. The other pieces of the set, some of which are attractive, are: Neptune and Amymone, by Vanloo; Jupiter and Europa, by Pierre; Pluto and Proserpine, by Vien; Cupids, by Vanloo; two Cupids, by Pierre; two Cupids, by Vien; Génies des Sciences, by Hallé; Mercury and Herse, by Pierre; Hippomenes and Atalanta, by Hallé; Corésus and Callirhoé, by Fragonard; Achilles Recognized, by Hallé; Silenus and Eglé, by Hallé; Triumph of Amphitrite, by Taraval; Bacchus and Ariadne, Jupiter and Leda, Clytie and Apollo, all three by Belle; Feast of Bacchus (Autumn), by Lagrenée.

Fifteen out of the twenty Gobelin Bouchers (all except the three Loves of the Gods, and the Rising and the Setting of the Sun just mentioned) were medallion tapestries like Coypel's Don Quixote set, with small pictures backgrounded by large decorative *alentours* (Plate XII, h). They are charming and marvelously decorative. England has more than its share, owing to the policy of the French government that officially encouraged the taking of orders in England by Neilson. Four of the fifteen picture scenes from the Story of Amintas and Sylvia: (1) Sylvia Freed by Amintas (left medallion of Plate XII, h). (2) Sylvia cures Phyllis of a Bee sting; (3) Love revives Amintas in the arms of Sylvia; (4) Sylvia flees from the wounded Wolf (right medallion of Plate XII, h). The other eleven are: (5) Vertumnus, and Pomona; (6) Aurora and Cephalus (Plate XII, g); (7) Neptune and Amymone; (8) Venus and Vulcan; (9) Venus rising from the waters; (10) Fishing; (11) Fortune Teller; (12) Jupiter and Callisto; (13) Psyche looking at Cupid asleep; (14, 15) small Cupid medallions.

Among pieces listed by Fenaille as in England are: Nos. 5, 6, 7, 8, at Croome Court; Nos. 5, 6, 7, 9, at Newby Hall; Nos. 5, 6, 7, 9, at Weston Park; Nos. 10, 11, Aske Hall; Nos. 5, 6, 8, 13, 14, 15, at Osterly Park; Nos. 1, 2, 3, 4, 11, at Welbeck Abbey in the collection of the Duke of Portland. Many of these were made with two medallions on one tapestry (Plate XII, h), and with supplementary small panels and furniture coverings. All of them were woven by Neilson on his improved low-warp looms. The Aske Hall pieces have stone-grey damassé ground, the Newby Hall ones mauve damassé ground, all the others crimson damassé ground. There is in the French Ministry of Marine a two-medallion piece on crimson damassé ground, made on high-warp loom by the younger Cozette in 1791; and in the Palais Bourbon three pieces on yellow ground, Nos. 5 and 6 one piece, Nos. 9 and 13 separately. Made by Neilson on crimson damassé ground were: Nos. 5, 6, 9, 13, at the Louvre; Nos. 5, 6, 8, 9, 12, at the Pavlosk Palace near Leningrad; No. 7 at the Berlin Kunstgewerbe Museum.

Sometimes the pictures were woven without *alentours,* as was the case with a set of ten for MM. Roux and Lambert, of Lyons, in 1779; and with Nos. 10 and 11 in the Bordeaux Bourse, each 4 feet by 4 feet 7, and signed Cozette, 1772. Sometimes they were woven separately to be inserted later (*Fenaille Gobelins* III, 267; IV, 294).

After the death of Boucher, Jacques made a new *alentour,* without the inside frame, and with the figure group of Boucher placed on a platform beneath a festooned canopy. The only known set, that in the Groult collection at Paris, includes Nos. 5, 6, 7, 8.

Vincent's Story of Henri IV which can be seen at Pau, and the Story of France by different painters, were originated in the latter half of the reign of Louis XVI. They are weak in design and inferior in weave. Callet's Four Seasons and Suvee's Feast of Pallas, though exaggeratedly neo-classic, shine by contrast.

PORTRAITS IN TAPESTRY

The eighteenth century had the bad taste to like isolated portraits in tapestry. Among those that have been preserved are Vanloo's Louis XV, Nattier's Marie Leczinska, Vanloo's Dauphin (later Louis XVI), Drouais' Marie Antoinette, all woven by Cozette and now in the Bordeaux Chamber of Commerce; Ducreux's Emperor Francis I, and Ducreux's Maria Theresa, woven by Cozette, at Versailles. The eighteenth century also had the bad taste to like small tapestries, and tapestries copied from easel paintings (Plate XVI, a, aa). Be it here recorded that the very qualities which make tapestry texture more effective than painting for the production of monumental pictures, tend to throw it out of scale for small work.

14

PLATE XII, b.—JANUARY. ONE OF MR. ROCKEFELLER'S GOBELIN MONTHS OF LUCAS

PLATE XII, C.—APRIL. ONE OF MR. ROCKEFELLER'S MONTHS OF LUCAS

PLATE XII, d.—OCTOBER.   ONE OF MR. ROCKEFELLER'S GOBELIN MONTHS OF LUCAS

PLATES XII, e, ea.—ON THE LEFT, ONE OF THE FAMOUS GOBELIN "NEW INDIES," AT THE QUIRINAL, SIGNED NEILSON EX. 1773. ON THE RIGHT, ONE OF THE GOBELIN "HUNTS OF LOUIS XV," SIGNED BY THE DESIGNER ON THE ROCK IN THE FOREGROUND OUDRY 1746; IN THE ROYAL ITALIAN TAPESTRY COLLECTION AT FLORENCE

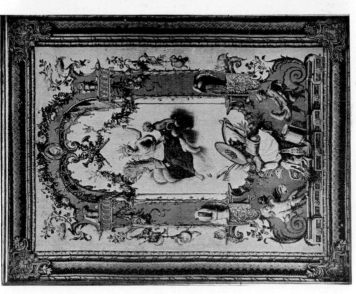

PLATES XII, f, fa.—ON THE LEFT, CERES, ONE OF THE QUIRINAL'S FAMOUS SET OF GOBELIN "SEASONS AND ELEMENTS," DESIGNED BY AUDRAN. ON THE RIGHT, ESTHER DRESSING, ONE OF THE FAMOUS STORY OF ESTHER SET IN THE ROYAL ITALIAN TAPESTRY COLLECTION AT FLORENCE, DESIGNED BY DE TROY

PLATE XII, g.—AURORA AND CEPHALUS, DETAIL OF ONE OF THE DUKE OF ALBA'S
GOBELIN BOUCHERS

PLATE XII, h.—GOBELIN-BOUCHER TAPESTRY, SIGNED BY THE WEAVER NEILSON EX. 1783, WITH TWO MEDALLIONS FROM THE STORY OF "AMINTAS AND SYLVIA". DUKE OF PORTLAND

PLATE XIII, a.—TRIUMPH OF CUPID, A LOUIS XVI AUBUSSON TAPESTRY CARTOONED
WITH BOUCHER, FRAGONARD AND TESSIER IN MIND. P. W. FRENCH & CO.

CHAPTER XIII

AUBUSSON TAPESTRIES

STRONG BLACKS, DAZZLING WHITES, LOOSE TEXTURE, SMALL SIZE
DUMONS, JULIARD, OUDRY, BOUCHER, LANCRET, HUET, REIMS
LILLE, NANCY

THE large number of ancient Aubusson tapestries in America has compelled me to develop this chapter at considerable length. My generalizations are based on Aubusson tapestries with which I am personally acquainted, and of which I have here given the exact location.

The historian of Aubusson tapestries was Monsieur Cyprien Pérathon. In the year-books of the Société des Beaux-Arts des Départments de la France, he published an iconography of ancient Aubusson tapestries, lists of Aubusson and Felletin weavers, special articles on Aubusson painters and inspectors and much other invaluable raw material, but without evolving order out of the chaos.

This chapter of mine is the first attempt to sketch the development of Aubusson tapestries, and to show how at different periods they differ from one another and from the tapestries of the Gobelins, Brussels, Oudenarde, and Beauvais.

Aubusson is a charming little city, delightfully situated in the mountains of Auvergne, 207 miles by rail south of Paris. It has long been famous for the production of inexpensive tapestries. The adjacent village of Felletin, which, to judge by the inventories of the sixteenth century, was first to develop the industry, trailed Aubusson in the seventeenth, and began to specialize on coarse verdures, leaving the more important *sets with personages* to Aubusson. An exception to the rule appears to have been the Felletin set of Illustrious Women; with gold, in six pieces, purchased by the Company of the Indies. in 1670, to send to the Far East.

A distinguishing feature of ancient Aubusson tapestries are the dazzling whites and the loose texture (Plates XIII, a, b). Also, the seventeenth century and early eighteenth Aubusson tapestries resemble those of Oudenarde in being too black (Plate XIII, ba). Possibly, even probably, this may have been due to a migration of Protestant weavers from Oudenarde to Aubusson, consequent upon the religious troubles of the Netherlands in the last half of the sixteenth century. But the contrasting whites of Aubusson tapestries of this period are distributed over larger surfaces than those of Oudenarde, and forced by hatchings into less abrupt and more effective contrast.

MADE IN 1619

In the archepiscopal palace at Reims there are four badly damaged pieces of tapestry ordered at Paris in 1619 from Gilbert Lombard, dealer, of Aubusson, and delivered in 1625. The field is in yellow fleurs-de-lis on blue, with picture medallion in the middle. The borders are of medium width, with white ground on which clusters of green foliage alternate with medallions some of which carry the arms of the Cathedral Chapter of Reims. The one of the tapestries illustrated on Plate 59 of *Sartor Reims,* with bottom border missing, is 14 feet high by 18½ feet long. The medallion carries the Assumption of the Virgin, standing on the heads of cherubs and borne aloft by four angels. In the choir of Notre Dame de Nantilly at Saumur is a Story of the Virgin, in 4 pieces and 8 scenes, dated 1619, very rough and crude, and as the inscription states, made at the expense of the parish.

The Cathedral of Angers has two pieces 4 feet 9 inches high, in 8 scenes, with united length of 49 feet, picturing the Story of Saint Saturnin, Archbishop of Toulouse, dated 1649 on two of the long French inscriptions in Roman capital letters. They were ordered by the Church of Saint-Mimbouf, of which they bear the arms as well as those of two donors.

The order was placed with René Jouaneau, tapestry dealer of Reims, and with François Pelerier, of Aubusson. These two tapestries are of poor design and faded.

The Tournon Lyceum has three pieces of a Life of Christ set, with wide borders that are more floral and less architectural than those of the Early Gobelins and contemporary Brussels. These resemble the "Jesus washing the Feet of the Apostles," at the Gobelins, which has lost all of its border except the inside moulding. The city hall of Vallon (Ardèche) has a set of Tasso's Jerusalem Delivered, in seven pieces, one of them signed DORLIAC AUBUSSON made about 1658. The borders are wide, with heavy moulding inside, and with a string of flowers twisting spirally around a pole in the field, which continued to be the favorite border motif at Aubusson for more than a century. While the contrast between the whites and blacks is strong, and the whites of the eyes are over-accentuated, as is common in Aubusson tapestries of the seventeenth century and later, the faces and forms and backgrounds are well composed, and the general effect is decidedly attractive.

As at the Early Gobelins, so at Aubusson, the Raphaelesque Psyche designs engraved by Agostino Veneziano were a favorite source. One of these, based upon the Betrothal of Psyche's Sisters, is in the collection of French & Co. The scene has been redrawn and amplified in the style of the seventeenth century. The number of personages has been increased from six to eleven. The burning brazier and the rich presents in the foreground have been added. Seated on the throne are Psyche's father and mother, both crowned. On the left, an Oriental king sues for the hand of the one of Psyche's sisters who stands by the father. On the right stands Psyche's other sister holding the hand of the king who has won her. Both sisters are provided for, but Psyche in the background is neglected. The goddess Venus, jealous of Psyche's extraordinary beauty, has put a curse upon her which seems to doom her to become an "old maid."

ALEXANDER AND JOAN OF ARC

When the Gobelins was reorganized in 1662, and the Beauvais factory established in 1664, plans were made to promote the industry also at Aubusson. The plans seem never to have been executed, although some artistic assistance was rendered in the form of full-size cartoons from the Gobelins, notably those of Lebrun's Elements. However, the designs of Lebrun that appealed most to Aubusson's customers were those of the Story of Alexander, which in abbreviated form was woven there over and over again, most frequently of all the Entry into Babylon of which many examples survive. The Musée des Arts Décoratifs has a small Alexander tapestry signed DAVBUSSON. RAYNAVD, with modern bottom border. This tapestry duplicates the right end of the Cleveland Museum's Entry into Babylon (Plate XIII, ba). Influenced by Lebrun's Alexander set was the designer of a set of Joan of Arc tapestries, based on Jean Chaplain's "La Pucelle, ou la France délivrée," published in 1656, with illustrations by A. Bosse, engraved by C. Vignon. Three of the set displayed in Notre Dame on May 14, 1922, at the services commemorating the Deliverance of France by the Maid of Orleans, were sold at the American Art Galleries on November 17 of the same year. In the first, Joan of Arc in full armor appeals to King Charles VII whose broken sceptre lies on the ground beside him. In the distance, soldiers and the city of Orleans. In the sky above, a winged figure of France holding a medallion that bears the title of the book. In another of the tapestries, Joan stands alone with background of fleurs-de-lis and forest. In the third, Charles VII, in armor and victorious, sees in a vision the martyred shepherdess. The tapestries are only 9 feet 2 inches high, with combined width of 22 feet 6. This calls attention to the fact that most Aubusson tapestries of the eighteenth and of the late seventeenth centuries are distinguished from those of the Gobelins and Beauvais by their *small size.* The height of those made for private purchasers and for stock ranges from 7 to 9½ feet.

Eighteenth century Aubussons at Angers are: a small Resurrection; a Marriage of Cana 7½ by 17 feet; a small Moses tapestry; a Last Supper 7½ by 17 feet; a John the Baptist, in six scenes, 9½ by 55 feet, with colours still bright and fresh, signed P. GRELLET; a Saint John the Evangelist in two scenes; a Story of Joseph in four scenes, 7¾ feet by 43; a Nativity, after Jouvenet, signed M.R.D.B. All are crude.

THE BEST PERIOD

Aubusson was greatly injured by the Revocation of the Edict of Nantes in 1685, as many of the best weavers were Protestants and left the country because it did not seem safe to stay: One of the best known of the emigrés is Pierre Mercier who located in Berlin (Chapter XIV). Aubusson also suffered more than its share during the hard times that prevailed in France in the last decade of the seventeenth century, even the Gobelins being shut down for lack of money in the royal treasury. Finally, in 1731, the government intervened positively and successfully. A dyer from the Gobelins was sent to Aubusson to reorganize the dyeing there, and a painter was appointed to superintend the production of new designs, and to spend at least three months of every two years in Aubusson. The first of the painters was Dumons, (1731–1755); the second, Juliard (1755–1780), who was succeeded by Ranson. Dumons and Juliard did splendid work. They not only painted cartoons themselves, but called in other painters to assist, notably Huet in the period of Louis XVI, and used freely all the suitable sketches and engravings that could be acquired inexpensively. As a result of their efforts, the best period of tapestry weaving in Aubusson is from 1740 to 1790. The ugly blacks disappear, leaving a rather agreeable dominance of whites and creams, enlivened by rosy reds. The coarse, loose texture, much cheaper to produce than that of the fine cloths of the Gobelins and Beauvais, is agreeable to the eye, and saves Louis XVI Aubussons from the paint-like flatness and hardness that began to be common elsewhere.

OUDRY

Almost as important in the regeneration of Aubusson as he had been in the regeneration of Beauvais, was Oudry whose Lafontaine designs were copied freely in both wall panels and furniture coverings. Furthermore, in 1761, the government sent the full-size cartoons of Oudry's Amusements Champêtres, Comedies of Molière, and Ovid's Metamorphoses, to Aubusson. By this time the Comedies of Molière must have been out of line with popular taste. At any rate I have never seen any Aubusson reproductions of them. But with the Metamorphoses it was different. Oudry's animal designs will never grow tame or old, and his very original versions of the Metamorphoses picture the scenes *all animals and no humans*. The Palace of Circe, (Plate XIII, c) shows a stately interior with the throne and wand of Circe and with monkey, parrot, tiger, bear, gazelle, and the boar into which one of Ulysses' companions has been transformed, but no personages. The Descent of Orpheus shows animals galore, but the lyre and the tambourine alone remind us of the Story. Actæon is rich with architecture and foliage but it takes the horn and spear to call our attention to the fact that the splendid stag whom the dogs attack is Actæon himself. Even Europa shows none of the charming maidens who usually dominate the scene, but, instead, cows on the seashore, and in the foreground a white bull looking eagerly for her who has bedecked him with flowers, while the caduceus of Mercury lying on the ground identifies the scene. (See *Arts and Decoration* of June, 1915). Three of the original set of eight was shown at Limoges in 1886; and two out of five belonging to French & Co., at the Philadelphia Tapestry Exhibition, 1915 (Nos. 45, 46 of the catalogue). One of the Limoges ones was signed

F. PICQVEAVX, who belonged to an old family of Aubusson paint-
er-weavers, and who was the King's assorter of wool and silk
at Aubusson from 1773 to 1786. M. Pérathon in speaking of
these tapestries, says: "They place François Picqueaux in the
first rank of Aubusson artists, and are justly considered as
the chef-d'oeuvre of the ancient Aubusson Tapestry Factory."

Inspired by Oudry and by Beauvais are many of the best
of the Aubusson verdures, among them the Dog pointing a
Pheasant, of the Braquenié collection and the Dogs chasing
a Rabbit, 9 feet 3 by 15 feet 8, lent by William Baumgarten
& Co. to the Cleveland Tapestry Exhibition, 1918 (No. 48 of
the catalogue). Oudry's Lion and Mouse on white ground
is No. 13 of the catalogue of the Buffalo Tapestry Exhibition,
8 feet by 6 feet 10, lent by Mrs. Frank H. Goodyear. Perhaps
by Dumons are the five Story of Diana tapestries from the
Château de Vares, 8 feet high, in the Williamson sale,
New York, 1911. Diana at the bath reflects Boucher; the
others, Oudry.

BOUCHER

However, judging by the tapestries that have survived,
Boucher was as easily first in popularity among Aubusson weavers, as among those of Beauvais and the Gobelins.
Again and again appear in auction sales, sets duplicating part of the Chinese set designed by Boucher and cartooned by Dumons for Beauvais. But in the Aubusson sets
we also find compositions that were not part of the Beauvais
set, sometimes based on other Chinese sketches by Boucher,
sometimes supplementary designs by other artists. There
are three of the Aubusson Chinese set 7 feet 7 inches high,
and without border, in the Martin Le Roy collection (Illustrated and described by M. Marquet de Vasselot in his splendid catalogue of the collection). The titles are Drinking Tea,
Gardening, and Fishing. The last of these is based on one
of the Boucher sketches at Besançon. The others though

similar in style do not look like Boucher. Other subjects that appear in a set of seven sold at the Hotel Drouot, May 5, 1905, are: Chinese Emperor's Audience, Chinese Dancing, Chinese Hunting, Chinese Fair, Rice Culture, Bird Seller; all but the last two, similar to the pieces of the same name in the Beauvais set. In the Vicomte de Curel sale, 1918, there were fine examples of Chinese Tea Drinking, and Chinese Dancing, 9 feet high, and 16 feet long, respectively, with narrow gilt-frame border. M. Alfred Lacaze's set of five adds another subject, Hunting with the Bow; the Count Lefebvre de Behaines' set of six, one of them double, adds the Toilet in a Park; the set of five sold at the Hotel Drouot December 21, 1916, adds the Flute Player, only 4 feet wide, and the Surprise of the Fisherman, only 3 feet 7 wide. A Chinese Tea Drinking, with the Flute Player attached at the right, was sold at Sotheby's November 12, 1920. A majority of these were probably made by Jean François Picon, one of the most notable Aubusson manufacturers of the last half of the eighteenth century, whose signature M. R. DAVBVSSON. PICON., M. Pérathon saw on three of a set belonging to M. Solanet. Two landscape *chinoiseries* sold at the Hotel Drouot on April 24, 1920, look more like Pillement, as does the *chinoiserie* landscape with turkeys in the foreground, signed by CONCEIX (Plate XIII, b) of which M. Braquenié has a duplicate signed DVMONTEIL. The four small figure pieces in the Baumgarten collection, with palm trees and without border, 5½ feet high, are another group of Aubusson design, echoing Boucher faintly (Plate XIII, d.)

An obvious imitation of the Gobelin-Boucher medallion tapestries are the Boucher medallion tapestries made at Aubusson, but with cream-white instead of crimson *alentour*, broken into pattern by strongly developed slits, and richly adorned with garlands of flowers and ribbons, and an occasional vase or trophy group. For example, one of these tapestries that I saw at Souhami's in Paris in 1921 had a pair of pendant garlanded medallions, with pendant musical trophy between,

ribbon-suspended above a vase full of flowers. One of the
medallion subjects, two children with a bird cage, is based on
Boucher; the other, a man and a woman in a garden, looks
more like Huet, who is responsible for the Huet-Boucher Pastoral set of Beauvais. Similar in style and execution is the
panel 7⅓ by 22½ feet, with three medallions and four trophies,
on diamond quadrille background strongly developed by diagonal series of slits, of the Williamson sale (New York, 1911).
Also similar are the four small medallion panels picturing the
Seasons, formerly lent to the Metropolitan Museum by Mrs.
Frederick H. Allen. Suggestive of Fragonard is the Triumph
of Cupid on Plate XIII, a, and its companion piece, the Bath
of Psyche.

Suggestive of Boucher's son-in-law Boudouin, are the four
gay panels 7½ feet high without border, formerly in the collection of French & Co., one of which pictures Cupid and
Psyche, with Cupid's bow and arrow hanging from a tree,
and a satyr peeking through the foliage. Altogether delightful are the various versions of Lancret's Four Ages. Dawson
had a set several years ago.

HUET

Favorite subjects of Jean Baptiste Huet were Country
Games and Rural Scenes. I attribute to him the Pastorals
in 8 pieces formerly in the Baumgarten collection (Plate
XIII, da). The resemblance between these and the Beauvais
Pastorals (Plate XI, fa), is obvious, especially in those Beauvais examples that have a fringed valance intertwined with the
flowers and palms above the figures (See plate on Page 433 of
Guiffrey Histoire). The subjects of the Aubusson Set are:
(1) Shepherd, (2) Shepherdess, (3) Morning, (4) Shooting (5)
Seesaw, (6) Playing Ball, (7) Dancing, (8) Evening. The set
averages 9 feet high, with combined length of 70½ feet. Two
of the pieces are very narrow, the Shepherd 19 inches wide,
the Shepherdess, 30. Playing Ball (Plate XIII, da) is 8 feet

wide. The widest two pieces are Morning (15 feet) and Evening (16 feet 3), both of which are closely related to sketches of Huet's that have been preserved. Similar in style and spirit are the four rather inferior Aubusson Pastorals in the Musée des Arts Décoratifs (Mérville Bequest), one of which the Sun Dial, is duplicated in the Braquenié collection, and in No. 833 of the Spetz collection sold at the American Art Galleries, January 17, 1925. Huet had an extraordinary knack at the truly rural. The cows of the piece last noted have striking character and individuality. Also attributed to Huet is the more ambitious Greek Drapery set of five pieces, with rug and furniture coverings to match, formerly in the collection of French & Co., called Greek because it spent a century in Greece before crossing the Atlantic, and Drapery because it has lambrequins at the top like the Baumgarten Pastorals (Plate XIII, da). One of the Greek Drapery set pictures the Fall of Phæthon, the other four are scenes from Fénelon's Story of Telemachus. One of the set is signed BABOVNEIX. The three large Telemachus pieces are: (1) Telemachus welcomed by Calypso; (2) Telemachus plays the Flute in Egypt; (3) Telemachus extolled before the Altar of Jupiter, by the Cretan Priest Theophanes. Three of the six Aubusson Pastorals formerly in the Ffoulke collection are hunting scenes. In the Braquenié collection, illustrated on page 509 of *La Renaissance de L'Art Français,* for September, 1923, is an attractive Aubusson tapestry without border, reproducing one of Vernet's "Harbor Scenes." There were five of the set lent by the Hayden Co. to the Brooklyn Tapestry Exhibition, 1914; and two lent by Alavoine to the Cleveland Tapestry Exhibition, 1918.

AUBUSSON RUGS

Owing to the production of many rugs in tapestry weave at Aubusson, the term Aubusson rugs has become synonymous with tapestry rugs. The few that have survived from the eighteenth century are not attractive. Most of those seen in auction rooms are of the nineteenth century.

REIMS, LILLE, AND NANCY

A manufacturer of Flemish origin active at Reims from 1627 to 1647 was Daniel Pepersack. His most important contract was with the Archbishop for a Life of Christ in 12 large pieces (18 feet 4 inches high), 14 small pieces, and 3 others, of which 17 still hang in the archepiscopal palace at Reims. The cartoons, of which 15 are preserved, were painted by Pierre Murgalet of Troyes. Pepersack's full name appears on several of the tapestries. Some of his weavers were French, notably Pierre Damour, of Paris. The style is that of the Early Gobelins, provincialized. The borders are wide and the coat-of-arms of the donor occupies the middle of the top border.

Active at Lille in the first third of the eighteenth century was Guillaume Werniers, whose widow continued to operate the factory after his death. She signed herself LA VEUVE DE G. WERNIERS. His tapestries are distinguished from the contemporary ones of Brussels, by the borders only, that are floriated more loosely and have stronger whites. One of his important sets was a story of Don Quixote in 8 pieces. Don Quixote made Knight, signed G. W., and L. F. with fleur-de-lis between (for Lille, France), was sold with the Spetz collection at the American Art Galleries, January 17, 1923.

At Nancy and its suburb Malgrange and the adjacent Lunéville, in the first quarter of the eighteenth century, Duke Leopold I of Lorraine had numerous tapestries woven to celebrate the warlike virtues of his father, Duke Charles V of Lorraine. Most of these tapestries are now in the National Austrian collection, as part of the inheritance of Duke Francis III of Lorraine, who as a result of his marriage with Maria Theresa became co-regent of the Austrian States and later Emperor Francis I. They look like contemporary Brussels tapestries except that the blues are harder and more brilliant.

There was formerly one of these Nancy tapestries in the Ffoulke collection, 12½ by 22 feet, picturing the "Triumphal Procession of Charles V, Duke of Lorraine." The earliest set contains five pieces and is signed C. M. E. NANCI. 1705, C. M. E. being the initials of the manufacturer Charles Mitté. One of the second set, that contains 23 pieces, and is based on the paintings of Charles Herbel († 1703), is signed FAICT A LA MALGRANGE EN *1725*. Besides these two sets there are many armorials displaying the arms of Duke Leopold and his wife, and a set of Months in 10 pieces. The first of the pieces combines January, February, and March, and is 15½ feet high by 45½ feet long, the largest tapestry still in one piece with which I am acquainted. Even the huge Berne Trajan and Herkinbald (Chapter IV) is only 14 by 41 feet.

PLATES XIII, b, ba.—ABOVE, CHINOISERIE LANDSCAPE, SIGNED M. R. DAVBVSSON C. CONCEIX. BELOW, TRIUMPHAL ENTRY OF ALEXANDER THE GREAT INTO BABYLON, COPIED FROM THE DESIGN OF LEBRUN, SIGNED DAVBVSSON A. GRELLET; IN THE CLEVELAND MUSEUM OF ART

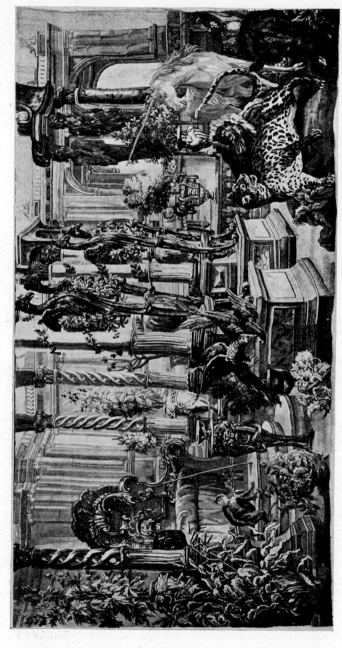

PLATE XIII, C.—PALACE OF CIRCE, WOVEN FROM ONE OF THE LARGE CARTOONS OF THE SET OF METAMORPHOSES PAINTED BY OUDRY FOR BEAUVAIS. P. W. FRENCH & CO.

PLATES XIII, d, da.—ON THE LEFT, TEA DRINKING, AUBUSSON CHINOISERIE, INSPIRATION OF BOUCHER AND PILLEMENT. ON THE RIGHT, PLAYING BALL, ONE OF A LOUIS XVI SET OF AUBUSSON "PASTORALS". WM. BAUMGARTEN & CO.

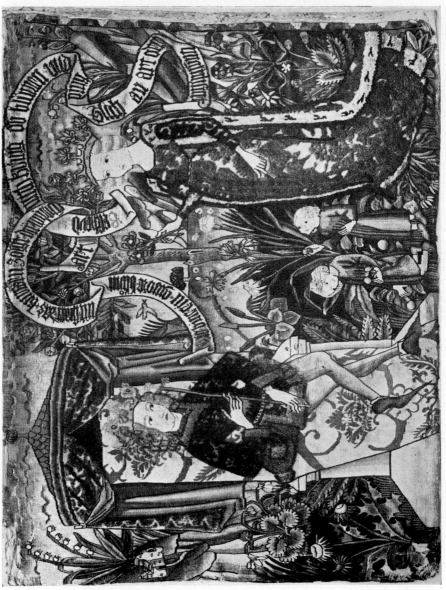

PLATE XIV. 8.—SOLOMON AND THE QUEEN OF SHEBA. A SMALL BUT BEAUTIFUL TAPESTRY, WITH VELVET CLOTHING

CHAPTER XIV

GERMAN AND SWISS TAPESTRIES

GERMAN AND SWISS GOTHIC TAPESTRIES, GERMAN IMITATIONS OF
FLEMISH AND FRENCH TAPESTRIES

GERMAN and Swiss Gothic tapestries are in a class by themselves. They are not an imitation of French Perfected Tapestries, but a thoroughly German product developed in Germany. They are not of monumental size, but have an average width of a little over a yard, with length of three yards or more. They were not often cartooned by skilful painters, and were never woven by highly trained weavers, such as created the masterpieces of Paris and Arras and Tournai and Brussels. They are usually provincial of design and crude of weave, having been made in convents and homes on small looms. The pictures were borrowed from the sources most available, manuscript and other paintings, and wood engravings, and stained glass windows, or even damasks and embroideries. The texture shows markedly the influence of embroideries. There are splendid collections at Nuremberg, and Basel, and Berlin, of which all Germans should be proud. The best books on German tapestries are *Schmidt Bildteppiche,* with many illustrations (Berlin, 1919) and *Burchardt Bildteppiche,* richly illustrated in colour and devoted mainly to the tapestries of the Basel Museum (Leipzig, 1923).

LOVE TAPESTRIES

At the head of Early German Gothic tapestries stands the so-called *Minneteppich* (Love Tapestry), in the Museum of Nuremberg. It is 4½ feet wide by 13 feet long, and shows groups of gentlemen and ladies in the costume of the Austrian

Tyrol of 1390, in social converse.   The foreground is carpeted with flowers and small plants, and there are castles in the background.   A little later than this is the long strip with the Story of William of Orleans and the Beautiful Amelie, at Sigmaringen.   Both tapestries have long scrolls with inscriptions in German.   Sometimes we find Garden of Love scenes, with one couple playing chess, another playing cards, another affectionately at luncheon, etc. as in the strikingly beautiful Engel-Gros tapestry of the Basel Museum, the design of which very rightly to Herr Burckhardt suggests the Master E. S. The weft is mostly wool with a little linen for the whites of the eyes, the playing cards and the head cloths; and a little silver on the chess-playing King.

THE KITE

Sometimes we have sets based ultimately on French romances, but directly on German versions.   Such a set is the Kite (*Der Busant*) illustrated and described by Betty Kurth in Volume XXXII of the *Austrian Jahrbuch*, one piece of which is in the Victoria and Albert Museum, another in the Nuremberg Museum, and two fragments in German private collections.   German inscriptions explain the different scenes. The story is quaint and the tapestry pictures are charming. The son of the King of England is sent to school in Paris. There he gets acquainted with the daughter of the King of France who has been betrothed against her will to the rich King of Morocco.   They fall in love and plight their troth secretly.   The English Prince goes back to England, promising to return in a year and elope with the French Princess on the day set for her wedding with the Moorish King.   He duly returns, with three fast horses, but disguised as a fiddler. The King invites him to play at the wedding.   He refuses, with the excuse that he has to set free a white dove, in accordance with a promise made a year ago.   Meanwhile the King

of Morocco arrives, and all the court go to greet him.   The
Princess, left alone and unwatched, slips out into the garden,
and rides off with the fiddler.   When the King of Morocco
asks for his bride, she cannot be found.   Meanwhile the elopers
reach an opening in the forest, and alight for a short rest.
They send their attendant to seek lodging in the nearest city.
The Princess falls asleep with her head in the Prince's lap.
While she sleeps, he takes two rings from her fingers.   A kite
swoops down from the sky and makes off with one of them.
The Prince throws sticks and stones at the kite, and starts
in pursuit.   He loses his way, and is unable to get back to the
Princess.   In mad despair he tears the clothes from his body,
and ranges the woods like a wild beast.   Meanwhile the Princess awakes, and after waiting long in vain, finds refuge with a
miller.   The pair suffer much before being finally united after
many years.   The tapestry in the Victoria and Albert Museum
begins with the Prince's return to England.   (Scene 1) His
parents, the King and Queen of England, receive him joyfully.
(Scene 2) The Prince orders his men to get him three fast
horses and a fiddle (Scene 3) His men bring him the three
fast horses and the fiddle.   (Scene 4) The Prince arrives in
Paris, and the King of France invites him to the wedding.
(Scene 5) The King of Morocco arrives and is welcomed by
the King and Queen of France.   (Scene 6) The Lovers elope.
The two fragments in private possession show the Princess
asleep in the Prince's lap; and the Kite in a Tree with the Ring
in its Mouth, while the Prince still wearing his crown, has
become a wild man, covered with long, shaggy hair.   All the
scenes have explanatory scrolls in German verse.

A favorite amusement of the fifteenth century was to mas-
querade as wild men.   Picturesque Wild Men tapestries are
those at Sigmaringen, Regensburg, Basel, and Brussels. Often
griffins, unicorns and other fabulous animals appear.

15

THE NINE PREUX

Sometimes the subjects are historical.   Probably the best-known German-Swiss tapestry is the Nine Preux (Plate XIV, c), with the coat-of-arms of the Eberler family of Basel (a boar's head) at the left of Judas' sword.   Only the right half of the tapestry remains.   Probably it was sometime divided between two heirs.   On the left, we have part of David with half of his inscription.   Next comes Judas, with sword-and-sphinx coat-of-arms; next Arthur with his three crowns on the flag at the end of his lance; next Charlemagne with half the Imperial eagle and the French fleurs-de-lis; next Godfrey de Bouillon, with the Cross of Jerusalem and a white cross-band on red.   King Arthur's scroll reads: *kunig. artus. min. macht. und. min. miltikeit. das. ich. alle. lant. erstreit* (King Arthur.   My power and my prowess so that I conquered every land).   The Orleans Museum has a Joan of Arc entering Chinon, with the German inscription: *Here comes the Virgin sent by God to the Dauphin in his land.*   Charles stands on the steps of the Castle to receive her.   Joan carries a pennant showing the Virgin and two angels, the inscription *Ihs Maria,* and three fleurs-de-lis.   The details of the composition, small animals in the foreground, fish in the moat, and foliage in both foreground and background, are naïvely archaic.

RELIGIOUS TAPESTRIES

Sometimes the subjects are religious (Plate XIV, ba). Here we have in the middle, three scenes from the Life of Christ: On the left, the Presentation in the Temple; on the right, His Entry into Jerusalem; in between, His Appearance to Mary Magdalen after Resurrection.   At each end of the tapestry are four Saints: On the left, (1) Saint Cecilia, with book; (2) Saint Elizabeth, with crown, a kettle, and bread; (3) John the Baptist, with lamb on book; (4) Saint Agnes with lamb at her feet.   On the right, (1) Saint Margaret of

Hungary, with lily and crown, and with the donor of the tapestry, a Dominican nun, at her feet; (2) Saint Dominic with star and lily; (3) Peter the Martyr, with knife and three head-wounds, crowned; (4) probably Saint Thomas Aquinas.

Mr. Charles Iklé has a Story of the Virgin, in six scenes, with silk and gold, 3½ by 11 feet. There were formerly in the collection of French & Co. two fragments, each with a scene from the Story of Saint Ursula, who found martyrdom in the third century A. D. at Cologne. The Basel Museum has the Story of Lazarus, 8½ by 12 feet, with the Jewish Temple of Jerusalem as pictured in 1491 by Anton Koberger, in the upper left corner, and a city in the distance more or less modeled after Basel. In the foreground of the tapestry, with four explanatory quatrains in German, are the two main scenes, Lazarus repulsed from the table of the Rich Man; and the Rich Man dying in Misery while his five heirs fight over the Inheritance. Above, we see vividly portrayed the agony of the Rich Man burning in Hell as he looks up to Heaven and sees Lazarus in Abraham's lap.

MORGAN QUEEN OF SHEBA

Small but uniquely beautiful is Solomon and the Queen of Sheba (formerly in the Morgan collection, and shown at the Burlington Fine Arts Club in 1906) with the velvet parts of the robes woven in the Ghiordes knot. The Queen is testing Solomon's wisdom. She holds in her hand two flowers, one of which is artificial. Before her are two children, one a girl, the other a boy. The game is for Solomon to tell which is the real flower, and which is the girl. The Queen's inscription reads: *Bescheyd mich kunig ob blumen und kind, Glich an art oder unglich sint* (Inform me King, whether the flowers and the children are of the same kind, or different). The King's inscription reads: *Die bine eine guote blum nit spart, Das knuwen zoigt die wiplich art* (The bee spares not a good flower. The kneeling shows the female kind). The Basel Museum has a degenerate Renaissance version of this dated 1561. In the sixteenth century many small tapestries continued to be made after fifteenth century German traditions. They were apt to be archaic and still saturated with Gothic, even when the costumes had turned Renaissance. By the end of the sixteenth century, however, little Gothic was left, as is illustrated by the six tiny Alsatian Life of Christ tapestries, 39 by 30 inches, in the Metropolitan Museum, with German inscriptions, and the weavers' monograms A R and I C M, and the dates 1592, 1595, 1598, or 1600. Two of them are based on Durer's Small Passion.

IMITATIONS OF FLEMISH AND FRENCH

None of the German imitations of Flemish and French tapestries are important. Among the various short-lived factories were those of :

I. Seeger Bombeck, a tapestry manufacturer from Brussels, at Leipzig and other places in Saxony, in the sixteenth century.

II. Hans van der Biest, also from Brussels, in Munich, at the beginning of the seventeenth century, made the great series of the Months, the Seasons, and the Triumphs of Otto von Wittelsbach, in the Munich Museum.

III. Pierre Mercier, from Aubusson, in Berlin at the end of the seventeenth century, six of whose Triumphs of the Great Elector designed by the Flemish painter Langefeld in imitation of the Gobelin Story of Louis XIV, are in the Royal Castle at Berlin.

IV. Jean Barraband, from Aubusson, in Berlin at the beginning of the eighteenth century.

V. Pierre Mercier, in 1714 moved from Berlin to Dresden.

VI. Charles Le Vigne, in Berlin, after Barraband's death, had fresh weavers imported from Brussels and Paris.

VII. Andreas Pirot, in Wurzburg, in the second quarter of the eighteenth century, made the large "burlesque" tapestries that still hang in the bedroom of Wurzburg Castle for which they were cartooned, (Plate 90 of *Schmidt Bildteppiche*) by the court painter Rudolf Byss, with Vernansal's Beauvais "Chinese Set" in mind.

VIII. In Munich, a plant founded by the Duke of Bavaria in 1718 lasted until after 1800, where was woven the great History of the Dukes of Bavaria, now in the Munich Museum; and later the Seasons, the Bacchus, the Flora, designed by the court painter Christian Winck, and now on the upper floor of the Munich Museum, in the Porcelain Room.

PLATES XIV, b, ba.—ABOVE, GARDEN OF LOVE, FRIEZE TAPESTRY (NARROW AND LONG, 3 FEET 4 BY 11 FEET 8) MADE AT BÂLE IN THE THIRD QUARTER OF THE FIFTEENTH CENTURY. FORMERLY IN THE ENGEL-GROS COLLECTION; NOW IN THE BÂLE MUSEUM. BELOW, PRESENTATION WITH OTHER SCENES, MADE IN BÂLE ABOUT 1490 IN THE BÂLE MUSEUM.

CHAPTER XV

ITALIAN TAPESTRIES

MANTUA, MILAN, FERRARA, FLORENCE, ROME

CONSIDERING the very great and almost necessary use of tapestry for the decoration of the bare, stucco walls of the Italian Renaissance, it seems strange to have to say that tapestry weaving in Italy was a borrowed art. During the fourteenth and fifteenth centuries the Italians imported most of their tapestries from the North. They also imported workmen to care for and repair them. Their attempts to have tapestries made at home were sporadic and unimportant.

The finest tapestries made in Italy in the fifteenth century were designed by Mantegna for the Gonzagas. They were used as a standard of comparison by a sixteenth century critic of Leo X's set of Flemish Acts of the Apostles after Raphael. That they were woven at Mantua by French Flemish weavers, is probable. With this group I associate Mr. Ryerson's Annunciation, formerly in the Spitzer collection (No. 1 of the Tapestries of the monumental catalogue). This Annunciation 4 by 7 feet is one of the finest small tapestries in existence. Though faded it still speaks eloquently. It is rich with gold, and is a marvel of high-warp weaving. The treatment of faces and hands is brilliant and distinctive. They have none of the dry hardness annoying in much tapestry flesh, but are alive with blood that flushes pink beneath the skin. The wool was not only loosely twisted—or perhaps untwisted as the weaver inserted it—but also loosely woven, incredibly so. Consequently the flesh surface is a soft and minutely fuzzy texture that contrasts strongly but agreeably with the stiff ribs of the ground surrounding. The freedom with which the threads have been manipulated to form eyes and other details is extraordinary. This tapestry is the creation of a great weaver, inspired by a noble cartoon.

In the sixteenth century the most important tapestry factories in Italy were those of Milan, Ferrara, and Florence. The set of Twelve Months completed in the first decade at the Milanese suburb of Vigevano for the Marchese Triulzio is still in the possession of the family. The designer was Bramantino (Wilhelm Suida in Volume XXV of the *Austrian Jahrbuch*) and the weaver was Benedetto da Milano, apparently an Italian, who signed on a pilaster at the right of January: EGO BENEDICTVS DE MEDIOLANO HOC OPVS FECIT CON SOCIIS SVVIS IN VIGLI. The borders are crowded with coats-of-arms of the family and their connections. In a medallion pendent from the top border is displayed the coat-of-arms of the Marchese, with his name and titles. In the upper left corner, the sun; in the upper right corner, the appropriate sign of the Zodiac. At the bottom, a Latin quatrain descriptive of the scene that is suitable to the season.

FERRARA TAPESTRY FACTORY

From Ferrara we have the two Grotesques in the Musée des Arts Décoratifs, the set of eight in the Cathedral of Ferrara picturing the Acts of Saint Maurelius and Saint George, the Story of the Virgin in the Cathedral of Como, and the Hercules slaying the Nemean Lion, now in America (Plate XV, a). The Hercules set to which this belongs, as well as a set of Ovid's Metamorphoses several of which are in the Museum of the Gobelins, were designed by Battista Dosso. The head weaver of the Ferrara Tapestry Factory (1536–1559) was Hans Karcher whose brother Nicolas Karcher left him in 1546 to go to Florence. Other tapestries that group themselves with these are the Moses set of the Cathedral of Milan, and the two Caesars, one of which was formerly in the Bauer collection at Florence, the other of which is in the Musée des Arts Décoratifs (Plate XV, c). There were formerly five of the

Moses set surviving, one a fragment consisting of only the upper third, but three were destroyed by fire at the International Exhibition of Milan in 1906. All the five pieces bore the Gonzaga arms in the middle of the top border, and one of them on each side of the coat-of-arms, had square medallions saying in Latin: William Duke of Mantua, Marquis of Mantua (who held these titles from 1550 to 1587). The fragment with its six cherubs is reminiscent of Giulio Romano's Children Playing. The borders of these tapestries were wide thick masses of foliage and fruit, with occasional serpents and fish, with medallions in most of the corners, and with masks in the middle of the side borders. Two of the complete tapestries had oval picture medallions in the middle of the bottom border; the other two, William, Duke of Mantua inscribed in Latin on square medallions.

MEDICI TAPESTRY FACTORY

The Medici Tapestry Factory (1546–1737) was established by Duke Cosimo I, with Nicolas Karcher and John Roost as master weavers. Karcher signed his monogram, John Roost, the picture of a Roast on a turnspit. The Medici coat-of-arms appears on many of the tapestries (Plate XV, b). The great period of the Medici Tapestry Works ended in 1574 with the death of Duke Cosimo I. The Royal Italian collection at Florence is rich in Medici tapestries. There are few elsewhere. Many hang in the Uffizi, the Pitti, and the Palazzo Vecchio, but more are in storage and inaccessible to visitors. In the Uffizi are the Months, in four pieces, by Roost and Karcher, after cartoons of Bachiacca. The Palazzo Communale at Genoa has a set of Months, two in each tapestry, that may be from the Medici Factory. Three of the finest tapestries made at the Medici Works are the Ecce Homo (Plate XV, b), Deposition, and Resurrection, by Nicolas Karcher, after Salviati, all rich with gold. Another impressive piece is the Entombment, by Roost, after Rossi. The most important set made by Roost and Karcher was the Story of Joseph, in twenty pieces, after Bronzino. These tapestries are much better in weave than in design. The compositions are too restless and broken, and *too sculptural*. During the last quarter of the century many religious subjects were woven after Allori. The Dante and Virgil of the Minneapolis Museum, though fresher in color, seems to group itself with the Metropolitan Museum's Moses striking the Rock which is signed in the bottom selvage by Bernardino van Asselt, who was active in the first half of the seventeenth century. The master weaver of highest reputation at the Medici works in the seventeenth century was the Frenchman, Pierre Lefebvre, who was called back to France by Mazarin, to reorganize the tapestry plant at the Louvre, and who later returned to Florence, leaving behind him his son Jean who became the first famous Lefebvre of the Gobelins. The Bathsheba at the Bath illustrated on Plate XV, da, is signed in the lower right corner of the panel, by the designer as well as by Lefebvre, D. ARTEMI PINX P. FEVERE PARISIIS EXTRAX 1663. There are three Æneas tapestries in the Hotel Biltmore, one of which is signed FEVERE.

BARBERINI TAPESTRY FACTORY

Especially interesting to Americans is the Barberini Factory in Rome, founded in 1633 by Cardinal Francesco Barberini, nephew of Pope Urban VIII. The Life of Christ in eleven pieces, designed by Romanelli and woven by Riviera, was formerly exhibited at the Metropolitan Museum, and now hangs in the Cathedral of Saint John the Divine, the gift of Mrs. John W. Simpson. Several of the pieces are signed IAC D.L.RIV. and all bear the arms of Urban VIII in each of the four corners—three golden bees, montantes, shaded with sable, posed two and one on azure field. In the middle of some of the top borders is the Sun, adopted by the Barberini as crest. Others have a plough drawn by two bees and guided by a third. The twelfth tapestry, a map of the Holy Land, though appropriate as a subject and woven by Riviera, is not part of the set. Mrs. Twombly has an Apollo set of five, after Poussin, made at the Barberini Works, and formerly in the Ffoulke collection. The Cleveland Museum has a set of eight Dido and Æneas tapestries, after Romanelli, made at the Barberini Works by M. WAVTERS who signed them, as did the artist. Mr. McLean has five Constantine tapestries signed RIVIERA.

In 1710 the manufacture of tapestries was revived at Rome by Pope Clement XI, with Jean Simonet as manager, and Andrea Procaccini, who later went to the Madrid Tapestry Works, as artistic director. From 1717 to 1770 Pietro Ferloni was manager and his signature appears on one of the five Jerusalem Liberated tapestries belonging to the Metropolitan Museum, and formerly in the Duke of Hamilton collection. Another of the set passed through the Marquand Sale, 1903, as a Louis XV Gobelin.

PLATE XV, b.—ECCE HOMO, A TAPESTRY RICH WITH GOLD, DESIGNED BY SALVIATI
AND WOVEN BY NICOLAS KARCHER IN 1549 AT THE MEDICI WORKS IN FLORENCE. ROYAL
ITALIAN COLLECTION, FLORENCE

PLATES XV, C, Ca.—ON THE LEFT, POMPEY'S HEAD BROUGHT TO CAESAR, ITALIAN TAPESTRY OF THE FIRST HALF OF THE SIXTEENTH CENTURY; MUSÉE DES ARTS DÉCORATIFS. ON THE RIGHT, DANTE AND VIRGIL, LARGE ITALIAN RENAISSANCE TAPESTRY, WITH SCENE FROM DANTE'S GREAT POEM; MINNEAPOLIS INSTITUTE OF ARTS

PLATES XV, d, da.—ON THE LEFT, MOSES STRIKING THE ROCK, LARGE TAPESTRY MADE AT THE MEDICI WORKS IN FLORENCE IN FIRST HALF OF THE SEVENTEENTH CENTURY BY BERNARDINO VAN ASSELT WHOSE SIGNATURE APPEARS IN THE BOTTOM SELVAGE; METROPOLITAN MUSEUM OF ART. ON THE RIGHT, DAVID SEES BATHSHEBA BATHING, MADE AT THE MEDICI TAPESTRY WORKS, SIGNED IN THE LOWER RIGHT CORNER WITH THE DATE 1663, AND WITH THE NAMES OF BOTH DESIGNER AND WEAVER

CHAPTER XVI

ENGLISH, SPANISH, AND RUSSIAN TAPESTRIES

BARCHESTON, MORTLAKE, VULCAN AND VENUS, ACTS OF THE
APOSTLES, HERO AND LEANDER, JOHN VANDERBANK, GOYA, RUSSIAN
INDIES AND COPIES OF PAINTINGS

PRACTICALLY all of the numerous tapestries listed in the
inventories of Henry V and Henry VIII came from across the
Channel. While some of the less important ones may have
been woven in England, by French-Flemish weavers, the first
English tapestry factory of any continuity appears to have
been established in the middle of the sixteenth century,
at Barcheston in Warwickshire, by Richard Hyckes, with
William Sheldon an English country squire as patron. A
tapestry in the Victoria and Albert Museum, 7 feet 8 by 13,
without border, and attributed to this factory (Page 48 of
Thomson English) bears in the centre the coat-of-arms of
Sir William Herbert, Earl of Pembroke. The design is one
of the Italian Grotesques so popular during the Renaissance
and later, modified by residence in Flanders. On each side
of the coat-of-arms are picture medallions showing Pride and
Luxury. Other armorial tapestries attributed to Barcheston
are the one at Chawton Manor which is dated 1564 and is a
record of the marriages of the Lewkenor family; and four at
Drayton House, Northamptonshire, bearing the arms, crests,
supporters, and motto of Robert Dudley, Earl of Leicester
and Warwick, and favourite of Queen Elizabeth. Later in
date are the three huge tapestry maps in the museum of the
York Philosophical Society, of Warwickshire, Worcester-
shire, and other English counties. Two of these are signed
Richard Hyckes, and one Francis Hyckes. All bear the
Sheldon arms. Also attributed to Barcheston are the Marquis

of Salisbury's Four Seasons, with large lightly clad figures in the centre, Venus for Spring, Ceres for Summer, Bacchus for Autumn, and Æolus for Winter, and with appropriate signs of the Zodiac above. In the background are personages engaged in the labours of the season. The wide border is crowded with tiny panels illustrating Latin inscriptions. The coat-of-arms in the middle of the top border is that of Sir John Tracey of Doddington in Gloucestershire (who was knighted by King James) impaling the arms of his wife, Anne Shirley of Isfield. The inspiration is Flemish-Italian, but the execution of both design and weave is English.

MORTLAKE TAPESTRY WORKS

The great name in the history of tapestry weaving in England is Mortlake. The great period is 1620 to 1636. For sixteen years Mortlake tapestries rivaled those of the Early Gobelins, and surpassed those of Brussels. After that the degeneration was rapid. The death of Charles I ended all hope of sufficient governmental and social support. The Mortlake Tapestry Works struggled on weakly until the reign of Queen Anne, and then gave up the ghost completely.

The success of Henri IV in establishing the Early Gobelins (Chapter IX) stirred England to imitation. A copy of the agreement made by Henri IV with Comans and Planche was secured, and the Mortlake plant was organized along similar lines. The proprietor was Sir Francis Crane, last lay chancellor of the Order of the Garter, and a prominent figure at the Courts of both James I and Charles I. To assist in financing the undertaking, Sir Francis was in August 1619 granted the fees of the making of three baronets. Arrangements were made by the King's agents abroad for the importation of Flemish weavers. In 1620 the secretary of the Flemish embassy at London reported to his sovereigns, Albert and Isabella, Archdukes of the Netherlands, that fifty had already arrived. Among them was Philip de Maecht of the Early

Gobelins, whose signature appears on both Gobelin and Mort-lake tapestries.

The man most responsible for the foundation of the Mort-lake Tapestry Works appears to have been "Steenie" the Marquis of Buckingham (Duke after May 18, 1623), bosom friend and mentor of the Prince of Wales and an art amateur of great experience and ability. He not only encouraged Charles to place generous orders at Mortlake, but also ordered tapestries made for himself. Payments, however, were less prompt than orders during the life of James I. During the absence of Charles and Buckingham in Spain in 1623, Sir Francis Crane complained to the King that his estate was wholly exhausted and credit spent, with £16,000 already put into the business and with return of only £2500. The Prince wrote from Madrid directing the payment of £700 for the Raphael Cartoons ordered from Genoa, and of £500 on the set of Twelve Months which he was anxious to have finished before his return to England. When the Prince came to the throne in 1625 as Charles I, Sir Francis Crane was rewarded for his patience. The King granted him £1000 a year "for the better Maintenance of the said Workes of Tapestries," and a second £1000 a year until the £6000 balance due on three sets of gold tapestry should be paid. The King also granted to Francis Cleyn, artistic director of the Mortlake Tapestry Works, a salary of £100 a year for life.

The first set of tapestries made at Mortlake was the Story of Vulcan and Venus in nine pieces, copied from a Brussels Renaissance set. It was begun on September 16, 1620 and finished on June 5, 1622. It was woven plain without gold except "in the piece of Apollo," and cost £2000. Three gold sets made later cost £3000 apiece. To the gold sets belong the Vulcan's Complaint to Jupiter formerly lent to the Metro-politan Museum by Baroness von Zedlitz; and the Gods dis-covering the Amours of Mars and Venus, in the Victoria and Albert Museum. Both are signed with the Mortlake mark, which is the red cross of St. George on a white shield, and with the monogram of Philip de Maecht. Both were finished by 1625 as shown by the badge of the Prince of Wales (the motto ICH DIEN, and three ostrich feathers enfiled by a coronet) in the middle of the top border. In the middle of the bottom border is a medallion probably adapted from the similar medallion of the Early Gobelins, four crossed sceptres tied with ribbon. The inscription SCEPTRA FAVENT ARTES, which should read SCEPTRA FOVENT ARTES (Sceptres, that is to say Kings, nourish the arts), is apparently a Mortlake addition. There are five of the pieces from one of the gold sets, in the National French collection. The piece in the Royal Swedish collection bears the arms of Buckingham overlaid with the arms of the King of Sweden. Pieces without gold are the three formerly lent to the Metropolitan Museum by Mr. Philip Hiss. Five of the Brussels Renaissance set from which the Mortlake set was copied were exhibited in Paris at the Union Centrale in 1876. All were enriched with gold, and all had the story told in Latin quatrains in the middle of the side borders (Illustrated in *L'Art* of the year 1881). The design suggests the inspiration but not the hand of Giulio Romano. It is more like the design of Mr. Stevens' Psyche set at the Metropolitan Museum.

The finest set of Mortlake tapestries in existence is Raphael's Acts of the Apostles, with gold, in the National French collection (Plate XVI, a). They were copied from the seven Raphael Cartoons now in the Victoria and Albert Museum (See Chapter XVIII, and Plates XVIII, j, ja), and have elaborately beautiful borders attributed to Van Dyck, with cherubs and with many picture medallions of the Life of Christ in bronze cameo, different in the different tapestries. In the middle of the top borders, is the Royal coat-of-arms supported by lion and unicorn and encircled by HONI SOIT QUI MAL Y PENSE. In the middle of the bottom borders is a medallion with Latin inscription, and with *Car. Re. Reg. Mortl.* (*Carolo rege regnante Mortlake*)=(*Mortlake, Charles reign-*

ing as King). The Latin inscription in the medallion of Curing the Paralytic (Plate XVI, a) is: DUM PETIT ARGENTUM, FIRMATA EST TIBIA CLAUDO.   NON DARE QUOD PETIT GRATIA MAIOR ERAT. (When the Paralytic asked for money, his leg was cured. To refuse what he asked was a greater favor). In the four corners of the tapestry, are cherubs holding a book with the symbol of an evangelist beside them—an angel in the upper left corner for St. Matthew, a lion in the upper right corner for St. Mark, an ox in the lower right corner for St. Luke, an eagle in the lower left corner for St. John. In the panel, St. John extends his arm over the head of the Paralytic, while St. Peter grasps the Paralytic's left arm. The architecture of the tapestry is rich and noble, and the hands of relief on the twisted columns are inspiring, with cupids and vines borrowed from ancient Rome. There are five Mortlake Acts of the Apostles tapestries, with later borders, at Forde Abbey, presented by Queen Anne to Sir Frances Gwyn.

Other sets made at Mortlake in the great period are the Naked Boyes (Children Playing), after Giulio Romano; the Twelve Months, also from sixteenth century designs; the Horses, and Hero and Leander, both designed by Francis Cleyn. There are five of the Hero and Leander set of six in the Royal Swedish collection. They are described in the 1656 inventory of the Swedish Kings tapestries as "beautiful tapestries of fine quality, new, enriched with gold and silver, which were given to His Royal Majesty (as a wedding present) by Count Johan (Axelstierna)." There is a full set of Hero and Leander, with different borders and made a little later, in the Lady Lever Art Gallery, Port Sunlight, near Liverpool, in England (Plates XVI, b, ba). A coarse and inferior "Hero casting herself into the Hellespont after the Death of Leander," from the collection of Mr. Charles Henry Allen, of Westham, Sussex, England, was sold at the Anderson Galleries on April 25, 1925. It had the Mortlake mark in the right selvage.
16

The death of Sir Francis Crane in 1636 ended the prosperity of Mortlake. His brother Captain Richard Crane could not even pay the men their wages, and a year after the death of Sir Francis, the King bought the plant which became "the King's Works." The King provided a subsidy of £2000 a year, and increased the salary of Francis Cleyn to £250 a year, out of which he was to pay his assistant. But the outbreak of the Great Rebellion in 1642 made it impossible for the King to keep up his payments. In 1649 he was put to death. Cromwell liked tapestries and had his bedroom at Hampton Court adorned with "five pieces of fine tapestry hangings of Vulcan and Venus." In 1653 he sent Mantegna's nine famous paintings of the Triumphs of Caesar to Mortlake that cartoons might be copied from them. The tapestries made from these cartoons were acquired by Charles II. During the reign of Charles II, Sir Sackville Crow tried to revive the industry, but failed, as did his successor Francus Poyntz. The tapestries of this period were poor.

Some of the Mortlake weavers set up for themselves in a small way. In 1671 William Benood of Lambeth made for the Countess of Rutland the six small Vulcan and Venus tapestries without border, now in Haddon Hall. From Lambeth came also a set of Classic Scenes, one of which is now in the Victoria and Albert Museum. It is inscribed in the lower border MADE AT LAMBETH, and is crude. The subject is the Elopement of Helen of Troy, redrawn from some Gothic version. A duplicate of this, together with another piece of this same set, the Slaying of Niobe's Children, were sold with the Spetz collection, New York, 1925. In 1686 Thomas Poyntz made three Months for the Queen's bedchamber in Windsor Castle.

The most successful English tapestry manufacturer of the period of Queen Anne was John Vanderbanc, who had charge of the Royal "Great Wardrobe" in Great Queen Street, Soho, from 1689 to 1727. He is represented in America by the Chinoiserie in the Metropolitan Museum (Plate XVI, c); by Lebrun's Air, and Water, copied from the Gobelins; and by the four famous Yale tapestries in the collection of French & Co. Closely related to the Chinoiserie through the flowers that enrich both, is the Baroque Grotesque presented by Duveen Bros. to the Victoria and Albert Museum in 1901.

The Air (Plate XVI, cb) after Lebrun is signed on the bottom selvage, IOHN VANDERBANC IN GREAT QUEEN STREET. In the middle of the top border, the arms of England. On the shield held by Juno's companion, Iris, the arms of Lord Gray for whom the tapestry was made, a Jacob's ladder with baton below and coronet above. In the Louis XIV original this shield bore the monogram of the King. The Yale tapestries belong to the so-called "Indian" group based on Chinese lacquer screens, and with Chinese or Hindoo personages. There are two of these "Indian" tapestries in the Victoria and Albert Museum, one of them signed IOHN VANDERBANC FECIT. There are also two at Belton House, and others at Adlington Hall, in Cheshire. The Yale tapestries get their name from having once been the property of Elihu Yale, to whom Yale University owes its name. Elihu Yale was born at Boston in 1648, returned with his parents to England in 1652, and in 1672 went to India where he became Governor of Madras and amassed a princely fortune. At the invitation of Cotton Mather, Elihu Yale in 1718 sent over a cargo of books, pictures, and other effects that were sold for the benefit of the struggling school in New Haven. Gratitude for the gift gave Yale its name. Elihu Yale had three daughters, the eldest of whom married the son of Baron Guilford. The tapestries left by her father remained in the possession of the Guilford family at Glemham, Suffolk, until sold at Sotheby's in July, 1924.

Other English tapestry weavers of the eighteenth century

were Stephen Demay, Bradshaw, Peter Parisot, and Paul
Saunders.   At Burley-on-the-Hill are the four Hero and
Leander, and the nine Acts of the Apostles tapestries, made
by Demay for the Earl of Nottingham.   Bradshaw's signature, STRANOYER above and BRADSHAW below the Mortlake
shield, appears on a hunting tapestry formerly in the Van
Straaten collection and on a sofa at Belton House (Illustrated
in colour opposite Page 150 of *Thomson English*).   Parisot
had a shop first at Paddington, later at Fulham, and enjoyed
the patronage of the Duke of Cumberland.   He flourished
briefly.   The most interesting item of his sale in 1755 was a set
of five tenières.   Though Paul Saunders of Soho belongs to
the washed-out school of the last half of the eighteenth century, there is charm about many of his French-inspired pieces
(Plate XVI, ca).   The Duke of Northumberland has a set of
landscapes, with peasants and ruins of Roman architecture,
signed P. SAUNDERS, SOHO, 1758, the design of which was attributed by Dr. Rock to Francesco Zuccharelli.

SPANISH TAPESTRIES

In 1720 the King of Spain, Philip V, encouraged Jacques
Vandergoten of Antwerp to establish in Madrid the Royal
Tapestry Factory that is still in operation.   The Vander-
gotens began by copying old sets of tapestries, among others
the Conquest of Tunis, and the Story of Cyrus.   One of the
most popular of the new designs was the Story of Don Quixote,
by Andrea Procaccini from the San Michele Tapestry Factory
of Rome.   But the reputation of the Madrid factory rests
mainly on the tapestries woven in the last quarter of the
eighteenth century from cartoons by Goya, and Goya's master
and father-in-law, Bayeu (Plates XVI, d, da, db).   Most of
the cartoons and tapestries are still preserved at the Escurial
and the Pardo.   Many of the tapestries, together with several
tenières, and several of the Don Quixote set, were shown in

the Tapestry Exhibition at the Hispanic Museum, New York, 1917. (See the catalogue for illustrations.)

RUSSIAN TAPESTRIES

Peter the Great in 1716 established an Imperial Tapestry Factory in St. Petersburg, with French weavers from Beauvais under Béhagle the son.   In 1717 Peter visited the Gobelins in Paris twice, and in commemoration of his visit received a set of the Indies. So we are not surprised to find that the most important tapestries surviving from the early period of the Imperial Russian Tapestry Works, in the Assembly Hall of Monplaisir Palace at Peterhof, are copies of the Indies, with Peter's monogram in the middle of the top border.   Later copies of two of the pieces, with the monogram of the Empress Elizabeth in the top border, and with AMERICA woven in Russian letters in the bottom border of one, and *Saint Petersburg, year 1759,* in the bottom border of the other, were sold at Hotel Drouot, March 5, 1918.   In 1720 most of the French weavers returned to France, and were replaced by Russians whom they had taught (See *Polovtsoff Russian*). In the latter half of the eighteenth century, the passion for making tapestries imitate paint texture prevailed here as in France (Plates XVI, e, ea).   Lent to the Metropolitan Museum by Miss Alice Einstein is a tapestry portrait of the Empress Elizabeth signed "Fait par Rondet a Petersburg, 1760," Rondet being one of five French weavers imported by Elizabeth to help revive the industry. There was formerly a portrait of Catherine the Great, on loan, in the Metropolitan Museum, signed P. BURG, 1811 G.; the final G. standing for *goda*, Russian for year; and not for Gobelins, as was formerly accepted.   In the Royal Swedish collection there are a number of tapestry portraits made in Russia, some of which are illustrated in *Boettiger Swedish*.   In the Moscow Museum of Arms and Armor there is one of Peter the Great dated 1840.   The Imperial Russian Tapestry Factory was discontinued in 1859.

PLATE XVI, a.—CURING THE PARALYTIC, ONE OF RAPHAEL'S ACTS OF THE APOSTLES WOVEN FOR CHARLES I AT THE
NATIONAL FRENCH COLLECTION

PLATES XVI, b, ba.—ON THE LEFT, LEANDER'S DEPARTURE. ON THE RIGHT, LEANDER'S ARRIVAL. FROM THE STORY OF "HERO AND LEANDER," DESIGNED FOR THE MORTLAKE TAPESTRY WORKS BY FRANCIS CLEYN. TWO OF THE SIX IN THE LADY LEVER ART GALLERY, PORT SUNLIGHT, NEAR LIVERPOOL, ENGLAND

PLATES XVI, c, ca, cb.—UPPER LEFT, LANDSCAPE CHINOISERIE, MADE BY VANDERBANC;
METROPOLITAN MUSEUM OF ART. UPPER RIGHT, THE SWING, MADE BY PAUL SAUNDERS
OF SOHO; RUCKSELIG. BELOW, AIR, DESIGN OF CHARLES LEBRUN, MADE AT THE BEGIN-
NING OF THE EIGHTEENTH CENTURY IN GREAT QUEEN STREET BY JOHN VANDERBANC.
P. W. FRENCH & CO.

PLATES XVI, d, da, db.—UPPER LEFT, "TINY GIANTS," DESIGN OF GOYA.
[UPPER RIGHT, "CHILDREN GATHERING FRUIT," DESIGN OF GOYA. BELOW,
"ORGEAT PEDLAR," DESIGN OF BAYEU. ALL THREE MADE AT THE MADRID
TAPESTRY WORKS IN THE LAST HALF OF THE EIGHTEENTH CENTURY, AND]
ALL NOW IN THE PALACE OF THE ESCURIAL

PLATES XVI, e, ea.—ON THE LEFT, PORTRAIT OF JEAN MALDERUS, BISHOP OF ANTWERP, DESIGN OF VAN DYCK. ON THE RIGHT, HANNAH AND SAMUEL, DESIGN OF REMBRANDT. TAPESTRIES COPIED FROM EASEL PAINTINGS, MADE AT THE ST. PETERSBURG TAPESTRY WORKS IN THE LAST HALF OF THE EIGHTEENTH CENTURY. BOTH IN THE COLLECTION OF MR. E. J. BERWIND

PLATES XVII, a, aa.—ON THE LEFT, HORIZONTAL RIBS. ON THE RIGHT, VERTICAL RIBS. NOTE HOW THE VERTICAL RIBS FATTEN AND DISTORT THE FACE AND THE ARM. BOTH TINY TAPESTRIES WOVEN AT THE GOBELINS FROM DESIGN OF DROUAIS BY COZETTE FILS (1764, 1763). THE FORMER IN THE LOUVRE; THE LATTER IN THE MUSEUM OF TOURS

CHAPTER XVII

TAPESTRY TEXTURE

PERFECTED TAPESTRIES VS. PRIMITIVE TAPESTRIES. RIBS, HATCH-
INGS AND SLITS. PERFECTED TAPESTRIES ALWAYS FULL OF HOLES
GOLD IN TAPESTRIES

THIS chapter analyzes the texture of Perfected Tapestries (Compare Chapter II). Before the fourteenth century there were no Perfected Tapestries. Before the fourteenth century there were Primitive Tapestries only.

The finest tapestries of ancient Egypt (Plate II, b), of the Saracenic Middle Ages, of ancient Peru, and of China, all belong to the group of Primitive Tapestries. It remained for the French of the fourteenth century at Paris and Arras to develop designers and weavers able to manipulate threads into the strongest and liveliest contrasts of form, color and tone that can be achieved on a flat surface. In the fourteenth century was developed the art of making huge picture cloths that hold the mirror up to human life powerfully.

Nearly all real tapestries have ribs, hatchings, and slits. Primitive as well as Perfected Tapestries have ribs, hatchings, and slits. But between the ribs, hatchings and slits of Primitive Tapestries, and the ribs, hatchings and slits of Perfected Tapestries, there is a world of difference.

The surface of all large Perfected Tapestries consists of *horizontal* lines in round relief (*ribs*), that are most prominent to the eye in *high lights*. These ribs are covered with fine threads that often combine themselves into *vertical* spires of colour (*hatchings*) in the *middle lights*. Heavy shadow effects are secured by means of holes (*slits*) often grouped in *diagonal* series. So that in addition to and superimposed

229

upon the contrasts found in the painted cartoon, we have horizontal lines in relief, contrasting with vertical lines in colour, and with diagonal lines in intaglio.

TAPESTRY RIBS

The ribs are the most obvious part of tapestry texture. They consist of coarse warps far apart, covered by fine wefts close together, in plain weave. Ribs by themselves are stupid. The surface of a plain rep is monotonous. But when artfully employed as on Plate XVII, ba, to bring the flesh of a portrait into relief, they fascinate.

On a large part of the surface of a tapestry the ribs are obscured, where the colour is dark or there are hatchings, or intricate colour pattern, or numerous slits. But contrast with the parts where the ribs are obscured makes the ribs all the more prominent where they are not obscured. They are most prominent in faces and hands and skies, and in the high lights of unfigured Gothic draperies.

The reduction in size necessary for book purposes does not usually leave the ribs visible in illustrations of tapestry. But on the face and bust of Danae (Plate XVII, ba), and on the sky of the landscape of Plate XVII, f, close inspection will reveal them, even without a magnifying glass. It will be noticed that in Danae the light surfaces push forward by contrast with the dark surfaces, and that in the landscape the dark surfaces push forward by contrast with the light surfaces. That is to be expected. We get this in drawing and painting. Light objects stand out against a dark background, and dark objects against a light background. What we do not get in drawing and the older school of painting, are ribs in the high lights that by line contrast vastly accentuate the distinction between foreground and background. And in modern painting, while the brush marks in the thick impasto of the high lights often carry out the same principle, the resulting contrasts are by no means as strong and convincing.

The position of the ribs is important. In all great tapestries they are horizontal. When vertical they distort the design. This I have illustrated on Plates XVII, a, aa. The two tiny tapestries are Gobelins by the same weaver from the same design. The tapestry on the left has horizontal ribs; the tapestry on the right has vertical ribs. The former is excellent. The latter is detestable.

TAPESTRY HATCHINGS

The power of tapestry hatchings is due to the fact that they have ribs to lean against. Hatchings as employed in painting and especially in line engraving are able to render service, but are feeble as compared with the hatchings of tapestry. First, it should be noted that tapestry hatchings are vertical spires of colour at right angles with the ribs. As the ribs are always horizontal in important tapestries, the hatchings in important tapestries are consequently always vertical. The moment you see the vertical hatchings on the drapery at the right of Plate XVII, c, you know that the ribs of that tapestry *must* be horizontal.

The main function of tapestry hatchings is to create middle lights intermediate in relief between shadows and high lights, and by line contrast push shadows and high lights violently apart. On Plates XVII, e, f, the clouds formed by hatching the light sky are intermediate in distance between the sky and the shadowed trees in the foreground. On Plate IV, d, the hatchings are in middle light, intermediate between the high lights in relief and the shadows in depression. On Plate XVII, a, the intermediate position of the hatchings in middle relief between high light and shadow is obvious, especially around the child's bonnet. In a word, hatched surfaces are almost always middle lights, whether dark on a light ground, or light on a dark ground.

What gives tapestry hatchings their extraordinary power is the way in which they contrast with the ribs. The strongest line contrast possible is that between horizontal and perpendicular. The strongest contrast in architecture is of vertical fluted columns with horizontal base and entablature, both accentuated by parallel mouldings. The strongest contrast in a room is of horizontal floor and ceiling with vertical walls. The strongest contrasts in engraving are groups of parallel lines perpendicular to each other, such as were employed so freely and skilfully by Piranesi. The architectural contrasts are in relief. The engraving contrasts are flat. Tapestry rib and hatching contrasts are both round and flat. The horizontal ribs are in *round relief,* and the vertical hatchings are in *flat colour.*

What accentuates the contrast of ribs with hatchings is that the hatchings obscure the ribs they cover, thus leaving middle light surfaces that look *unribbed,* which by contrast *forces* the ribs of both shadows and high lights, especially of high lights. The vertical hatchings of tapestry middle lights are like the columns of architecture that push the entablature (high lights) one way and the base (shadows) the other way.

This creates the inimitable deep folds of Gothic tapestry draperies, at the right of Plate XVII, c, and on Plates IV, h, i, j, ja, jb, k, ka, l.

Even where the draperies are patterned (Plate XVII, b) hatchings are still used to force contrast between shadow and high light, always with an effect that is multiplied by contrast with the ribs of the high lights.

TAPESTRY SLITS

Slits skilfully placed are the most vital part of Perfected Tapestries. In Primitive Tapestries they are automatic and of little value, though usually numerous and *very noticeable.* In Perfected Tapestries they are planned with extraordinary intelligence to strengthen diagonal straight and curved outlines, and to introduce spots and blocks of vibrant shadow where spots and blocks of shadow help the design. In Primitive Tapestries they come where it is easier for the weaver to introduce them, than to leave them out. In Perfected Tapestries they come where their introduction makes more work for the weaver. Consequently lazy and ignorant weavers always tend to revert to Primitive weaving.

Unfortunately it is impossible to illustrate slits adequately in any material except tapestry. My halftones by substituting spots of black ink for the actual holes of tapestry lose most of the powerful effect. But in the foliage of Mrs. Harold Pratt's Early Gothic "Annunciation" (Plate XVII, c) which is one of the finest examples still surviving of supreme tapestry texture, I think the reader will have little difficulty in distinguishing some of the slits. Especially prominent are those that mark the main ribs of the wide leaves; that model the knots of the tree trunks; and that outline some of the spiky leaves at the bottom of the tapestry. Less obvious, though vivid in the actual tapestry, are the slits that line the leaves of the Golden Tree on Plate XVII, d. Wonderfully clear, even in the halftone, are the slits that model the foliage and the field of the tree in one of Mr. Rockefeller's Months of Lucas (Plate XVII, f), and give life to the lad climbing the tree. Note how the tree with its wealth of slits comes opaquely forward by contrast with the ribbed sky that is comparatively free from slits, though saved from opaqueness by the few that there are.

The tree of Plate XVII, d, appears on the right of Plate XVII, e. Here the reduction is so great that only the largest slits of the foliage are visible. But the effect of all of them is seen in the strength of the modeling. Also, the furrows of the ploughed field below are so powerfully separated by slits, that in the tapestry the slits can be distinguished from across the room by anyone who knows what to look for. Also, the mountains in the distance are forced into lively relief by the slits that mark the different ridges.

FINE TAPESTRIES FULL OF HOLES

All fine tapestries are full of holes. No tapestry that is not full of holes can possibly look right or be right. One reason that many modern tapestries look flat, and stupid, and boardlike, is that the slits are inserted automatically and often in the wrong place, and then *carefully sewed up after the tapestry leaves the loom.* Of course the *long* slits should be sewed up, *loosely,* from the back, without exposing an offensive series of *rentraiture* threads over the face of the slit. When the slit is sewed up properly, the line of it is stronger than the other lines between ribs, as it should be. When the slit is broken by the sewing-up threads, it is weaker than the other lines between ribs, thus weakening the line of demarcation between the two colours.

Slits are of prime importance in modeling flesh. Tapestry faces and hands are hopelessly monotonous and shapeless unless developed boldly by the use of slits. The reason that many ancient Gothic tapestries have stupid faces is that ignorant repairers have with the needle eliminated the slits, and with the slits the modeling.

One of the most splendid illustrations of a slit-modelled face is that of King Arthur on Plate III, a. Mr. Mackay's tapestry, of which this face is a detail, dates from the last quarter of the fourteenth century. In technique and texture it is superior to any other tapestry that has survived from the fourteenth century. There are no faces in the Angers Apocalypse that equal it. Even in my illustration the slits that model the eyes and brow and nose and mouth are visible. Those that give life to the hair and beard though richly present in the tapestry are obscured in the illustration. Those that outline and border the jeweled collar, and those that separate the fingers are prominent.

Another face shaped by slits into form and character is that of King Priam on Plate V, a. This is a detail from Mr.

Mackay's brilliant middle-of-the-fifteenth century tapestry Hector and Andromache of the famous Trojan War series. My illustration has been fortunate in indicating the slits that outline and model the eyes and nose, and take away solidity from hair and beard. Clearly marked also are the slits that line the bottom of Priam's headdress, and that set forth the jeweled band around its crown.

Another portrait that gets its character from the artfully left slits is that of King Priam on Plate XVII, b. This tapestry is of later date and later texture than Hector and Andromache, and a century later than King Arthur. The texture, though refined to the extreme and able to express delightful delicacies of gradation and contrast, lacks the boldness and freedom of the texture of King Arthur. No longer do the wefts achieve variation by wandering diagonally or even in diagonal curves. Strictly they are held to the vertical position, and to absolutely regular parallelism. But what they miss by having lost freedom of direction is largely compensated for by increased power of expression due to an even freer placing of slits than in King Arthur. Effects that in Early Gothic tapestries were secured by twisting wefts, are in Late Gothic tapestries often secured by twisting series of slits.

Note, in the face of King Priam on Plate XVII, b, the slits that model the eye, opening in curves below it, as well as the slits that shape the mouth, and the little group of slits bringing the nose prominently forward. Note also the line of slits at the right of the nose, separating it definitely from the rest of the face.

The face of Danae on Plate XVII, ba, being in profile, less modeling for roundness and fewer slits are necessary. But even here, the eye, the nose, the chin, are by slits shadowed apart from the adjacent flesh, while the atmospheric quality of the shoulders above, and of the space between arm and breast, is due to the vibrancy of the slit-stippled surfaces.

Groups of faces that testify to the power of properly placed slits are those on Plates V, d, e, g.

Without the highly developed use of slits, hands are flat and flabby, like those of most modern tapestries. A fine example of a slit-modeled hand is that of Priam on Plate XVII, b. Here the lines of slits are so prominent that they are obvious even in my halftone. Note how the hand and fingers are outlined and shadowed with slits giving the feel of bones that hold, of flesh that softens, and of veins that darken. Note also the hands in Plates V, d, e, g.

In the development of hair and beard, skilfully placed slits are imperative. By the use of slits, hair is given the fascinating softness and looseness and openness of actual hair. The hair of Danae on Plate XVII, ba, and the hair and beard of Priam on Plate XVII, b, are almost as lacelike as the foliage of Plates XVII, c, f.

Slits are important in the weaving of patterned robes. While some of them come automatically in the weaving, the automatic ones seldom come sufficiently, and not always where they should. Priam's robe and the drapery behind his head on Plate XVII, b, are alive with tiny slits that outline the design, and at the same time give it atmosphere and vibrancy.

While many tapestries that are full of holes are bad, it may be regarded as an axiom that *no tapestry that is not full of holes is worth while.* A Perfected Tapestry lighted from the front and seen from the back, shines like the midnight sky through thousands of tiny holes. Seen from the front it is stippled with thousands of tiny black spots, and with short black lines that are slits.

Ribs, hatchings and slits! These in skilful combination give Perfected Tapestries their wonderful texture and vibrant atmosphere, making large Gothic tapestries superior to any other monumental form of flat art. Tapestry texture is the most necessary part of tapestries, and tapestries that attempt on the loom to substitute paint texture are bound to miss the mark, as do most modern tapestries.

TAPESTRY MATERIALS

The texture of tapestries varies according to the materials employed. Wool makes an elastic *warp* that adapts itself to refinements of weft-placing, but unless handled with great care, is apt to produce cloths of crooked shape. Linen and cotton warps are stiffer and easier to keep even. For *wefts,* wool is the fundamental material. Without wool, Perfected Tapestries could never have been created. Silk which shows to such advantage in satins, damasks, and brocades, is stupid when used by itself in tapestry, and entirely flat and inefficient in the interpretation of large pictures. Chinese tapestries demonstrate the best that can be accomplished with all-silk wefts.

Silk tapestries are much thinner than woolen ones. The thickest tapestries are those made entirely of coarse wool.

In Early Gothic tapestries the ribs are farther apart, and consequently flatter and less pronounced than later. The wefts being of two strands *loosely* spun, show flat and double. The lines formed by wefts, slits, and ribs, are much coarser, in Gothic tapestries than thereafter.

The basis of tapestry texture is line contrast. Whoever tries to make great tapestries in paint texture is sure to fail.

Modern woolen yarns are too soft and fuzzy. Most modern tapestries have too even a surface. The ribs are too close together.

While many Early Gothic tapestries had weft surfaces entirely of wool, French weavers soon discovered that the use of *silk and wool* gives opportunity by contrast of materials to heighten the powerful contrasts of ribs, hatchings and slits. Though the proportion of silk to wool varies at different periods and places, it may be laid down as a general principle that tapestry faces and hands and other flesh are in wool, except where touched with red silk to accentuate lips and complexion; and that écru and dull and dark colours are apt to be in wool, while delicate golden-yellows, blues, greens, and roses are apt to be in silk. Sometimes the faces of Late Gothic and of Renaissance tapestries were touched up with pastels, as is shown by Flemish Renaissance government and craft regulations permitting it under restrictions. But as a rule tapestries in all ages have relied upon loom contrasts. An important exception are Chinese silk tapestries whose blacks are often put in with the brush. Another exception are German Gothics that occasionally secure variety of texture by outlining eyebrows and other details with embroidery, and inserting blocks of velvet in Oriental rug knot.

As the records show, gold was used lavishly in fine tapestries of the fourteenth century. But owing to the fragility of the gold tinsel, the earlier large tapestries enriched with gold have perished. Mr. Rockefeller's Unicorn set shows the brilliant effects that Gothic weavers understood how to secure with a little gold. The highest point of gold weaving, with understanding of how to take advantage of gold-and-metal and silk-and-metal contrasts, was attained in religious tapestries like the Mazarin, and the Royal Spanish Virgin Late Gothic picture cloths made in Brussels under Philip and Joanna (1496–1506); and in Early Renaissance Van Orleys, like Mr. Philip Lehman's Last Supper, made a little later at the same place under Margaret of Austria. The gold and the silver were used in the form of silk threads spirally wound with silver ribbon, the silver being gilded for gold, and sometimes losing most of the gilding with time. The gold effects are most apt to be found in the garments of the personages, (Plate S, d, of *Subscribers' Edition*), in jewelry and armor (Plate VIII, a), in the columns and arches of architecture, and in the lettering of names. Gold requires supreme skill on the part of the weaver. Gold and silver inserted casually or carelessly or unintelligently, spoil a tapestry. Gold as employed in most

Renaissance tapestries adds shine and sheen while obscuring the design. This is obvious in those of the Medici Works at Florence, as well as in those of the Royal Spanish collection from Brussels. The gold of Mortlake tapestries has usually gone black because of the poor gilding of the silver ribbon. The last important attempt to use gold in tapestries was in Louis XIV Gobelins. In some of them gold was inserted effectively, but sparingly and without inspiration.

An interesting feature of tapestry texture is that tapestry pictures go all the way through. The picture on the back, after shaving off the loose loops of thread that mark the transition of bobbin from block to block of the same colour, *is the same as the picture on the face,* except of course that it is left-handed. Two of the Seven Sacraments tapestries in the Metropolitan Museum of Art are mounted wrong-side out. I find that few members of my tapestry classes are able to tell *which,* until specially instructed. Nevertheless, most tapestries do show differences in detail between face and back, usually small but often significant. The back of a tapestry, even when clipped close, is apt to be unkempt as compared with the face.

DEGENERATION OF TAPESTRY TEXTURE

Gothic designs lend themselves to tapestry texture. In Gothic designs, grounds are tipped up and forward so that the middle-ground figures, and sometimes the figures all the way up to the top of the tapestry, as in the Metropolitan Museum's Rose Garden tapestries, are like columns continuing the vertical lines of the figures of the foreground. In Gothic tapestry designs, *vertical lines are dominant.* The line structure of tapestry texture makes it efficient to create in Gothic designs the vigorous contrasts necessary in monumental pictures. Only in Late Gothic tapestries do horizontal lines due to Italian influence, begin to upset the clarity of Gothic composition, and weaken the contrasts of ribs, hatchings, and slits.

17

At the end of the fifteenth century tapestry texture began to degenerate. The tapestries of coarse weave no longer have the vigor of the earlier ones. Many of the tapestries of fine weave have faces utterly without character. After 1510 the degeneration is rapid. The Dreicer Crucifixion in the Metropolitan Museum is hack work as compared with the Virgin tapestry of the Altman collection. The Notre Dame de Sablon set of the Spitzer collection (Plate 79 of *Hunter 1912*) is rough and crude as compared with the great Gothic Credo and Salvation sets. The Vatican Acts of the Apostles after Raphael, despite its gold and despite the genius that inspired the cartoons, is far inferior to the monumental Gothic religious tapestries.

The difference is a difference mainly of texture, though largely caused by the different character of the designs. Renaissance cartoons are not as suitable as Gothic for reproduction in tapestries. The lowering of the skyline and the development of perspective produce compositions harder to handle in tapestry technique than in paint technique.

In the seventeenth century, designs become Baroque and sculptural. Heavy shadows take the place of texture and colour contrasts. Baroque designs are less suitable than any others for reproduction in tapestry.

The best tapestries of the seventeenth century are Louis XIV Gobelins. In them the exaggerations of Baroque are refined under the early sixteenth century Italian Renaissance influence that reasserted itself in France at the beginning of the reign of Louis XIV. This influence was felt in Brussels largely by reflection from the Gobelin (For example, the New York Public Library's Parnassus).

The best tapestry texture of the eighteenth century is that of Beauvais-Bouchers. The Beauvais weavers seem by the decorative compositions of Boucher to have been thrilled to outdo themselves. On a tiny scale they redeveloped many of the effects of Gothic tapestry texture.   At the Gobelins also, especially as illustrated in Mr. Rockefeller's Months of Lucas, the weavers were inspired to make tapestries of texture far superior to those of the original Months of Lucas of the Brussels Renaissance.

The period of Louis XVI saw another degeneration of tapestry texture, and the final one.   The passion for gentleness and flatness and simplicity, made strong contrasts unpalatable. Since then no great tapestries have been made.

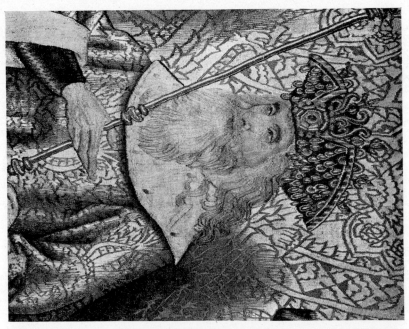

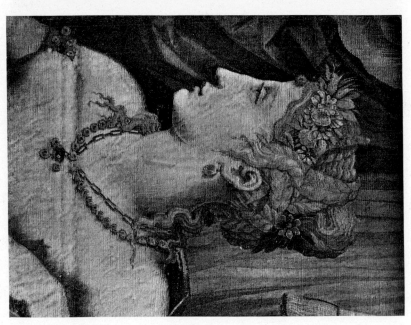

PLATES XVII, b, ba.—ON THE LEFT, DETAIL, PORTRAIT OF PRIAM, FROM ONE OF A SET OF FOUR GOTHIC HELEN OF TROY TAPESTRIES; DUVEEN BROS. ON THE RIGHT, PORTRAIT OF DANAE, FROM THE FRENCH RENAISSANCE DANAE TAPESTRY OF THE FONTAINEBLEAU MYTHOLOGICAL SET IN THE NATIONAL AUSTRIAN COLLECTION

PLATE XVII, C.—FOLIAGE DETAIL FROM MRS. HAROLD PRATT'S EARLY
GOTHIC "ANNUNCIATION"

PLATE XVII, d.—THE GOLDEN TREE, DETAIL FROM ONE OF A SET OF FOUR HELEN OF TROY TAPESTRIES; DUVEEN BROS. NOTE ESPECIALLY THE STEPPED SLITS OF TRUNK AND FOLIAGE

PLATE XVII, e.—LANDSCAPE DETAIL OF ONE OF MR. ROCKEFELLER'S GOBELIN MONTHS OF LUCAS

PLATE XVII, f.—TEXTURE DETAIL FROM TAPESTRY OPPOSITE

PLATES XVIII, a, aa, ab.—FIFTEENTH CENTURY MANUSCRIPT
PICTURES OF THE NINE PREUX, WITH THEIR COATS-OF-ARMS: HECTOR,
ALEXANDER, CAESAR, JOSHUA, DAVID, JUDAS MACCABEUS, ARTHUR,
CHARLEMAGNE, GODFREY DE BOUILLON

CHAPTER XVIII

TAPESTRY DESIGN

DESIGNS OF GOTHIC TAPESTRIES. AUTHORS VS. PAINTERS. LITERARY
SOURCES OF THE DESIGNS. DESIGNERS AND CARTOONISTS, AND THEIR
SIGNATURES. JEAN DE BRUXELLES *ALIAS* JEAN DE ROME. OWNERS
AND DONORS. ARMORIALS. PORTRAITS. COSTUMES. FLORA AND
FAUNA. STYLES OF DESIGN

PERFECTED TAPESTRIES are an aristocratic art. They were
developed in the fourteenth century for nobles and kings
whose language and culture were French. Only in churches
and cathedrals could the multitude see them.

Perfected tapestries were not a popular art based on folk
tales, and created by provincial artists and weavers. They
were a rich man's art elaborated for the decoration of palatial
castles, and for the delectation and comfort of the aristoc-
racy. They adorned the walls, and kept out the cold.

The stories and the designs were based on the illustrated
books of the period, mainly French but sometimes Latin, books
so expensive that only millionaires and monasteries could
afford them.

The common people did not count. They were like the
dumb beasts of the field. Though the home language of many
of the designers and weavers was Flemish, we never find Flemish inscriptions on Gothic tapestries. The designers were
working not for themselves, but for aristocrats who desired
to extend the influence and memory, *not* of the artists and
weavers, but of themselves. Gothic tapestries pictured vividly
the life of the French nobility of the period, and this just as
much when the stories are ancient as when they are modern.
Typical illustrations of this are Mr. Rockefeller's Unicorn set,
and the great Trojan War group. The personages in both

are knights and ladies of the fifteenth century, with an air of antiquity given to the Trojan War series by occasional archaicisms.

While the common people did not count, the Church did. The language of priests and of the learned professions was Latin. Often on tapestries made for cathedrals and convents, and sometimes also on religious tapestries made for private chapels and palaces, the inscriptions were in Latin alone. Often inscriptions were in both Latin and French—French at the top of the tapestries and Latin at the bottom, as in the Trojan War group. Often the inscriptions were in French alone.

However, there was a popular side to Gothic Religious Tapestries, which affected also the design of Gothic Historical and Country Life tapestries. This popular side was a spectacular side. It was a side due to the influence of the stage —of the mystery plays that in the fifteenth century were even more popular than the movies are now, and vastly more thrilling. What could possibly grip an audience of believers who were also sinners, like a vivid portrayal of Adam by his sin bringing woe upon us all; the prophets of the Old Testament foretelling the arrival of a Saviour to redeem Man; Christ born of a Virgin giving His life on the Cross that we might be saved; all this with awe-inspiring stage scenery—God, Himself with angels in Heaven above; Satan and his devils in Hell below, with flames spouting out of the mouth of Hell; the Earth a wide platform, with different sections marked each with its name—Paris, Rome, Jerusalem, Egypt, the Wilderness—and with scenery painted to suggest landscape and architecture. Just as in the eighteenth century, the scenery of Opera gave "pep" and charm to the pictures of Boucher and Coypel, so in the fifteenth, the scenery and action of the stage put passion and conviction into the huge cloths of the Credo and Salvation sets (See Chapter IV).

The conventions of Gothic tapestry design were wonderfully suited to the capabilities of the tapestry loom. Nowadays the earnest and enthusiastic efforts of the personnel of the Gobelins are exhausted in the effort to reproduce cartoons which are considered successful in proportion as they conform to the paint technique of the moment. In the fourteenth and fifteenth centuries, designers and weavers avoided what was hard to do in tapestry, but with marvelous ingenuity took every advantage of the extraordinary possibilities of tapestry texture. Cartoons were produced utterly different from, *though possible because of,* the paintings of the period, by painters whose job it was, not to glorify themselves, but to get results. Backgrounds were tipped up as on Plate V, c, so that there were no empty expanses of air and sky. Ornament was applied to all plain surfaces so that every inch of the surface was interesting.

AUTHORS VS. DESIGNERS

The AUTHOR of Gothic tapestries was not the painter who made the original sketches or executed the full-size cartoons. It was the writer who composed the scenario and the inscriptions (Plates XVIII, f, fa). What was true of tapestries was also true of Gothic illuminated manuscripts, and in accordance with the precedent set by them. The AUTHOR who composed the text and printed it in beautiful letters with his own hand, was vastly more important than the painter who under the AUTHOR's direction did the illustrations. The AUTHOR was the originator, and the creator, and the architect, to whom credit for the book or the set of tapestries was allowed as a matter of course (Plate XVIII, b). The painter played the part of the modern illustrator of a popular novel, or of the photographer who records on the film the ideas of the AUTHOR of the scenario, as made into pictures by the actors of the cinema. In later centuries as the AUTHOR's function came more and more to be assumed by the painter, the story interest of tapestries declined. They began to look like what they

were—pictures based on reference books, instead of on scenarios composed by literary masters. Nowadays the ignorance
of many painters and some critics, regards as a virtue the
absence from pictures of illustrative interest.

LITERARY SOURCES OF THE DESIGNS

The stories on which Gothic tapestries were based, were
Romantic stories. This applies quite as much to Historical
and Religious tapestries as to those that have their origin
in the Chanson de Roland and other *chansons de geste*.

These *chansons de geste* (Consult *Bédier Épiques*) were
not assemblages of popular songs and tales from the time of
Charlemagne. They were imaginative creations, full of religious fervor, inspired by the contemporary crusades against
the Saracens—especially those of Southern France and Spain
—with whom all other non-Christian enemies were more or less
confused. From the age of Charlemagne, the *chansons de geste*
borrowed little but the names of the principal personages, and
an historic background strangely unlike the real one. Charlemagne and his knights they transformed into eleventh and
twelfth century crusaders, with the customs and costumes of
the eleventh and twelfth centuries.

The monasteries on the road to Spain, whose prosperity
depended upon visits of pilgrims and crusading knights, were
hotbeds of Romance. Local legends were by French poets
expanded into long romances that not only glorified the reputation of the monasteries for sanctity and good works, but
often attributed their foundation and endowment to the piety
of Charlemagne and his entourage. The Army and the Church
were thrilled by a common ambition—to crush the Saracens
and recover the Holy Places. So far was the Present—and
even the Future—projected into the Past, that the single short
campaign of Charlemagne in Spain was floriated into several
long ones, and he was made to conduct adventuresome expeditions (that have no basis in fact) to Constantinople and even

to Jerusalem. Also Charlemagne, who had been as much German as French, with the accent on the German, was transformed into a French monarch, whose deeds glorified France and whose heart was French.

What the *chansons de geste* sang, French crusaders justified. Latin remained the international language of the Church, but French became the international language of Society and of Chivalry. The Normans made French the aristocratic language of England and Sicily and Southern Italy. The leadership of the Crusades for the recovery of Jerusalem was so largely French that for centuries the people of the Eastern Mediterranean designated Westerners as Franks. The French romances were recited, even before translation, in Italy and Germany, as well as in Spain and England. Some of the *chansons de geste* were composed, not in the French of Paris, but in the French of Normandy and England.

Ancient history was rewritten in the style of the *chansons de geste*. But with less imagination and with more history. Much of the history, however, was already romantic, made so by the Greeks of the Orient, Latin translations of whose works supplied material to French poets.

The great Gothic Alexander tapestries are based not on the classic writers of Greece and Rome, but on the second century fabulous Greek history of Alexander by the Pseudo-Callisthenes, as developed by French poets from versions in Latin. The great Gothic Trojan War tapestries are based, not on Homer, but on Benoit de Sante Maure's twelfth century Roman de Troie, that claimed as its sources Dictys the Cretan and Dares the Phrygian, the former a Greek, the latter a Trojan, reputed eyewitnesses of the events they chronicled.

However, the authors of fifteenth century tapestries were apt to use, *not* the original poems of the twelfth and thirteenth centuries, but fourteenth or fifteenth century versions, edited and abbreviated or expanded, with the addition of other material assembled from heterogeneous sources. As is indicated by the "Death of Philip" scene, the AUTHOR of the Doria Alexander tapestries used, *not* the early thirteenth century poem of Lambert le Tort, Alexandre de Bernay, and Pierre de Saint Cloud, published at Stuttgart in 1846 by H. Michelant, but some fifteenth century compilation such as Jean Wauquelin's *Livre des conquestes et faits d'Alexandre le Grant* made for Philip the Good's relative, the Count d'Etampes (Page 143 of *Doutrepont Bourgogne*) or, availing himself of the resources of the library of the Duke of Burgundy—among them the great fourteenth century Latin Encyclopedia of Vincent de Beauvais—did his own selecting and editing from numerous manuscript volumes.

The scenes of the Gothic Trojan War tapestries, while following in a general way the original text of Benoit de Sainte Maure's Roman de Troie, as well as the abbreviated and modified text of the fourteenth century French prose version, differ here and there from both to such an extent as to indicate that the AUTHOR of the tapestries (See the last scene of Plate V, c) leaned on later versions such as the French translation of Guido da Colonna's *Historia Destructionis Troiæ,* itself plagiarized from Benoit de Sainte Maure; perhaps also on Jacques Millet's *Mystère de Troie* (Pages 567–574 of Volume II of *Julleville Mystères*); copies of both of which were in the library of Philip the Good (Page 486 of *Doutrepont Bourgogne*).

The authors of Gothic religious tapestries found much material in the Vulgate, extracts from which appear on the scrolls of the Prophets in the great Gothic Salvation and Credo series (Chapter IV). But they found more in the voluminous Latin theological literature in prose and verse, as well as in the fourteenth century Latin Encyclopedia of Vincent de Beauvais, and in the picturesque Lives of the Saints, many of which had been developed locally to spread the glory of churches and monasteries founded by, or consecrated to, aforesaid Saints. A popular version of the more important of these Lives was Giacomo da Voragine's thirteenth century *Legenda Aurea* (Golden Legend), which was accessible in French translation. The Golden Legend was employed especially in the creation of provincial religious tapestries, where the AUTHOR was one of the local priests or monks. Other popular sources were the *Speculum Humanæ Salvationis* (Lutz and Perdrizet, Mulhouse, 1907) and the *Biblia Pauperum* (Heitz and Schreiber, Strasburg, 1903) whose illustrations can be seen reproduced in the Reims Virgin and in the La Chaise Dieu Christ (Pages 249, 251 of *Mâle Fifteenth*). The Lives of the Saints, in Latin, are accessible in the New York Public Library, in the monumental tomes published by the Bollandist Fathers at Antwerp and Brussels, in the seventeenth century and later. The Angers Apocalypse was based on illustrated manuscripts of the Apocalypse, one of them lent for the purpose to the Duke of Anjou, by the French King Charles VI.

As the Renaissance approached tapestries became less and less Romantic. Writers like Jean Lemaire de Belges continued to use the medieval sources. The Beauvais Kings of Gaul, with views of French cities in the background, is based on one of his books that continues the Romantic traditions of the Gothic Past. But the tendency was away from Romance and Religion, back to the ancient classic authors as we know them, and to allegorical patchwork like that of the Spanish Honors and Moralities. The Apocalypse tapestries of the Royal Spanish collection are dead and stupid, compared with the Early Gothic Apocalypse of Angers.

During the sixteenth and seventeenth centuries, tapestries become constantly less Romantic and less Christian, and constantly more Pagan and more Classic.

In the eighteenth century the ancient stories again had life put into them (De Troy's Esther, Boucher's Loves of the Gods, Boucher's Psyche). The last was based on Lafontaine's charming version of the Psyche story anciently told in Latin by Apuleius. Lafontaine also supplied other up-to-date material in his Fables, which were pictured delightfully by Oudry. (Chapter XI). Another author favored by eighteenth century tapestry designers of Brussels and Madrid, as well as by Charles Coypel at the Gobelins, was Cervantes, whose Don Quixote is immortal.

Contemporary and recent history was also a source for authors and cartoonists, especially when they wished to glorify the deeds of Kings and Nobles. (Tunis set, and Victories of the Archduke Albert, in the Royal Spanish collection; Victories of the Duke of Alba, in the collection of the Duke of Alba; Story of the King in the great Louis XIV set of the Gobelins).

Petrarch, with his *Laura,* fathered not only the Gothic Triumphs in the National Austrian collection, and those of entirely different design at Hampton Court and in the Victoria and Albert Museum, but also Renaissance sets on the same subject, notably the one in the Royal Spanish collection. To Petrarch's *Africa* we owe Giulio Romano's Scipio, so often woven at the Gobelins, as well as in the sixteenth and seventeenth centuries at Brussels. Xenophon's Cyropedia gave numerous different sets on the Story of Cyrus the Great.

During all these periods Ovid's Metamorphoses were pictured repeatedly, by Oudry and by Boucher as well as by the designers of the Renaissance. Notable Renaissance examples are the Vertumnus and Pomona sets in the Royal Spanish and National Austrian, and French & Co. collections. The last of these sets is the one that was formerly in the Berwick and Alba collection.

DESIGNERS AND CARTOONISTS

Our information about the designers and cartoonists of Gobelin tapestries is almost complete (Chapters IX, XII; and *Fenaille Gobelins*). We are fairly well informed about the designers of ancient Beauvais tapestries (Chapter XI). We know much about the design sources, and something about the cartoonists of Aubusson tapestries (Chapter XIII). We are able to identify the designers of many of the important Renaissance and seventeenth century sets of Brussels (Chapters VIII, X). There are also still in existence many of the small sketches—Giulio Romano's Scipio, and at least one of his Children Playing (Plate XVIII, ia); Bernard van Orley's Pavia (Plate XVIII, i) and Hunts of Maximilian; some of Rubens' Achilles, and other sets by Rubens. There are also preserved some of the full-sized cartoons, principally of Gobelin and Spanish tapestries; but the most important are those of Raphael's Acts of the Apostles at the Victoria and Albert Museum; (Plates XVIII, j, ja; VIII, f); next in importance, the Decius paintings of Rubens in the Liechtenstein collection. But about the names as well as the personalities of the designers and cartoonists of Gothic tapestries, we are woefully ignorant.

Thanks to the brilliant work of the late Jules Guiffrey, the cartoonist of the Angers Apocalypse was established as the King's painter, Hennequin de Bruges. Joseph Destrée revealed Jean de Bruxelles, *alias* Jean de Rome, as the designer, and Maitre Philippe as the cartoonist, of the Brussels Cinquentenaire Museum's Herkinbald. We know that Philip the Good's great set of the Golden Fleece, no longer in existence, was cartooned by Baudouin de Bailleul. We know that the Louvre's "Saint Luke painting the Virgin" was copied from one of Roger van der Weyden's paintings still in existence, and we have literary evidence to prove that the Berne Museum's Trajan and Herkinbald was based on now destroyed paintings of the same master. We have the names of other Gothic painters who are known to have designed and cartooned tapestries. We have small colour sketches at the Louvre, which have been claimed as the original sketches for the great Gothic Trojan War series, but which seem to me rough copies.

Nevertheless, the pictures of most Gothic tapestries are anonymous. We can compare them with manuscript illustrations to which they show relationship, and with paintings that they resemble in style, but the results of such comparison are small. The technique of Gothic tapestries is so different from paint technique, as to indicate that the full-size cartoons were made by painters of special knack and training, among whom were probably some of the painters of the Gothic manuscripts and easel paintings that have come down to us. My identification of Gerard David as the designer and cartoonist of the Spanish Virgin set, is merely a suggestion. But I read with interest and respect what Joseph Destrée has to say about Juste de Ghent and Maitre Philippe.

JEAN DE BRUXELLES *ALIAS* JEAN DE ROME

Here we have the Atlantis of the Tapestry World. As is known by everybody, many Gothic tapestries have long inscriptions made up of series of letters that do not combine into words, and that are apparently ornamental only. It has been asserted that wherever in such tapestries, whether dating from 1460 or 1520, we find the letters ROM, MOR, IRON, ROEM, ROOM, REOON, etc.; we have the signature of the painter who appears, several times on the account books of Margaret of Austria as Jean de Bruxelles, and once as "Jean de Bruxelles otherwise called Jean de Rome." Monsieur F. de Mély bolsters up the theory by finding IAN ROME on a manuscript painting of the *Heures de la Princesse de Cory*. Göbel on Page 407 of Volume I of his *Wandteppiche* makes a rather futile attempt to explain the double name, Jean de Bruxelles *alias* Jean de Rome. Many of the supposed signatures were reproduced by Thiéry in his *Inscriptions et Signatures de Jean de Bruxelles* (Louvain 1907). Marquet de Vasselot and Hermann Schmidt have handled the theory with discretion, but more sympathetically than it deserves. The only adequate and reasonable presentation of the facts was by Joseph Destrée in his *Maitre*

Philippe à propos de Jean de Bruxelles dit van Room (*Brussels, 1904*). Plates XVIII, e, ea, show two instances, where the letters do really seem to suggest a signature. The incorrect spelling is held to help the theory, because testifying to the ignorance of the weavers.

To me it seems probable that the Jean de Bruxelles mentioned in the accounts of Margaret of Austria was Jean Mostaert, who was crowded out as court painter in 1518 by Bernard van Orley. If Mostaert was responsible for the Brussels Herkinbald and similar tapestries from 1506 to 1516, it is easy to understand why he was replaced by the designer of the great Van Orley Passion set. Mostaert's relations to Margaret of Austria had long been so close ("Nostre aimé maitre Jean de Bruxelles" in 1516) as to explain why he should —once only and that in 1510—be jokingly addressed as Jean de Bruxelles, otherwise called "de Rome."

I should not be surprised to have it develop later that Van Orley worked at first *under* Mostaert. Several of the Brussels tapestries made about 1515 suggest the arrival of a cartoonist with more ability than the head designer, and some of the faces look like Van Orley's work.

OWNERS AND DONORS

The owner or donor for whom important work was executed often perpetuated his memory as the First Cause of the Tapestries, by having his name appear in an inscription (See the Beauvais Saint Peter set, Chapter IV; Mortlake Vulcan and Venus, Louis XIV Story of the King); his coat-of-arms woven into the cloth (See the Louis XIV set, and also the Angers Apocalypse, the Brady Visit of the Gipsies, the Reims Virgin, and the Reims Saint Remi, and many Gobelins made for the King); or his portrait, with that of his wife if he had one, introduced as the most effective signature of all (See the Kahn "Training the Falcon," the Valencia marriage tapestry at the Musée des Arts Décoratifs, the Notre

Dame de Sablon tapestry in the Brussels Cinquentenaire Museum, the Pierre de Rohan musical tapestry at Angers, the Brussels and Gobelin Months of Lucas). I suspect that the bearded personage in the last scene of Plate XVIII, fa, and the man labeled PHILIEP in the Brussels Deposition, may also be portraits of the donor.

ARMORIALS

Often tapestries were decorative armorials, without story or personages (Plate XVIII, c); the two Margaret of Austria armorials at the Bruges Toison d'Or Exhibition, 1907; many Gobelins, the Duke of Alba's Columbus tapestries (Plate XVIII, ha). Sometimes the monogram also appears (Plate XVIII, d). The monogram is common on the shields in the border corners of Gobelins made for the King. The monogram still testifies to the fact that Mr. Rockefeller's Months of Lucas (Plates XII, b, c, d) were made for Alexander, Count of Toulouse, son of Louis XIV and Madame de Montespan. Sometimes ancient personages bear their coats-of-arms (Plates III, b; XVIII, g). Compare the manuscript pictures of the Nine Preux on Plates XVIII, a, aa, ab.

PORTRAITS

Sometimes we find portraits of contemporaries; Francis I and many others in the Naples Pavia set, and in the Fontainebleau set of the National Austrian collection; the whole Habsburg family in the Brussels Cinquentenaire Museum's Notre Dame de Sablon; Louis XII and Philip the Handsome and others in the Valenciennes Tournament tapestry (Plate XVIII, ba); Charles V and many others in the Tunis set of the Royal Spanish collection; Maximilian and Charles V in the Louvre Hunts of Maximilian; Louis XIV and many others in the Gobelin Story of the King; Louis XV and many others in the Hunts of Louis XV.

Sometimes we find portraits of the designer; Vermeyen

in the Tunis set, Oudry in the Hunts of Louis XV. Sometimes we find the signature of the designer: L. VAN SCHOOR on Louis XIV Brussels, *F. Boucher* on Beauvais-Bouchers, *I. F. Romanelli* on the Medici Story of Dido, *Oudry* on the Hunts of Louis XV.

COSTUMES

Costumes help to distinguish tapestries of different periods. In the Gothic tapestries all fine gentlemen were clean-shaven—Philip the Good, Charles the Bold, Charles VII, Henry VI, Henry VII, Louis XI, Maximilian. In the middle of the fifteenth century they wore short hair and long-pointed shoes. Towards the end of the century the hair lengthened and the shoe-toes shortened and rounded. Beards in Gothic tapestries were used only on ancient or provincial personages, and not always then.

In the sixteenth century all gentlemen wore full beards (Charles V, Francis I, Henry VIII, Henri II). At first the beards and the toes of shoes were absurdly wide, sleeves and knickerbockers balloon-shaped and full of slashes, as were also breast and back of coats, and even shoes. About the middle of the century, beards became pointed, degenerating into goatees in the first half of the seventeenth (Richelieu), with moustaches prominent. Louis XIV who set the fashion in the last half of the century was cleanshaven, and wore long flowing curls that degenerated into a wig, with age.

In Gothic tapestries, even those picturing ancient history, most of the personages looked just like contemporaries. In Renaissance tapestries, ancient personages, and sometimes contemporary ones, were pictured in what they thought the ancient Romans wore. In the seventeenth century, the Classicism continued, but in the eighteenth century the ancients were up-to-dated again, only to relapse into pseudo-antiquity in the period of Louis XVI.

The flora of Gothic tapestries is contemporary and vivid,

18

as is the fauna, even the mythical animals.   The favorite tex-
tile pattern on tapestries of the last half of the fifteenth century was the pomegranate, with actual pomegranate trees
introduced into out-of-door scenes.   The flora of the sixteenth
and seventeenth centuries is more formal, and larger in scale,
and less interesting.   The flora of the eighteenth century is
fascinating, especially as drawn by Boucher and Jacques
and Tessier.

The designs of the different periods, as stated elsewhere,
are *line* style, with flat colour, in Gothic tapestries, *paint* style,
in Renaissance tapestries, *sculptural* style in seventeenth century tapestries, and again *paint* style in eighteenth century
tapestries.   This means that the shadows of seventeenth century tapestries are too heavy, while the relief effects of Gothic
tapestries are secured, not by the tones and colours of the
painter, but through the extraordinary contrasts introduced
on the loom by Tapestry Texture.

PLATES XVIII, b, ba.—ABOVE, CONTEMPORARY MANUSCRIPT PORTRAIT OF PHILIP THE GOOD AND HIS YOUTHFUL SON CHARLES THE BOLD, SHOWING A BOOK PRESENTED BY ITS AUTHOR. BELOW, VALENCIENNES TOURNAMENT TAPESTRY WITH PORTRAITS OF LOUIS XII AND PHILIP THE HANDSOME

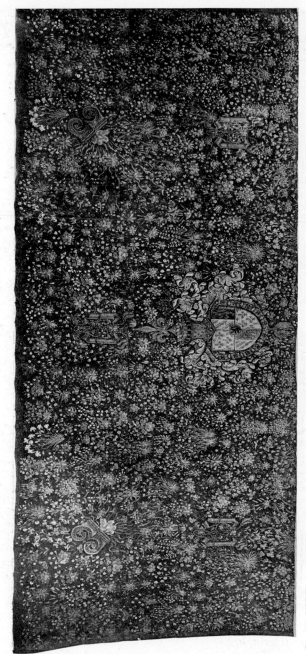

PLATE XVIII, C.—GOTHIC VERDURE ARMORIAL TAPESTRY OF CHARLES THE BOLD, IN THE BERNE MUSEUM. NOTE THE DOUBLE = C MONOGRAMS, AND THE FLINTS STRIKING FIRE

PLATE XVIII, d.—DETAIL OF TAPESTRY OPPOSITE, SHOWING DOUBLE=C MONOGRAM OF
CHARLES THE BOLD

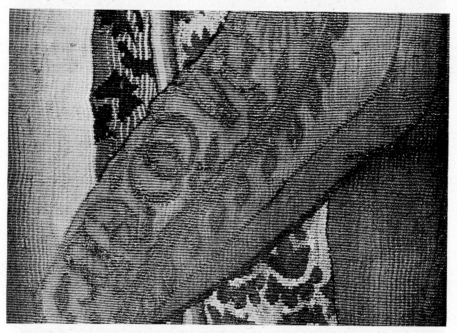

PLATES XVIII, e, ea.—SO–CALLED SIGNATURES OF THE PAINTER JEAN DE ROME, OTHERWISE JEAN DE BRUSSELS. ABOVE, DETAIL "ROEM" FROM THE PAYNE "CRUCIFIXION WITH SUBORDINATE SCENES" OF THE METROPOLITAN MUSEUM OF ART. BELOW, DETAIL "REOON" FROM "ESTHER AND AUGUSTUS," A LATE GOTHIC TAPESTRY RICH WITH GOLD IN THE COLLECTION OF DUVEEN BROS.

PLATES XVIII, f, fa.—ABOVE, "INFAMY," ONE OF THE "HONORS" SET OF TAPES-
TRIES IN THE ROYAL SPANISH COLLECTION, SHOWING ON THE RIGHT THE PORTRAIT
OF THE AUTHOR. BELOW, "CAPTURE OF RABBAH," ONE OF THE "STORY OF DAVID"
TAPESTRIES IN THE CLUNY MUSEUM, SHOWING ON THE RIGHT PORTRAIT OF THE
AUTHOR WITH TWO COMPANIONS

PLATES XVIII, h, ha.—ON THE LEFT, HONEYMOON SCULPTURE PORTRAIT OF THE EMPEROR CHARLES V AND HIS WIFE
ISABELLA OF PORTUGAL; CHÂTEAU DE GAESBECK. ON THE RIGHT, ONE OF THE SET OF TWELVE CHRISTOPHER COLUMBUS
ARMORIAL TAPESTRIES ACQUIRED BY THE PRESENT DUKE OF ALBA FROM THE FAMILY OF COLUMBUS. THE PLACE ILLUSTRATED
IS PANAMA AS SHOWN BY THE INSCRIPTION UNDER THE COAT-OF-ARMS

PLATES XVIII, i, ia.—ABOVE, BERNARD VAN ORLEY'S SKETCH IN THE LOUVRE FOR ONE OF THE BATTLE OF PAVIA TAPESTRIES. BELOW, GIULIO ROMANO'S SKETCH IN THE SALTING COLLECTION OF THE VICTORIA AND ALBERT MUSEUM FOR ONE OF THE "CHILDREN PLAYING" TAPESTRIES

PLATES XVIII, j, ja.—TWO OF THE FAMOUS RAPHAEL CARTOONS IN THE VICTORIA AND
ALBERT MUSEUM. ABOVE, CURING THE PARALYTIC (SEE PLATE XVI, a, FOR ONE OF THE
MORTLAKE TAPESTRIES WOVEN FROM IT). BELOW, SACRIFICE AT LYSTRA

PLATE XVIII, k.—MAKING A SET OF FIVE CARTOONS. UPPER RIGHT CORNER, THE
FIRST SMALL COLOR SKETCH. ON THE LEFT, ONE OF THE PANELS COMPLETED. ON
THE RIGHT, MEDALLION OF ANOTHER PANEL, DRAWN BUT NOT COLORED. EDGEWATER
TAPESTRY LOOMS

PLATE XVIII, 1.—CARTOON PAINTERS AT WORK. ON THE RIGHT, MR. KLEISER, PROPRIETOR AND
DIRECTOR OF THE EDGEWATER TAPESTRY WORKS

PLATE XIX, a.—HIGH-WARP LOOM AT THE GOBELINS. THE WEAVER PULL-
ING THE LEASHES (*lisses*) WITH HIS LEFT HAND, TO FORM THE SHED THROUGH
WHICH WITH HIS RIGHT HAND HE IS PASSING THE POINTED BOBBIN (*broche*),
FROM LEFT TO RIGHT

CHAPTER XIX

TAPESTRY MANUFACTURE

HIGH WARP VS. LOW WARP, SIGNATURES OF MANUFACTURERS
REPAIRING AND CLEANING TAPESTRIES

AMONG modern tapestry factories at which I have studied
the process of tapestry weaving are those of Baumgarten,
of the Herter Looms, and of others in New York; the Gobelins,
Beauvais, and Aubusson, and others in France; Merton in
England, one in Brussels, two in Rome, and the Royal Tapestry Works in Madrid. The illustrations used in this chapter
are from the Gobelins; and from the Edgewater Tapestry
Looms at Edgewater, New Jersey, where the making of inexpensive tapestries in loose texture has been developed to a
high degree of excellence.

The process at all of these factories is practically the same,
except that some of the factories use high-warp looms, while
others use low-warp looms. High-warp looms are used at
the Gobelins, Merton, Madrid, and Rome; low-warp looms,
elsewhere. While the French call high-warp looms *haute lisse*
looms, *lisse* means not warp but *leash* (See below). High-
warp looms have the warp in a perpendicular position, winding up as completed on the lower roller, and unwinding from
the upper roller (Plates b, ba). Low-warp looms have the
warp in a horizontal position, winding up as completed on the
roller next the weaver, and unwinding from the other roller
(Plate XIX, d). Neither high-warp looms nor low-warp
looms have mechanical power or shuttle. Both are manipulated entirely by the weaver and both are *bobbin* looms, as
contrasted with *shuttle* hand looms, and with power looms.

At this point it should be noted that high-warp looms are

not necessarily tapestry looms. For example, Oriental rug looms are high-warp looms. A majority of the *haute lisse* looms mentioned in documents of the fourteenth and fifteenth centuries, produced fabrics not tapestry.

The object of both high-warp looms and low-warp looms is the same—to hold the warps parallel and taut, and to facilitate the passing of the bobbins. While it is possible to weave a tapestry by passing the bobbin to the left alternately over and under the warp threads, and back to the right alternately under and over, the passing goes quicker when a shed between the odd and even warps, with the odd warps next to the weaver, is formed for the passage of the bobbin to the left, and a reversed shed with the even warps next to the weaver, for the passage of the bobbin back. On the high-warp loom the first shed is formed by a stick between the odds and evens, and the second shed by pulling with the left hand leashes that draw the even warps through the odd warps to the side next the weaver (Plate XIX, a). This leaves only the right hand free for passing the bobbin back.

The low-warp loom is mechanically an improvement on the high-warp loom. In the low-warp loom (Plate XIX, d) there are two sets of leashes, one set attached to the odd warps and worked with the left foot, the second set attached to the even warps and worked with the right foot. Push the right foot down, letting the left foot up, and the first shed is formed. Push the left foot down, letting the right foot up, and the second shed is formed. The width of shed made by working the treadles of the low-warp loom is much greater than that made by the left hand on the high-warp loom. The low-warp loom is much faster than the high-warp loom, when the passes are long. The high-warp loom might be described as an all-hand loom, the low-warp loom as a hand-and-foot loom.

TAPESTRY WOVEN WRONG SIDE

On both looms, tapestries are woven wrong side next to the weaver. While a tapestry can be woven face next the weaver, the process is slow and awkward. The weaver needs the bobbins next him. The *low-warp weaver* has to judge what he has woven *from the wrong side only,* which is obscured by floating threads and bobbins. Bits of the face he can see only imperfectly in a tiny mirror through the warps. Here is the great artistic advantage of the high-warp loom. The *high-warp weaver* has only to go around to the front of his loom to see the face of his tapestry. This helps not only the weaver, but especially the foreman and the artistic director in their efforts to keep track of the weaver's work. Mistakes and imperfections are easily seen and quickly rectified. On most low-warp looms the face of the tapestry is first seen after the tapestry has been completed and demounted from the loom. While the small iron low-warp looms now used at Beauvais allow the warp to be revolved to a perpendicular position during the weaving, the preparations involved are elaborate and time-consuming.

An important difference between high warp and low warp is in the position of the cartoon. The high-warp weaver usually works with a full-size colour model behind him, or over him, and with the outline of the design inked on the warps. The low-warp weaver has his large cartoon under the warp, close up and facing it, so that no inking of the warp is necessary. The tapestry being woven face down, the low-warp weaver consequently reverses the direction of the design in weaving, so that cartoons for the low-warp loom have to be painted left-handed in order to make them come out right-handed. But at Beauvais they have a transparent tracing under the warp, made from the coloured cartoon beside the weaver, and reversed by being placed face down. On high-warp looms the weaver gets his colour by looking at a cartoon that is distant from the warp. On most low-warp looms, the weaver gets both design and colour from a cartoon that is close up against the warps (Plate XIX, c). So the high-warp process as regards colouration is much freer and more dependent upon the weaver's skill.

LOW WARP FASTER

While low-warp weaving is faster, high-warp manipulation of the wefts is more completely under the weaver's control. The high warp is far superior for the first interpretation of an intricate design. When the design is intricate and the texture is coarse the high-warp is not only easier but faster. When the design is coarse and the texture is fine, the low warp is twice or three times as fast. The high-warp loom is primarily and in its origin a loom for the coarse threads of wool. The low warp is primarily and in its origin a loom for the fine threads of silk. I am certain that the development of the texture of Perfected Tapestries in the fourteenth century took place on the high-warp loom, and I believe that some of the degeneration of tapestry texture in the sixteenth century was due to the general substitution of low-warp looms for high-warp looms. I do not mean to say that wonderful tapestries cannot be woven on low-warp looms by weavers familiar with high-warp traditions. But I maintain that the tendency of the low warp is to eliminate the refinements of tapestry texture, and I believe that the revival of the ancient art depends upon the revival of ancient tapestry texture, best studied by reproducing details of masterpieces from actual masterpieces that are still in perfect condition, upon the high-warp loom. However, the difference between high-warp cloths and low-warp cloths is general and not specific. Intrinsically they are alike. The skilful low-warp weaver can reproduce most of the effects characteristic of the high warp; and the patterned parts of a tapestry such as damassé grounds he can do better.

HIGH-WARP TEXTURE SUPERIOR

Perhaps the clearest illustration is from tapestries of a set made at the Gobelins in the last half of the eighteenth century. I refer to Mrs. Dixon's fine Don Quixote tapestries formerly in the Morgan collection, inherited by the King of Spain from his grandfather, and long exhibited on loan at the Metropolitan Museum. Four of the tapestries are high warp, one is low warp. While the ornamental parts of the low-warp tapestry are better, the medallion pictures of the four high warps are incomparably superior. The texture of the low-warp medallion is too smooth and flat. The high-warp medallions have irregularities and refinements that give life to the faces and strength to the contrasts. They look less like the cartoons, but have more of the vigor that is apparent in Gothic tapestries. In other words, the texture of the low-warp tapestry is more like that of painted pictures and of damasks, while the texture of the four high-warp tapestries is the texture of Perfected Tapestries.

The tapestries made at the Gobelins on high-warp looms in the reign of Louis XIV are immeasurably superior to those made on the low-warp looms. The first interpretations of great sets like the Story of the King were invariably entrusted to the managers of the high-warp shops. A superlative example of eighteenth century Gobelin high-warp texture is Mr. Rockefeller's set of ten Months of Lucas (Plates XIII, b, c, d; XVII, e, f). I doubt if the refinements of texture shown on Plate XVII, f, could be successfully reproduced on the low warp. Beauvais-Bouchers show the low-warp loom at its highest point in the eighteenth century. They possess many texture refinements peculiar to the Beauvais Tapestry Works at this period.

I do not think that low-warp looms became common for large picture tapestries until near the end of the fifteenth century. Perhaps the so-called Louis Douze tapestries of Brussels are their first important production. The great Mazarin and similar gold tapestries I attribute to high-warp looms. During the sixteenth century, the low warp reigned at Brussels. Raphael's Acts of the Apostles (Plate VIII, fa) was woven on low-warp looms. The fact that the cartoons (Plate VIII, f) were painted left-handed, makes this certain. Meanwhile France clung to the more primitive and less profitable high-warp loom. The institution of tapestry weaving at the Gobelins at the beginning of the seventeenth century was an effort to establish Flemish low-warp weaving in Paris. Both before and after the Gobelins became a State institution in 1664, high-warp and low-warp looms were used there side by side. Beauvais founded in 1664 represents another influx of Flemish low-warp looms and weavers, although Béhagle probably employed high-warp looms for some of his greatest sets. Since the eighteenth century, the Gobelins have used high-warp looms only.

Sometimes tapestries were woven in two or more pieces, and sewed together after leaving the loom. The few instances of this before the eighteenth century are principally of bottom borders, or top and bottom borders, made separately from the rest of the panel. In the last quarter of the eighteenth century at the Gobelins, we have Don Quixote and Boucher small medallion pictures sometimes woven separately from the damassé backgrounds that frame them. Two of the small Boucher pictures woven for separate use are the "Fortune Teller" and "Fishing" in the Bordeaux Bourse. At Beauvais some tapestries were woven in half a dozen separate pieces, and sewed together after weaving (Plate XI, ga).

GOTHIC MANUFACTURERS

Gothic tapestries were not signed by the manufacturer. If his name appears, it is as part of an inscription. For instance, one of the lost panels of the Saint Piat and Saint Eleuthère set (Plates III, e, f) at Tournai had a French inscription reading in translation: *These cloths were made and completed in Arras by Pierrot Fere, in the gracious month of December, 1402.* Also, a lost panel of the Saint Anatoile set—two of which belonging to the Salins Museum are now in the Louvre, one in the museum of the Gobelins, and a fragment with portrait of Saint Anatoile in the Demotte collection—bore the inscription: "These fourteen pieces of tapestry were made and constructed at Bruges in the shop of Jehan Sauvage in the year 1501."

Most of the information we have about Gothic merchants and weavers comes from inventories and other ancient records on paper. The account books of the Duke of Anjou in the fourteenth century show that Nicolas Bataille of Paris received 1000 francs apiece for the famous Angers Apocalypse tapestries (Plates III, c, ca, cb, cc, d). Other tapestries sold by Bataille were: Story of Hector, to the Duke of Anjou; Story of Theseus and the Golden Eagle, to the Duke of Touraine; Story of Penthesilea, to the Duke of Orleans; Gentlemen and Ladies, Godfrey de Bouillon, Shepherds and Shepherdess, Bertram de Claiquin, to the Duke of Burgundy. Other important tapestry sales of the period were of: Roman de la Rose, Shepherdesses, Ladies leaving for the Hunt, Conquest of Babylon by Alexander the Great, Nine Heroines (*Preuses*), Charlemagne, Esau and Jacob, Percival le Gallois, Château de Franchise, Bertrand du Guesclin, Hector of Troy, by Jacques Dourdin, to the Duke of Burgundy; Story of the Credo with the Twelve Prophets and the Twelve Apostles, Coronation of the Virgin, Dourdon, the Duke of Beauvais, Destruction of Troy, Boudouin de Sebourc, Charlemagne going to the aid of King Jourdain, by Jacques Dourdin, to the Duke of Orleans; Passion of Our Lord, Judas Maccabeus, Story of the Credo, Roman de la Rose, Nine Heroes and Nine Heroines, Life of Saint Denis, Jason and the Golden Fleece, by Pierre de Beaumetz, to the Duke of Burgundy. Most of these tapestries were enriched with gold.

During a large part of the fifteenth century, the French Duke of Burgundy had more power, wealth and glory than his liege lord, the King of France. The finest tapestries were made not for Charles VII but for Philip the Good. Due perhaps to the fact that the Bishop of Tournai was very close to Philip, the most important tapestries of the middle of the fifteenth century were made in Tournai. In 1449 Philip ordered the Story of Gideon, a set of eight tapestries to hang in the chapter hall of the Order of the Golden Fleece, from Robert Dary and Jean de l'Ortie, tapestry manufacturers of Tournai. The tapestries were to cost 8960 gold crowns, to have a total area of 1120 aunes (630 square yards), to be executed in wool and silk, gold and silver, and to be delivered in four years. This would indicate an average size of 18 feet high by forty feet long. It was certainly one of the most important, if not the most important, set of tapestries made in the fifteenth century. It was displayed in 1468 at Bruges, on the occasion of the marriage of Philip's son, Charles the Bold, to the English princess, Margaret of York; at Brussels in 1498 at the baptism of Eleanor, daughter of Philip the Handsome, and elder sister of the Emperor Charles V; again at Brussels in 1555, when Charles V abdicated. It disappeared at the end of the eighteenth century.

In 1459 Philip bought from Pasquier Grenier of Tournai a story of Alexander enriched with gold and silver and measuring about 400 square yards. It included bed draperies in addition to the six wall panels, and cost 5000 gold crowns. The two Alexander tapestries in the Doria Palace at Rome (Plates V, k, ka) each 15 by 33 feet, may be part of this set. The apparent absence of gold would not necessarily prove the contrary. Gold tended to disappear almost as quickly as dark brown from Gothic tapestries made before 1480, and where it is still found is often restoration. In 1461 Philip bought from Pasquier Grenier six Passion of Our Lord tapestries rich with gold and silver for 4000 gold crowns. The average size was about 15 by 27 feet, and there were Latin inscriptions in gold on black. In 1462 Philip bought six Story of Esther tapestries from Pasquier Grenier. The Esther tapestries at Saragossa are probably part of this set or of a duplicate set. In 1462 Philip bought of Pasquier Grenier three Knight of the Swan (*Chevalier au Cygne*) tapestries, which are undoubtedly related to the fragment in the Cracow Katharinenkirche (12 by 18 feet), and the smaller fragment in the Vienna Museum of Art and Industry. In 1472 the magistracy of Bruges bought of Pasquier Grenier a Trojan War Tapestry to present to Charles the Bold. This almost certainly was part of the famous Trojan War group described by me in Chapter V.

Towards the end of the fifteenth century Brussels supplanted Tournai as the great tapestry-weaving centre. Tournai was pro-French and does not appear to have got on well with Philip the Handsome, grandson of Charles the Bold. In 1497 Tournai presented to Philip the Handsome six chambers of tapestry (*room sets*) to induce him to withdraw the edict forbidding the sale of Tournai tapestries in territory controlled by him. In 1505 Philip the Handsome bought of Jean Grenier of Tournai a Story of Banquet in six pieces (Plate IV, m), a room set of Vine Dressers, and a room set of Woodchoppers, which he took with him on his trip to Spain.

The finest tapestries of the end of the fifteenth century such as the Mazarin and the other religious tapestries similarly rich with gold, were made at Brussels during the married life of Philip the Handsome, and Joanna the Mad, daughter of Ferdinand and Isabella of Spain. To the same period and a little later belong the so-called Louis Douze tapestries, strong in blue-greens and apt to be confused in composition. While the draperies are strongly hatched and splendidly effective, most Louis Douze tapestries are obviously commercial degenerations of great tapestries like the Salvation and Credo groups (Chapter IV) and Mr. Mackay's David and Bathsheba. A great tapestry manufacturer of this period was Peter Van Aelst of Brussels who was Philip the Handsome's Chamberlain, and later made for Pope Leo X the famous Acts of the Apostles tapestries after Raphael (Plate VIII, fa). The Brussels gold tradition was worthily continued in the Early Renaissance Van Orley tapestries rich with gold.

SIGNATURES OF MANUFACTURERS

We have now reached the period when the manufacturer's signature becomes usual on tapestries. In 1528 it was ordered that henceforth all tapestries made in the Netherlands should bear the mark of the city and of the maker. The mark of Brussels, a red shield between two golden B's (standing for *Brussels, in Brabant*), continued to appear in the bottom selvages of tapestries made in Brussels for three centuries. During the rest of the sixteenth century the maker's signature was commonly his monogram, put in the right selvage near the bottom. During the seventeenth century and early eighteenth, the maker's initials or full name were woven into the bottom selvage.

The most successful Brussels tapestry manufacturer of the sixteenth century was William Van Pannemaker. He made for the Emperor Charles V the great Tunis set commemorating the Emperor's expeditions to Africa, and for the Duke of Alba, his Victories, both sets rich with gold and silver. Pannemaker's receipt to the Duke of Alba's agent, in Flemish with translation in Spanish, and signed by Pannemaker's own hand, is still preserved by the family and I have been allowed to have a photograph of the document which I hope to publish later.

The best accurate lists of tapestry signatures are those in *Birk Austrian* and *Baldass Austrain, Valencia Spanish, Boettiger Swedish,* and *Garde Meuble* (See index of books in Chapter XXII). Pannemaker's monogram, a left-handed *P* growing out of a W, the *P* sometimes being triangular like the mark of the Cross appears on hundreds of tapestries notably on the Tunis, Abraham, Apocalypse, and Capital Sins sets of the Royal Spanish collection; and on the Arms of Charles V, Deadly Sins, and Garden Views, of the National Austrian collection. Other monograms of important Brussels Renaissance tapestry manufacturers are those of François Geubels, Antoine Geubels, Nicolas Leyniers, Marc Cretif. Jan Raes of Brussels in the first quarter of the seventeenth century sometimes signs both monogram in right selvage and name in bottom selvage. (For instance, Mrs. Wheaton Vaughan's Samson and Delilah tapestries). Seventeenth century Brussels signatures often found are those of G. V. D. STRECKEN and I. V. LEEFDAEL (on the Cleopatra tapestries of the Metropolitan Museum); H. REYDAMS and E. LEYNIERS (on Mr. Hinckle Smith's monumental Judith set); at the end of the century, I. DE VOS (on the New York Public Library's Parnassus); and A. AVWERCX (on Abundance, No. 43 of the Philadelphia Tapestry Exhibition 1915).

Early Gobelin signatures are P with fleur-de-lis for Paris, and the monograms of Frans Van der Planken, Philip de Maecht who later signed at Mortlake, Hans Taxis (on the Diana set at the Morgan Memorial in Hartford); Alexander de Comans (on the Rinaldo and Armida formerly in the Hampton Shops collection); Raphael de la Planche on Mr. Albright's Diana tapestry that was No. 69 of the Buffalo Tapestry Exhibition 1914.

Signatures at the Gobelins after 1662 when it became a State institution are those of the proprietors of the different shops. G or GOB, with a fleur-de-lis, takes the place of Paris. Names that occur on the bottom selvage of tapestries in the French National collection are IANS; sometimes the monogram of Lefebvre, sometimes the name spelled out, sometimes the initials L. F.; AUDRAN (See Mr. Rockefeller's Months of Lucas), MONMERQUÉ, D. LA. CROIX (Delacroix), MOZIN, D. L. F. (Delafraye), E. LEBLOND, I. SOUET, NEILSON, COZETTE (See Mr. Mackay's Don Quixote set). There were several Jans, Lefebvres, Leblonds, Audrans, and Cozettes, son succeeding father. Of the weavers named above Jans, Lefebvre, Monmerqué, Audran and Cozette used high-warp looms, the others low-warp looms, except the elder Cozette who began on the low warp and ended on the high warp. Many Gobelin tapestries were not signed.

Beauvais signatures are those of the proprietors, BÉHAGLE, BESNIER, (Senator Clark's Fountain of Love), A.C.C. (Andre Charlemagne Charron) on Mrs. Hutton's Bacchus and Ariadne, D. M. (De Menou) on Mr. Mackay's Vasco da Gama set. Consult Chapter XI for signature of Béhagle.

The present mark of the Gobelins is a G impaled by pointed bobbin (*broche*). This draws attention to the fact that the high-warp bobbins (Plate XIX, a) are pointed at one end while low-warp bobbins are blunt at both ends. Also, the ends of Aubusson bobbins are round, while those of Beauvais are hexagonal. In a modern tapestry factory at Brussels I saw bobbins spade-shaped at one end, and was told that they were copies of ancient ones. The reason high-warp bobbins are pointed is that the pointed ends are used in pressing down the threads.

Anciently tapestries were measured in aunes (English ells). The Flemish aune was 27 inches, the French aune 46¾ inches.

The Flemish aune was used at Flanders and at Beauvais; the French aune at the Gobelins and elsewhere in France. Commercially the French *square* aune was figured as equivalent to three Flemish square aunes.

The great centres of tapestry weaving at different periods were: Paris and Arras in the fourteenth century and early fifteenth; Tournai in the middle of the fifteenth; Brussels at the end of the fifteenth and through the sixteenth; the Gobelins and Brussels in the seventeenth; the Gobelins, Beauvais, Brussels, and Aubusson in the eighteenth.

PLATES XIX, b, ba.—ON THE LEFT, BEHIND A HIGH-WARP LOOM. ON THE RIGHT, IN FRONT OF A HIGH-WARP LOOM. BOTH AT THE GOBELINS

PLATE XIX, C.—LOW—WARP TAPESTRY WEAVING AT EDGEWATER. THE WEAVER WITH HIS LEFT HAND HAS FORCED THE WARP THREADS APART SO THAT THE FIGURE ON THE CARTOON BENEATH IS CLEARLY SEEN

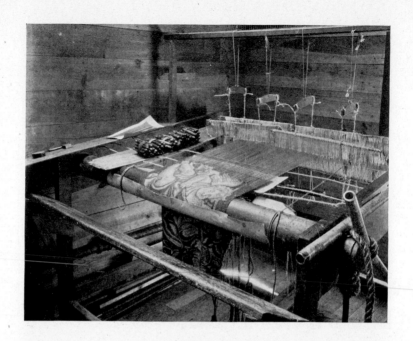

PLATES XIX, e, ea.—ABOVE, SUPPLEMENTING AN ANCIENT FRAGMENT ON A SMALL LOW-WARP LOOM. BELOW, FRICTION LEVERS BIND THE ROLLERS AND KEEP THE WARP TAUT, JUST AS THEY DID FIVE HUNDRED YEARS AGO

PLATES XIX, f, fa.—ABOVE, SPINNING WHEEL, AND SPOOLS OF WOOLEN THREAD.
BELOW, BOBBINS WOUND WITH WOOL OR SILK, AND STOCK OF YARN

PLATE XIX, g.—JARS AND FIRKINS OF DYE MATERIALS. COFFEE GRINDER TO PULVERIZE THE COCHINEAL

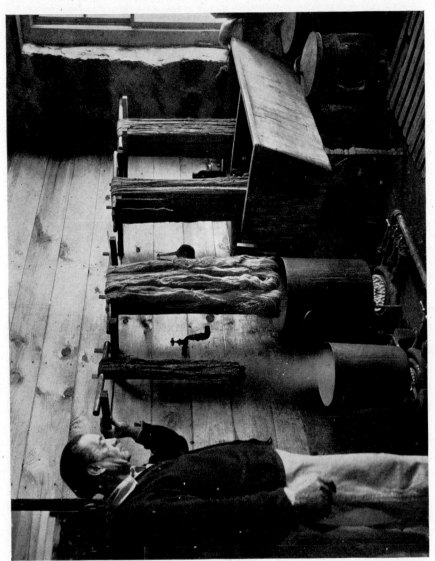

PLATE XIX, h.—THE DYER AND HIS VATS

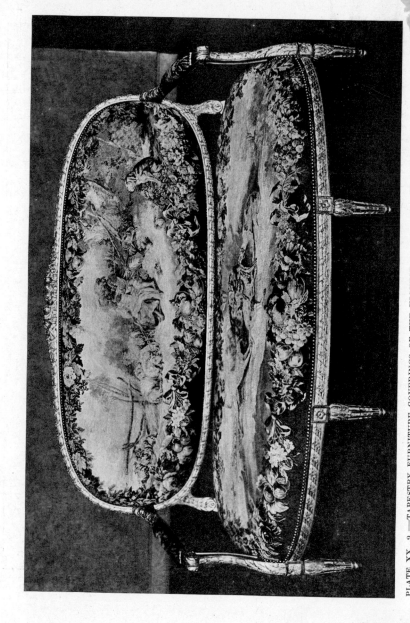

PLATE XX, a.—TAPESTRY FURNITURE COVERINGS OF THE HIGHEST CLASS AND MADE AT THE GOBELINS. BACK BY BOUCHER, SEAT BY OUDRY. FLORAL BORDERS BY TESSIER. DUVEEN BROS.

CHAPTER XX

TAPESTRY FURNITURE COVERINGS

IN THE Gothic fourteenth and fifteenth centuries pillow and cushion tops, as well as bed draperies, were often woven as part of room sets of tapestry, and also separately. The evidence is literary only. In the Renaissance sixteenth century, and in the early seventeenth century, coverings for sofas and chairs were woven in floral and grotesque designs like the borders of Late Renaissance tapestries. Much of the Renaissance tapestry now found on furniture consists of borders and small grotesque panels cut up and turned from their original purpose. In the seventeenth century tapestries were less common on furniture than velvets, damasks, brocades and embroideries. We have, however, a number of ancient tapestry examples both French and Flemish.

The great century for tapestry furniture coverings was the eighteenth. Furniture came into more general use than ever before, and seats and backs were upholstered for everybody. France set the pace; Flanders was a poor second. From England we have a number of good sets made by weavers who had been at Mortlake, and by their pupils, and by immigrant French weavers.

The low-warp loom is most efficient on floral and ornamental designs, and on a small scale. Most of the furniture coverings of the first half of the eighteenth century were made at Beauvais on low-warp looms, and a few of the finest on low-warp looms at the Gobelins in the third quarter of the century by Neilson.

Oudry and Boucher who set the pace in the designing of wall tapestries, also surpassed in the designing of furniture tapestries. Oudry's illustrations of Lafontaine's Fables were extremely popular on the backs of chairs and sofas, usually

19   271

with floral designs on the seats; but were before long often supplanted on the backs by Boucher's dainty pastorals with figures, and sought refuge in the seats. At the same time Oudry designs often appeared on both seat and back (Plates XX, e, ea, f) and many all-floral seats and backs were made.

Famous all floral sets are the one in the National Austrian collection, with screens and Boucher picture-medallion wall tapestries to match; and the Duke of Cumberland's set which has just arrived in America, as fresh as the day it was made, never having been used. Both of these sets were made by Neilson at the Gobelins. Several important Beauvais sets from the designs of Salembier (Plate XX, g) are also now in America.

The finest set of furniture coverings ever made is the one in the possession of Sir George Cooper, with Boucher pictures on both seat and back, woven for Madame de Pompadour by Neilson at the Gobelins. Almost as fine is the set illustrated (Plates XX, a, b, c), with Boucher pictures on the back and Oudry Lafontaine pictures on the seat. The floral borders by Tessier are indescribably rich in colour and texture and in design are unsurpassed. Note how wonderfully flowers and fruit soften the foreground on the seats.

The example set at Beauvais and the Gobelins was followed at Aubusson, from which we have many attractive sets with white ground, especially in the period of Louis XVI, with Boucher and Oudry designs copied and developed by Huet and others.

Other designers of Beauvais furniture tapestries were Leprince and Casanova; for the Gobelins, Charles Coypel, Fontenay, Perrot, Eisen, Jacques, and Tessier.

PLATE XX, b.—ONE OF THE CHAIRS BELONGING TO THE SET OF WHICH
PLATE XX, a, SHOWS THE SOFA. DUVEEN BROS.

PLATE XX, C.—ANOTHER OF THE CHAIRS BELONGING TO THE SET OF WHICH
THE SOFA IS ILLUSTRATED ON PLATE XX, a. DUVEEN BROS.

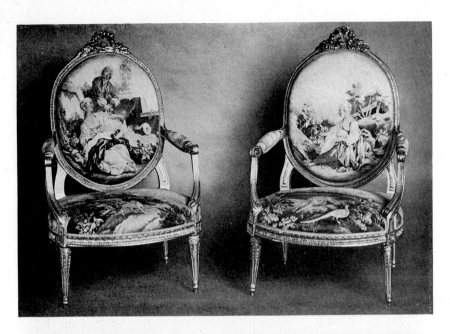

PLATES XX, d, da.—BEAUVAIS TAPESTRY FURNITURE COVERINGS IN THE LOUVRE;
BACKS BY BOUCHER, SEATS BY OUDRY

PLATES XX, e, ea.—BACK AND SEAT OF A SET OF BEAUVAIS TAPESTRY FURNITURE COVERINGS DESIGNED BY OUDRY. ON THE LEFT, THE FOX BANQUETS THE CRANE. ON THE RIGHT, THE CRANE BANQUETS THE FOX. DUVEEN BROS.

PLATE XX, f.—SOFA OF A SET OF FURNITURE COVERINGS DESIGNED BY OUDRY AND WOVEN AT BEAUVAIS. THE SEAT AND BACK OF ONE OF THE CHAIRS ARE ILLUSTRATED ON THE OPPOSITE PAGE. DUVEEN BROS.

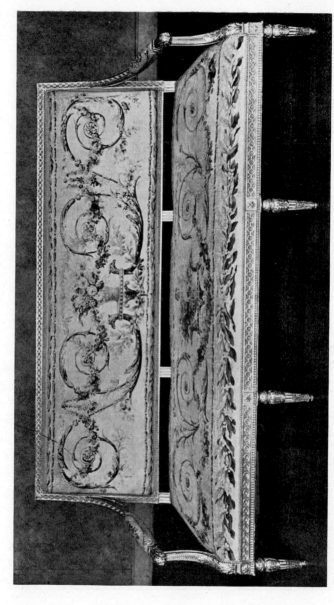

PLATE XX, g.—BEAUVAIS SOFA, ONE OF A SET OF LOUIS XVI TAPESTRY FURNITURE COVERINGS DESIGNED BY
SALEMBIER. IN THE COLLECTION OF DUVEEN BROS.

CHAPTER XXI

MODERN TAPESTRIES

I AM very much in sympathy with what Monsieur Geoffroi and Monsieur Ajalbert are trying to do at the Gobelins and at Beauvais. They are employing the best French painters to originate cartoons that shall be as representative of French art of today as were the cartoons of Louis XIV and Louis XV, and of the Gothic fourteenth and fifteenth centuries, representative of French art of those periods. I feel they deserve so much credit for what they have already accomplished that I do not wish to criticise them for what they have as yet failed to accomplish.

The Gobelins is the artistic centre of tapestry weaving. From the paint point of view the designs used at the Gobelins are superior. There is none of the bad drawing so common elsewhere. Often the colours have real tapestry strength, and sometimes the compositions have real tapestry power. Yet none of them equal in tapestry merit the compositions developed for Merton by Burne-Jones and William Morris, and one or two of their immediate followers. The weave, however, of modern Gobelins is distinctly better than that of the best picture cloths of Merton. The design of the Merton verdure in the Metropolitan Museum is better than the weave. The finest Morris-Jones tapestries are the Holy Grail set of twelve made for Stanmore Hall, Middlesex. It was part of the Stanmore Hall sale at Sotheby's July 16, 1920 (Plates 129, 131, 133, of *Hunter 1912*). The modern Gobelin tapestry that I like best is Gorguet's "Vertumnus and Pomona" (1903). It was a great advance over Jules Lefebvre's "Nymph and Bacchus" (1888). Charming with its flowers and Gothic lettering, but not overstrong, is the "Joan of Arc" set by J. P. Laurens, exhibited at San Francisco in 1915 and at

Brooklyn in 1918 (Illustrated in the catalogue). Charming but out of balance and out of scale are Jean Verber's "La Belle au Bois Dormant" and "Le Petit Poucet"; also Raffaelli's "La Bretagne," Anquetin's "La Bourgone," and especially Chéret's "Printemps," "La Danse" and "Le Dejeuner sur l'Herbe." More interesting in subject than in execution are Toudouze's historical panels, in the Court of Justice at Rennes; and Willette's "Salut à Paris." Blanc's "Les Armes de la Ville de Paris" is excellent, but might have been woven more in accordance with the capabilities of tapestry texture. Braquemond's "L'Arc en Ciel," and Madame Cazin's "Diane," show how not to do it. They look like weak imitations of the Brussels Renaissance Poésies (Ganymede, Andromeda, Marsyas, Icarus, Polixena) in the Royal Spanish collection. Maurice Taqoy's furniture coverings, made at Beauvais for the Compagnie des Arts Français, are up-to-date in style and altogether fascinating. They are like what Oudry might do if he were still alive.

The making of tapestries at Aubusson is hampered by the failure of the French Government to coöperate sufficiently with the industry. The local museum, which should be rich with ancient tapestries of an inspirational type, is shamefully neglected. Most of the weavers have no opportunity to study the great examples of the past. Even the large manufacturers do not show sufficient initiative in training the men who sit at the loom. Aubusson is at its best in the reproduction of eighteenth century furniture coverings.

Some of the best weaving in the world is done in a small way at Paris, mostly in connection with the repairing and cleaning of tapestries. Unfortunately too many of the weavers regard the copying of paintings in paint technique as the summit of their ambitions.

The rugs made at the Royal Tapestry Factory in Madrid are so good that the tapestries ought to be better.

Of the three principal tapestry plants in New York, the

Baumgartens have made the best reproductions of Gobelin Bouchers; the Herter Looms have employed the most original designs; the Edgewater Factory has been most successful in weaving for the trade, and in developing texture that without having all the refinements of ancient Gothic texture, avoids the boardlike surface of many modern tapestries. Many of the Edgewater tapestries are superior to many of the inexpensive tapestries of the sixteenth, seventeenth and eighteenth centuries. The furniture coverings in the style of cross stitch needlework are admirable.

As for the "fake" Gothics said to be made in Spain—well, that is another story. They come nearer than any other modern tapestries to achieving the texture of Perfected Tapestries. They are good enough to be sold honestly.

The trouble with most modern tapestries is not their newness. They look better new than they do ten years later. The faults are fundamental.

It would seem to go without saying that designs should fit the process. Textiles depend for expression upon the threads of which they are composed. These threads being coloured and toned from light to dark are able by contrast of colours and of light and shade to simulate many of the effects of paint. But their peculiar and principal power is, by contrast of threads, which are lines in relief, to secure the line effects that are suggested by the flat lines of engraving but realized only in textiles.

Modern tapestries look weak and are weak. They employ the line contrasts that are shared by tapestries with the other textiles, but few of them go far beyond the primitive stage in the utilization of the line contrasts that are peculiar to tapestries, and that were developed to perfection in Gothic tapestries. (Consult Chapter XVII.)

The characteristic feature of tapestries—that which makes them the wonderful things that they are—cannot be put on paper or canvas. While it can be suggested in small colour sketches in oil, to put it into full-size cartoons is impossible. We have no right to blame tapestry designers for not making cartoons that look like tapestries. The tapestry part is up to the weaver. But we have the right to insist that tapestry designers shall create compositions lending themselves to interpretation in tapestry texture, which give opportunity for the free employment of tapestry technique, and which do not call for the imitation of paint technique and of stunts that are peculiarly the glory of the painter.

I repeat, *we have the right to insist that tapestry designers shall create compositions lending themselves to interpretation in tapestry texture.* This means that the compositions shall be well covered, like the compositions of great Gothic tapestries (Plates IV, f, g, i, j, l, n; V, b, c, j; VI, a, b, f, m)—human figures and trees and buildings architecturally arranged with a maximum of vertical and a minimum of horizontal effects, with a minimum of shadows and a maximum of large line and colour contrasts—adjacent personages in contrasting colours, personages in the foreground pushed forward by personages and architecture in the middle-ground, personages and architecture in the middle-ground; pushed forward by personages and architecture and landscapes, on a smaller scale, in the upper ground. The designs as a whole should be silhouetted, without attempt at sculptural presentations in the round. Tapestry texture can take flat designs and, through the magic of the bobbin, produce relief effects far stronger on a large scale than those of brush and chisel.

The colour should be strong. Grays should be produced by the blending of bright colours, and not by the thinning of weak ones. One of the great faults of most modern tapestries is tameness of colour.

Even if we had brilliant modern tapestry designs we have not the weavers competent to interpret them. And if we had weavers competent to interpret them we have no factories where the transformation into tapestry technique would be

permitted. Oudry, at the Gobelins in the middle of the eighteenth century, took the heart out of tapestry weavers by
ordering them to copy the full-size cartoons exactly, without
introducing the modifications that make a tapestry *different*
from the cartoon, and superior to it. Oudry set a precedent
that was fatal. Within thirty years his ideas were dominant
at both the Gobelins and Beauvais, and have been dominant
there ever since. When I asked my late lamented friend,
Monsieur Jules Guiffrey, Administrator of the Gobelins, why
no great tapestries were being made at the Gobelins, he
replied: "The painters won't let us."

I believe there are many weavers, at the Gobelins and elsewhere, who would be competent to interpret great tapestry
designs boldly, if they were encouraged to study and imitate
the technique of the middle of the fifteenth century. It would
help them to copy some of the great fifteenth century tapestries
that have not been spoiled by the repairer—copy literally I
mean, with the same number of ribs to the inch, with warps
and wefts of the same size spun in the same way out of similar
fibres, and with only the same colours in the dyepot. The
details illustrated on Plates S, e, f, i, j, l, q, t, of the *Subscribers' Edition,* and on Plates XVII, b, f, are a liberal education in tapestry texture.

PLATES XXI, a, aa.—ABOVE, MODERN AMERICAN VERDURE WITH COAT—OF—ARMS.
EDGEWATER TAPESTRY LOOMS. BELOW, DETAIL OF SAME

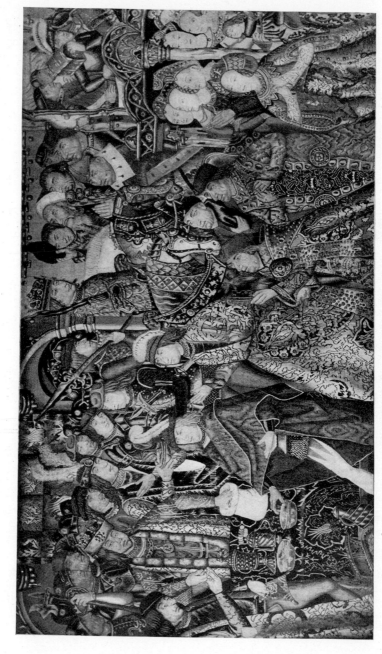

PLATE XXI, b.—BRENNUS, BRITISH KING OF GAUL. A GOTHIC TAPESTRY FROM THE THIRD QUARTER OF THE FIFTEENTH CENTURY. DUVEEN BROS.

PLATE XXI, C.—ARRIVAL OF PSYCHE AT CUPID'S PALACE, ONE OF MRS. RICE'S PERFECT SET OF FIVE BEAUVAIS—BOUCHERS

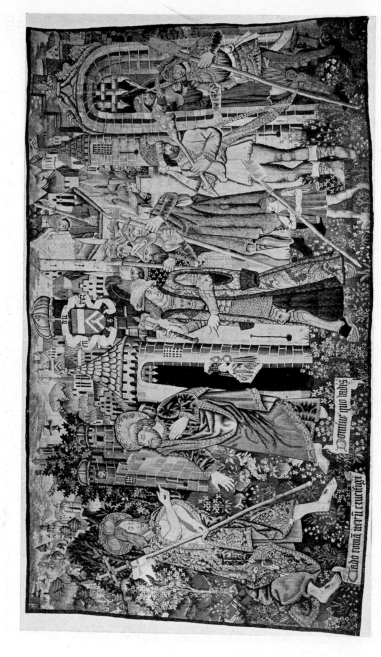

PLATE XXI, d.—QUO VADIS, ONE OF A SET OF GOTHIC SAINT PETER TAPESTRIES, MADE IN THE THIRD QUARTER OF THE
FIFTEENTH CENTURY. FORMERLY IN THE BLANCHET COLLECTION. JACQUES SELIGMANN & SON

PLATE XXI, c.—YOUTH, ONE OF THREE BRILLIANT GOTHIC TAPESTRIES FROM THE CHÂTEAU DE CHAUMONT. IN THE COLLECTION OF DUVEEN BROS.

PLATES XXI, f, fa.—ABOVE, PIERRE DE ROHAN SINGS TO HIS WIFE'S
PLAYING, A GOTHIC TAPESTRY MADE ABOUT 1510; CATHEDRAL OF
ANGERS. BELOW, ADORATION OF THE MAGI, A GOTHIC TAPESTRY
FROM THE MIDDLE OF THE FIFTEENTH CENTURY; BERNE MUSEUM

PLATE XXI, g.—AUTUMN, ONE OF THE SET OF FOUR GOBELIN SEASONS OF LUCAS THAT ADORN THE WALLS OF THE BROOKLINE TRUST CO.

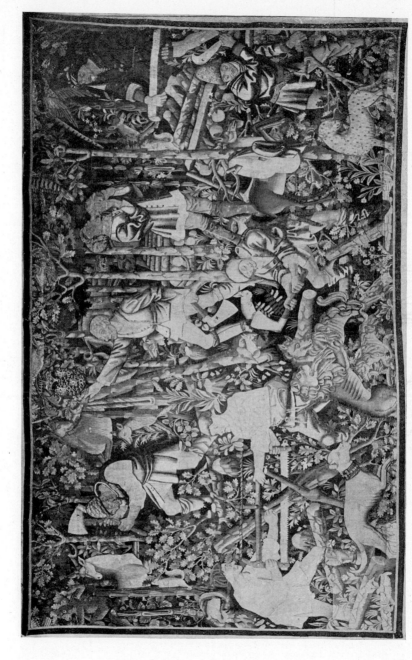

PLATE XXI, h.—THE WOOD CUTTERS, A GOTHIC TAPESTRY FROM THE MIDDLE OF THE FIFTEENTH CENTURY, IN THE MUSÉE DES ARTS DÉCORATIFS. THE COAT-OF-ARMS IS THAT OF ROLIN, CHANCELLOR OF PHILIP THE GOOD

CHAPTER XXII

PUBLIC COLLECTIONS AND TAPESTRY LITERATURE

THE most important public collections of tapestries to be seen are:

In FRANCE: *Gothic,* at Angers, the Louvre, Cluny Museum, Reims; *Late Gothic* and *Gothic-Renaissance* religious sets, at Angers, Saumur, La Chaise Dieu, Aix-en-Provence, the Gobelins. *Gobelins,* at the Louvre, the Gobelins, Fontainebleau, Chantilly, Pau.

In SPAIN: *Gothic,* at Saragossa, Palencia, Zamora, Burgos. *Late Gothic* rich with gold, the Royal collection in Madrid, and Saragossa. *Flemish Renaissance,* the Royal collection in Madrid. *Spanish eighteenth century,* the Escurial and the Pardo.

Most of the world's Late Gothics rich with gold, are in the Royal Spanish collection. Many of the finest earlier Gothics are in Spanish cathedrals. The only set of fourteenth century Gothics is at Angers.

In ENGLAND: *Gothic* at the Victoria and Albert Museum, and Hampton Court. *Flemish Renaissance,* at Hampton Court. *Mortlake,* at the Victoria and Albert Museum, and at the Lady Lever Museum, Port Sunlight, near Liverpool.

In SWITZERLAND: *Gothic,* at Berne; *German-Swiss Gothic,* at Basel and Zurich.

In GERMANY: *German Gothic,* at Nuremburg, Regensburg, and Berlin. *Flemish Renaissance,* in Berlin.

In the UNITED STATES: *Gothic,* in the New York Metropolitan Museum, and the Boston Museum of Fine Arts. *Flemish Renaissance,* in the New York Metropolitan Museum, and the Boston Museum of Fine Arts. *French* and *Flemish seventeenth century,* in the New York Metropolitan Museum. *Beauvais-Bouchers,* in the New York Metropolitan Museum.

In AUSTRIA : *Flemish Renaissance,* and *Flemish seventeenth and eighteenth century; Gobelins,* and *early eighteenth century Lotharingian,* in the National Austrian collection at Vienna and Schönbrunn.

In SWEDEN : *Gobelins, Mortlake,* and *Flemish seventeenth century,* in the Royal Swedish collection, at Stockholm.

In ITALY : *Late Gothic, Flemish Renaissance, Gobelins,* at the Vatican; *Gobelins, Beauvais-Bouchers,* at the Quirinal; *Florentine Renaissance* and *Florentine seventeenth century, Flemish Renaissance, Gobelins,* in the Royal Italian collection at Florence.

Spain stands first in the possession of great Gothic tapestries. The United States comes next but with nearly all the important pieces in private possession. Spain is first for Flemish Renaissance tapestries rich with gold; and Austria, second. France is many times first for Gobelins. The finest full-size tapestry cartoons are those of Raphael at the Victoria and Albert Museum. The most important ancient sketches of Gothic tapestries are those of the Trojan War set at the Louvre.

DESCRIPTIVE LIST OF BOOKS REFERRED TO IN THE TEXT
AND SOME OTHERS THAT THE STUDENT WILL
FIND INTERESTING

ALBA, 1877 — Sale Catalogue of the Collection de S. A. le Duc de Berwick et Alba, including 75 tapestries, among them three of the Van Orley Passion set rich with gold, and six of the great Gothic Salvation set.

ALFASSA MAXIMILIAN — Les Tapisseries des Chasses de Maximilien, By Paul Alfassa. The best work on the subject. In the *Gazette des Beaux-Arts,* 1920, Volume LXII, pp. 127–140, 233–256.

ANDERSON MORTLAKE — A Short Account of the Tapestry Works at Mortlake. By John Eustace Anderson. It reproduces King James' copy of the agreement made by Henri IV with Comans and Planche. The only copy of this is type-written, and in the Library of the Victoria and Albert Museum.

ARCHIVES — Catalogue illustré des Cliches Photographiques des Archives de la Commission des Monuments Historiques. Many tapestry photographs that can be purchased.

ARTS DÉCORATIFS, 1907 — Les Chefs-d'Oeuvre du Musée des Arts Décoratifs. Shows some of the Tapestries. Paris, 1907.

ASTIER SCIPIO — La Belle Tapisserie du Roy. By Colonel d'Astier. An exhaustive study of Scipio tapestries. Paris, 1907.

AUSTRIAN INDEX — Die Wiener Gobelinssammlung. Verzeichnis der Photographien. Indexes by (1) factories, (2) manufacturers, (3) designers and cartoonists, (4) subjects of the photographs of all the tapestries, including many photographs of details, in the National Austrian collection. Indispensable.

BADIN BEAUVAIS — La Manufacture de Tapisseries de Beauvais depuis ses origines jusqu'a nos jours. By Jules Badin. Much valuable raw material. Paris, 1909.

BALDASS AUSTRIAN — Die Wiener Gobelinssammlung, drei hundert Bildtafeln mit beschreibendem Text und wissenschafthchen Anmerkungen. By Ludwig Baldass. Three hundred illustrations, with critical description, of tapestries in the National Austrian collection. Vienna, 1920.

BAILLIE-GROHMAN — Sporting Art, from the fifteenth to the eighteenth century. By William A. Baillie-Grohman. Illustration and description of the Hunts of Maximilian and other hunting tapestries. London, 1919.

BÉDIER ÉPIQUES — Les Légendes Épiques, recherches sur le formation der Chansons de Geste. By Joseph Bédier. The best book on Chansons de Gestes. Paris, 1914–21.

BERTAUX SARAGOSSA — L'Exposition Retrospective de Saragosse. By Emile Bertaux. Tapestries of the Saragossa cathedrals illustrated and described at considerable length. Saragossa and Paris, 1908.

BIRK AUSTRIAN — Inventar der in Besitze der Allerhochsten Kaiserhauses befindlichen Niederlander Tapeten und Gobelins. By Dr. Ernest Ritter von Birk. In the *Austrian Jahrbuch* 1882, 1883, 1884, 1885.

BODENHAUSEN DAVID — Gerard David und seine Schule. By Eberhard Freiherr von Bodenhausen. The best book on the subject. Munich, 1905.

BOETTIGER SWEDISH — Svenska Statens Samling af Vafda Tapeter. By Dr. John Boettiger. In Swedish and French.

BRITTANICA TAPESTRY — Tapestry, in the eleventh edition of the Encyclopedia Brittanica. By Alan S. Cole. An excellent article well illustrated. December, 1911.

BRUGES, 1907 — Chefs-d'Oeuvre d'Art Ancien a l'Exposition de la Toison d'Or, at Bruges in 1907. Illustrates the Esther and Ahasuerus tapestries of the Cathedrals of Saragossa, and many important Burgundian portraits.

BRUSSELS, 1910 — L'Art Belge au XVII siècle, mémorial de l'Exposition d'art ancien à Bruxelles en 1910.

BRUSSELS, 1905 — Tapisseries et Sculptures Bruxelloises a l'Exposition d'art ancien bruxellois, organisée a Bruxelles au cercle artistique et littéraire, de juillet à octobre, 1905. By Joseph Destrée. Plates I to XXXI are of Tapestries.

BRUSSELS, 1880 — Les Tapisseries Historiées à l'Exposition Belge de 1880. By Alphonse Wauters.

BUFFALO, 1914 — The Buffalo Tapestry Exhibition. With important illustrations. In (Buffalo) *Academy Notes,* October, 1914.

BURKHARDT BASEL — Gewirkte Bildteppiche des XV und XVI Jahr hunderts im Historischen Museum zu Basel. By Rudolf F. Burckhardt. The best book on German Swiss tapestries. The many colored illustrations are of the first order, and the text is valuable and interesting. Leipzig, 1923.

CALVERT SPANISH — The Royal Spanish Tapestries. By Albert F. Calbert, with 277 illustrations. London, 1921.

CHANSON DE ROLAND — La Chanson de Roland. Texte critique, traduction et commentaire, grammaire et glossaire. By Léon Gautier. Tours, 1920.

CLUNY, 1883 — Catalogue by E. du Somérard. Describes the David and the Unicorn sets, and others.

CONCORDANCE — Concordantiarum universæ scripturæ sacræ Thesaurus. By Peultier, Etienne, Gautois, and others of the Society of the Jesuits. A concordance to the Vulgate, with full lines quoted. Indispensable in studying religious tapestries.

COX LYONS — L'Art de décorer les Tissus. Illustration of tapestries in the Lyons Museum.

CRICK-KUNZIGER — Guillaume de Hellande's Tapestries. By Marthe Crick-Kunziger. In the *Burlington Magazine,* November, 1924. With note by George Leland Hunter, in the *Burlington Magazine,* April, 1925.

DEMOTTE GOTHIC — La Tapisserie Gothique, with preface by Solomon Reinach. The finest book ever published on Tapestries. There are 100 large and magnificent illustrations in color, of precious Gothics. Demotte. Paris, 1925.

DERLEYEN REGENS-BURG — Die Altdeutschen Wandteppiche im Regensburger Rathause. By Friedrich von Derleyen and Adolf Spamer. Some of the illustrations are in color. Regensburg, 1910.

DESTRÉE CINQUENTE-
NAIRE Les Tapisseries des Musées Royaux du Cinquente-
naire. By Joseph Destrée and Paul van den Ven.
Well illustrated. Brussels, 1910.

DESTRÉE GOES Hugo van den Goes. By Joseph Destrée. Brussels,
1914.

DESTRÉE ROME Maitre Philippe auteur de Cartons de Tapisserie, à
propos de Jean de Bruxelles dit Van Room. By
Joseph Destrée. Brussels, 1904.

DOUTREPONT
BOURGOGNE La Littérature Francaise à la cour des Ducs Bourgogne. By Georges Doutrepont. Paris, 1909.

FARCY ANGERS Histoire, et Description des Tapisseries de la Cathe-
drale d'Angers. By L. de Farcy. Indispensable.
Lille and Angers, undated.

FENAILLE GOBELINS État générale des Tapisseries de la Manufacture des
Gobelins depuis son origine jusqu'a nos jours (1600–
1900). By Maurice Fenaille. An elaborate descriptive and illustrated inventory of tapestries made at
the Gobelins and Fontainebleau. The best work of
the kind ever published. In five volumes, with
splendid index. Paris, 1903–1923.

FFOULKE The Ffoulke Collection of Tapestries. Many tapestries described, and 74 illustrated. New York, 1913.

FRIEDLANDER ORLEY Bernaert van Orley. By Max J. Friedlander, in the
Prussian Jahrbuch, 1908, 1909. The only important
work on Van Orley as designer of tapestries and
as painter.

GAYLEY MYTHS The Classic Myths in English Literature and Art.
By Charles Mills Gayley. Indispensable in studying
mythological tapestries.

GEOFFROY GOBELINS Les Gobelins, avec 42 illustrations sans texte et 110
illustrations dans le texte. By Gustave Geoffroy,
Director of the Gobelins. Illustration of ancient and
modern Gobelins. Paris, 1924.

GÖBEL TAPESTRIES This is *Göbel Wandteppiche* translated into English
and abbreviated. In one volume. New York, 1914.

GÖBEL WANDTEPPICHE Wandteppiche, die Niederlände. Illustrations of 508
tapestries. Volume I, Text; Volume II, Plates. Shows
wide acquaintance with Tapestry Literature and
Tapestry Photographs. Good indexes. Leipsic, 1923.

GONZAGA LUZIO — Gli Arazzi dei Gonzaga restituiti dall' Austria. Illustration and description of the Raphael's Acts of the Apostles Tapestries, originally in the Gonzaga collection at Mantua, but alienated to Vienna in 1866 by order of Emperor Francis Joseph, and returned to Italy as one of the results of the Great War. Bergamo, 1919.

GOYA TAPICES — Los Tapices de Goya. By D. G. Cruzada Villaamil.

GROSCH NORWEGIAN — Gamle Norske Billedtaepper. By H. Grosch. Text in Norwegian and German. Color plates of twelve ancient tapestries made in Norway. Berlin, 1901.

GUERIN CHINOISERIE — Le Chinoiserie en Europe au XVIII Siècle. By Jacques Guérin. With illustration of Vernansal's Chinese set made at Beauvais, and of Boucher's Chinese sets made at Beauvais and at Aubusson. Paris, 1901.

GUICHARD GARDE MEUBLE — Les Tapisseries Décoratives du Garde Meuble. By Ed. Guichard, with text by Alfred Darcel. Splendid illustrations of Tapestries in the National French collection. Paris, undated.

GUIFFREY BIBLIOGRAPHY — La Tapisserie, bibliographic critique de la Tapisserie dans les differents pays de l'Europe, depuis ses origines jusqu'a nos jours. Paris, 1904.

GUIFFREY GOBELINS — Les Gobelins and Beauvais. By Jules Guiffrey. A brief but useful illustrated book on the factories and tapestries of the Gobelins and Beauvais.

GUIFFREY GOMBAUT — Les Amours de Gombaut et de Macée. By Jules Guiffrey. A study of the Gombaut and Macée set in the Museum of Saint-Lô. Paris, 1882.

GUIFFREY HISTOIRE — Histoire de la Tapisserie. By Jules Guiffrey. A fine pioneer work, with excellent index. Tours, 1886.

GUIFFREY SEIZIÈME — Les Tapestries du Douzième à la Fin du Seizième Siècle. By Jules Guiffrey.

HAVARD GOBELINS — *Les Manufactures Nationales*, Les Gobelins, Sèvres, Beauvais. By Henry Havard et Marius Vachon. Paris, 1889.

HISTOIRE GÉNÉRALE — Three huge and unwieldy volumes: French Tapestries, by Guiffrey; Flemish tapestries, by Pinchart; Italian, German and English tapestries by Müntz. Much raw material. Some important illustrations. Paris, 1874–1884.

HOENTSCHEL MORGAN — Volume I of the illustrated catalogue of the Collections Georges Hoentschel acquises pas M. J. Pierpont Morgan. Plates LX to LXXII are of Tapestries. Paris, 1908.

HUNTER ACHILLES — Achilles Tapestries designed by Rubens, with especial reference to the three in the Boston Museum of Fine Arts. By George Leland Hunter. In the *International Studio,* December, 1913.

HUNTER APOSTLES — The Acts of the Apostles Tapestries, after Raphael. By George Leland Hunter. In the *International Studio,* 1913.

HUNTER CHICAGO — Tapestries in the Chicago Art Institute. By George Leland Hunter. In *House Beautiful,*

HUNTER CLEVELAND — The Cleveland Tapestry Exhibition. By George Leland Hunter. In *American Magazine of Art,* February, 1919.

HUNTER ENCYCLOPEDIA — The article on *Tapestry* in the New International Encyclopedia, New York, 1907.

HUNTER, 1912 — Tapestries, their Origin, History and Renaissance. By George Leland Hunter. New York and London, 1912.

HUNTER EXHIBITIONS — The Tapestry Exhibitions of New York and Buffalo. By George Leland Hunter. In *Arts and Decoration,* November, 1914.

HUNTER EXHIBITIONS — Catalogues of the Tapestry Exhibitions of Brooklyn, 1914; Avery Library, 1914; Buffalo, 1914; Philadelphia, 1915; Cleveland, 1918; Detroit, 1919. By George Leland Hunter.

HUNTER GODS — The Loves of the Gods, most famous of the six splendid sets of Beauvais-Boucher tapestries. With illustration of the Metropolitan Museum's "Venus and Vulcan." In *Arts and Decoration,* March, 1923.

HUNTER GOLD — Tapestries rich with Gold. By George Leland Hunter. With illustrations of three of Bernard Van Orley's great Passion set; Mr. Philip Lehman's Last Supper; the Road to Calvary, and Gethsemane, of the Royal Spanish collection. In *Arts and Decoration,* December, 1922.

HUNTER METAMOR-
PHOSES

The Metamorphoses of Ovid. By George Leland Hunter. Illustration and description of an Aubusson set of Oudry's Metamorphoses. In *Arts and Decoration,* June, 1915.

HUNTER METROPOLI-
TAN

Tapestries at the Metropolitan Museum. By George Leland Hunter. In the *International Studio,* February, 1912.

HUNTER MUSEUMS

Tapestries in American Museums. By George Leland Hunter. In the *International Studio,* 1913

HUNTER PARNASSUS

Parnassus, a tapestry in the New York Public Library. By George Leland Hunter. In the *Bulletin* of the Library, August, 1915, and separately as a pamphlet.

HUNTER ROMANTIC

The Romantic Interest of Tapestries. By George Leland Hunter. With important illustrations. In the *Brooklyn Museum Quarterly,* March, 1914.

HUNTER SACRAMENTS

Burgundian Tapestries in the Metropolitan Museum. By George Leland Hunter. This article established the facts about the Metropolitan Museum's Seven Sacraments. In the *Burlington Magazine,* December, 1907.

HUNTER TEXTILES

Decorative Textiles. An illustrated book on coverings for furniture, walls and floors, including damasks, brocades and velvets, tapestries, laces, embroideries, chintzes, cretonnes, drapery and furniture trimmings, wall papers, carpets and rugs, and illuminated leathers. By George Leland Hunter. Chapters XII to XVI, on Tapestries. Philadelphia, 1918.

JOURDAIN DE BLAYE

Amis et Amiles and Jourdains de Blaivies. Edited by Konrad Hofman. Erlangen, 1882.

JUBINAL TAPISSERIES

Les Anciennes Tapisseries Historiées. By Achille Jubinal. Ninety-nine large plates in line, hand colored, from drawings by Victor Sansonnetti, of famous Gothic tapestries. The text is interesting. Paris, 1838.

20

JULLEVILLE MYSTÈRES   Les Mystères. By L. Petit de Julleville. Paris, 1880. The best book on the French Gothic religious theatre.

KANN, 1907   Volume II of the catalogue of the Rodolphe Kann collection. Illustration of Boucher's Noble Pastorale, and Oudry's Comedies of Molière.

KOCH KUNSTWERKE   Kunstwerke und Bücher am Markte. By Gunther Koch. Esslinger, 1915.

KURT BUSANT   Mittelhochdeutsche Dichtungen auf Wandteppichen des XV Jahrhunderts. By Betty Kurt. A study of the "Story of the Kite" (*Busant*) tapestries at the Nuremberg, and Victoria and Albert Museums; also, of the "Queen of France and the Faithless Marshal" in the Nuremberg Museum. Good work. In the *Austrian Jahrbuch,* 1915.

KURT TOURNAI   Die Blutzeit der Bildwirkerkunst zu Tournai. By Betty Kurt. Brilliant and indispensable study of Gothic tapestries made at Tournai. In the *Austrian Jahrbuch,* 1917.

LAFONTAINE FABLES   Fables de Lafontaine, *avec les Figures d'Oudry.* Réimpression de l'edition Desaint et Saillant, 1755. Oudry's famous illustrations of Lafontaine's Fables, many of which were woven over and over again into chair and sofa tapestry seats and backs at Beauvais and Aubusson, and also into seats at the Gobelins. Lévy, Paris, 1886.

LAFONTAINE PSYCHE   Les Amours de Psyché et de Cupidon. By Jean de Lafontaine. With lithographed reproductions of Agostino Veneziano's engravings of the Story of Psyche, from sketches made in the studio of Raphael. Didot, Paris, 1825.

LAROUSSE DICTION-NAIRE   Grand Dictionnaire Universel. By Pierre Larousse. Indispensable. Paris, 1866 to 1876.

LAROUSSE LITTERATURE   Histoire de la Littérature Francaise, illustrée. By Joseph Bédier and Paul Hazard. Convenient in studying the literary sources of Gothic and other French tapestries. Paris, 1924.

LÉGENDE DOREE   La Légende Dorée, par Jacques de Voragine. Traduite du Latin. Gosselin, Paris, 1843.

LOEB METAMORPHOSES Ovid Metamorphoses, Latin text, with English translation by Frank Justus Miller. Indispensable in studying mythological tapestries. London and New York, 1916.

LESSING JACOB Die Wandteppiche aus dem Leben des Erzvaters Jacob. By Julius Lessing. Large illustrations of the set of ten Story of Jacob Renaissance tapestries formerly in Bologna, now in a German private collection.

LESSING WANDTEP-PICHE Wandteppiche und Decken des Mittelalters in Deutschland. By Julius Lessing and Max Creutz. With large illustrations, some in color, of medieval German tapestries. Berlin, 1872.

LOEB PSYCHE Apuleius, the Golden Ass, being the Metamorphoses of Lucius Apuleius. Latin text, with English translation. Contains the Story of Psyche, as told by the Old Woman. London and New York, 1919.

MADRID, 1893 Catálogo General of the Exposicion Historico-Europea, 1892–1893. Contains much information not elsewhere accessible about tapestries of the Spanish cathedrals, and of the Spanish Royal collection. Madrid, 1893.

MÂLE THIRTEENTH L'Art Réligieux du Treizième Siècle en France. By Emile Mâle. Important for Vincent de Beauvais and other sources of Gothic religious tapestries. Paris, 1902.

MÂLE FIFTEENTH L'Art Réligieux de la Fin du Moyen Age, en France. By Emile Mâle. Indispensable for sources of Gothic Religious Tapestries. Paris, 1908.

MARILLIER TROJAN The Tapestries of the Painted Chamber. By H. S. Marillier. In the *Burlington Magazine,* January, 1925. With note by George Leland Hunter in the *Burlington Magazine,* April, 1925.

MARTIN LE ROY, 1908 Volume IV of the splendid, illustrated catalogue of the collection of Martin Le Roy of Paris. By Marquet de Vasselot.

MEYER ALEXANDER Alexandre le Grand, dans la Littérature Francaise du Moyen Age. By Paul Meyer. Indispensable in studying the Story of Gothic Alexander tapestries. Paris, 1886.

MICHELANT ALEXANDER Li Romans d'Alixandre, par Lambert li Tors, et Alexandre de Bernay. Edited by Heinrich Michelant. Stuttgart, 1846.

MIGEON MAXIMILIAN Les Tapisseries des Chasses de Maximilien, au Musée du Louvre. Two large plates in color, and 12 in héliogravure, of the Tapestries, besides halftones of the original small sketches.

MIGEON TISSUS Les Arts du Tissu. By Gaston Migeon. Pages 168 to 349 are devoted to the history of Tapestries. Paris, 1909.

MUNTZ LOUIS DOUZE La Tapisserie, l'Époque de Louis Douze. Illustration of the Hunolstein and Kermaingant collections. By Eugene Muntz. In Les Lettres et Les Arts, August, 1886. Library of the Metropolitan Museum, 156.3; M 926.

MUNTZ TAPESTRY A Short History of Tapestry. By Eugene Muntz, translated by Louisa J. Davis. London, 1885.

MUNTZ TAPISSERIE La Tapisserie. By Eugene Muntz. Paris, 1882.

MUNTZ VATICAN Les Tapisseries de Raphael au Vatican, et dans les principaux musées ou collections de l'Europe. By Eugene Muntz. Paris, 1897.

POLOVTSOFF RUSSIAN Some Notes on the St. Petersburg Tapestry Works. By A. Polovtsoff and V. Chambers, in the *Burlington Magazine,* 1919.

PRIMITIFS 1904 Illustrated catalogue of the Exposition des Primitifs Français au Palais du Louvre, Pavillon de Marsan. Nos. 259 to 286, 260 *bis,* are tapestries.

RICCI MORGAN Catalogue of Twenty Tapestries from the J. P. Morgan collection. By Seymour de Ricci. Paris, 1913.

ROMAN DE TROIE Le Roman de Troie par Benoit de Sainte Maure. Edited by Leopold Constans. Société des Anciens Textes Français. Paris, 1904.

ROTHSCHILD TESTA-MENT Le Mystère du Vieil Testament, publié avec introduction, notes et glossaire. By Baron James de Rothschild. Société des Anciens Textes Français. Paris, 1878.

ROZZI ARAZZO L'Arte Arazzo. By G. B. Rossi. Milan, 1907.

SARAGOSSA, 1917 — Illustrated catalogue of the Exposicion celebrada en la antique Lonja de la Ciudad, of Los Tapices de Zaragoza, containing many of the marvelous tapestries in the collection of the Saragossa cathedrals.

SARTOR REIMS — Les Tapisseries, Toiles Peintes et Broderies de Reims. By M. Sartor. The best book on the tapestries of Reims. Reims, 1912.

SCHMIDT BILDTEPPICHE — Bildteppiche, Geschichte der Gobelin-wirkerei. By Hermann Schmidt. The best book on German tapestries, with abbreviated treatment of others. Well illustrated. Berlin, 1919.

SCHUMANN TROJAN — Der Trojanische Krieg. Illustration and description of the eight fifteenth century color sketches, now in the Louvre, of part of the great Gothic Trojan War set of Tapestries. Dresden, 1898.

SOIL TOURNAI — Les Tapisseries de Tournai; les tapissiers et les haute lisseurs de cette ville. By Eugene Soil. Lille, 1892.

SOMZÉE, 1901 — Illustrated sale catalogue of the famous Somzée collection, containing many important tapestries.

SPILIOTTI RUSSIAN — An article in Russian on the Imperial Russian Tapestry Factory. In the magazine, *Treasures of Art in Russia,* 1903.

SPITZER, 1890 — The finest of art catalogues. The 23 tapestries are described by Müntz, and 7 of them are illustrated in color. Others of the tapestries are illustrated in the Sale Catalogue. Paris, 1893.

SUBSCRIBERS' EDITION — A special edition of this volume, at an advanced price, in special binding; with four extra colour plates, and 16 extra plates in doubletone, of important tapestries in America.

SUIDA TRIULZIO — Jugendwerke von Bramantino. By W. Suida. In the *Austrian Jahrbuch,* 1904. Shows that the Triulzio tapestry Months were designed by Bramantino.

TAPICES DEL REY — Los Tapices de la Casa del Rey N. S. By Elias Tormo Monzo and Francisco J. Sanchez Canton. Tapestries of the Royal Spanish collection illustrated and described. Indispensable. Madrid, 1919.

THOMSON ENGLAND — Tapestry Weaving in England. By W. G. Thomson. The best book on the subject. London, 1914.

Thomson History   A History of Tapestry from the earliest times until the present day. By W. G. Thomson. Has fine color illustrations of two of the Duke of Devonshire's Gothic Hunting tapestries, and useful indexes. London, 1906.

Union Centrale, 1876   Catalogue of the Fifth Exhibition of the Union Centrale des Beaux Arts Appliqués. Nos. 253 to 409 are tapestries, many of them of prime importance.

Valencia Spanish   Tapices de la Corona de España. By Count Valencia de Don Juan. Tapestries of the Royal Spanish collection illustrated and described. Indispensable. Madrid, 1903.

Valeri Vigevano   Volume IV (on le arti industriali, la letteratura, la musica) of La Corte di Lodovico il Moro. By Francesce Malaguzzi Valeri. Milano, 1923.

Vatican History   The Vatican, its history, its treasures. Pages 231 to 250 on the Gallery of Tapestries. Illustrated. New York, 1914.

Victoria and Albert, 1914   Catalogue of Tapestries in the Victoria and Albert Museum. By A. F. Kendrick. Illustrated.

Versailles, 1910   Tapisseries des Gobelins exposées au Palais de Versailles, en 1910. Plates I to XII illustrate the set copied after Mignard's paintings at St. Cloud; plates XIII to XXIV, Coypel's Old Testament.

Vulgate   Biblia Sacræ, vulgatæ editionis. Indispensable in studying religious Tapestries. Pustet, at Ratisbon and Rome, 1922.

Wauters Brussels   Les Tapisseries Bruxelloises. By A. Wauters. Brussels, 1878.

Weese Berne   Die Cäsar-Teppiche. With four large color plates. By Arthur Weese. Berne, 1911.

Wood Credo   Credo Tapestries. By D. T. B. Wood. In the *Burlington Magazine,* 1920, Volume XXIV, pp. 247–254, 309–316.

Wood Salvation   Tapestries of the Seven Deadly Sins. By D. T. B. Wood. In the *Burlington Magazine,* 1912, Volume XX, pp. 210–222, 277–289.

Wurzbach Lexicon   Niederländsches Kunstler-Lexicon. By Dr. Alfred von Wurzbach. The best dictionary of the painters of the Netherlands. Vienna, 1906.

INDEX

A

Abraham, 13, 128, 133, 267

Achilles, 75, 76, 77, 78, 87, 154, 177, 189, 251

Adlington Hall, 225

Aelst, Peter van, 121, 130, 133, 266

Ainard Collection, 84

Aix-en-Provence, 160, 176

Alavoine collection, 176, 202

Alba, Duke of, 79, 80, 136, 150, 181, 250, 254, 266

Albert and Isabella, Archdukes, 3, 220, 250

Albright, Mr. John J., 127, 140, 267

Aldred, Mr. J. E., 103

Alexander, Mrs. C. B., 33, 175

Alexander the Great, 18, 46, 83–85, 86, 145, 147, 155, 177, 247, 248, 264

Alentours, 182, 183, 189, 190, 200

Aliaga, Duchess of, 134

Allen, Mr. Charles Henry, 223

Allen, Mrs. Frederick H., 201

Altman collection, 124, 127, 174, 240

Amiens, 44

Anet, Chateau d', 138

Angers, 17, 21, 22, 45, 46, 54, 104–105, 137, 194, 196, 249, 251, 253, 254, 263

Anitchkoff Palace, 182

Anjou, Duke of, 21, 249, 253

Apocalypse, 17, 20, 21, 24, 25, 135, 249, 251, 253, 263, 267

Architecture, 20, 23, 26, 42, 50, 55, 57, 61, 64, 68, 79, 88, 90, 125, 128, 132, 138, 167, 168, 169, 172, 175, 223

Arnault, 162

Arthur, King, 17–21, 24, 25, 115, 116, 207, 234, 235

Arras, 1, 17, 24, 25, 229, 269

Aske Hall, 190

Asselt, Bernardino van, 216

Assisi, Don Franciso d', 183, 186

Astor, Major J. J., 93

Atherton, Mrs. Ray, 136

Aubusson, 12, 99, 101, 147, 193–204, 251, 257, 258, 269, 272, 274

Aubusson Rugs, 202–203

Audran, designer, 181, 182

Audran, weaver, 151, 180, 183, 188, 268

Augustus, 44, 58, 90, 113–114, 115, 154

Aune (ell), 268–269

Austrian, 69, 70, 132, 133, 135, 137, 138, 140, 149, 152, 154, 156, 158, 162, 181, 203, 254, 267, 272

Authors, 41, 59, 60, 111, 245–250

Auwercx, 156, 267

B

Babouneix, 202

Bachaumont, 166

Bacri collection, 64

Bailleul, Baudouin de, 251

Baker, Mr. Geo. F., 173, 174, 176

Bale (Basel), 205–210

Balloch Castle, 152

Barberini, 216–217

Barraband, Jean, 210

Barcheston, 219–220

Bardac collection, 106

Barney collection, 136

Bataille, Nicolas, 21, 263

Bauer collection, 214

Baudouin, 138, 201

Baume, Count Guillaume de la, 89

Baumgarten & Company, Wm., 156, 199, 200, 201, 257, 275

293

Destrée, Joseph, 27, 122, 251, 252
De Troy, 187, 249
Devonshire, Duke of, 101
Diana, 135, 136, 138, 140, 141, 143, 145, 181, 186, 199, 267
Dixon, Mrs. Fitz-Eugene, 183, 185, 261
Dollfus collection, 126
Don Quixote, 100, 176, 181, 185, 189, 203, 226, 250, 261, 262, 268
Doria, Palazzo, 84, 86, 180, 181, 248, 264
Donádelle Rose, Count, 133
Dourdin, Jacques, 263
Drake, Mr. Alexander W., 108
Dreicer collection, 45, 124, 240
Dresden, 180, 210
Drouais, 191
Dubreuil, Toussaint, 140, 144, 146
Dulcinea del Toboso, 183
Dumons, Jean Joseph, 170, 197, 199
Durmonteil, 200
Duveen, Sir Joseph, 31, 44, 54, 58, 103, 105, 108, 225

E

Edgewater Tapestry Looms, 257, 275
Eells, Mr. Howard P., 144
Egyptian, 7, 8, 9, 11, 12, 15
Einstein, Miss Alice, 227
Elizabeth, Empress, 227
Elizabeth, Queen, 219
Ell (see *aune*)
Elysée, Palace de l', 150
Engel-Gros collection, 115, 206
Enghien, 137
Erlanger, Baron d', 155
Escurial, 226
Esther, 46, 55, 58, 112, 115, 116, 124, 187, 188, 249, 265
Eucharist, 64, 68, 123
Eugénie, Empress, 182
Evangelists, with symbols, 70, 118, 149, 223

Exhibitions—Avery Library, 1914, 127; Brooklyn, 1914, 202; Brooklyn, 1918, 147; Bruges, 1902, 41; Bruges, 1907, 254; Brussels, 1905, 41, 127; Brussels, 1910, 154; Buffalo, 1914, 127, 140, 154, 199, 267; Cleveland, 1918, 141, 144, 170, 174, 188, 199, 202; Franco-British, 1921, 82, 93; Hispanic Museum, 1917, 227; Limoges, 1886, 198; Madrid, 1892, 79, 86; Musée des Arts Decoratifs, 1923, 186; Notre Dame, 1922, 196; Paris, 1876, 24; Paris, 1880, 40; Philadelphia, 1915, 154, 156, 157, 161, 198, 267; Primitifs Francais, 1904, 24, 106; San Francisco, 1915, 147; Union Centrale, 1876, 222.

F

Farcy, L. de, 21
Faust, Mr. Edward A., 60
Felletin, 137, 138, 193
Fénelon, 162, 163, 202
Ferdinand, Archduke Franz, 157, 182
Ferdinand, Emperor, 128, 129
Ferdinand and Isabella, 50, 56, 113, 123, 265
Fere, Pierrot, 263
Ferloni, Pietro, 217
Ferrara, 133, 135, 214, 215
Fishing, 148, 165, 170, 175, 176, 180, 199, 200, 262
Florence, 61, 63, 95, 106, 118, 122, 135, 140, 147, 150, 154, 161, 186, 214–216
Fontainebleau, 186, 254
Fontenay, 182, 272
Forde Abbey, 223
Fortuny, 50
Foucquet, Jean, 107
Foulke collection, 127, 142, 180, 202, 204
Fouquet, 140, 145, 149, 157